Digital Home Recording

Tips, Techniques, and Tools
for Home Studio Production

Jon Chappell, Editor

Backbeat
Books
San Francisco

Published by Backbeat Books
600 Harrison Street, San Francisco, CA 94107
www.backbeatbooks.com
email: books@musicplayer.com
An imprint of the Music Player Group
Publishers of *Guitar Player*, *Bass Player*, *Keyboard*, and other magazines
United Entertainment Media, Inc.
A CMP Information company

CMP
United Business Media

Copyright © 2003 by United Entertainment Media, Inc. All rights reserved. No part of this book covered by copyrights hereon may be reproduced or copied in any manner whatsoever without written permission, except in the case of brief quotations embodied in articles and reviews. For information, contact the publishers.

Distributed to the book trade in the US and Canada by
Publishers Group West, 1700 Fourth Street, Berkeley, CA 94710

Distributed to the music trade in the US and Canada by
Hal Leonard Publishing, P.O. Box 13819, Milwaukee, WI 53213

Cover Design: David Hamamoto
Text Design and Composition: Michael Cutter
Proofreading: Richard Maloof

Library of Congress Cataloging-in-Publication Data

Digital home recording : tips, techniques, and tools for home studio
production / Jon Chappell, editor.
    p. cm.
Includes index.
  ISBN 0-87930-732-3 (alk. paper)
  1. Sound—Recording and reproducing—Digital techniques. 2. Sound
studios. I. Chappell, Jon.

TK7881.4 .D535 2002
621.389'32'0285—dc21

                                        2002038358

Printed in the United States of America
03 04 05 06 07   5 4 3 2 1

Contents

Introduction

When the first edition of *Digital Home Recording* was released in 1998, it was unsurpassed in comprehensiveness and savvy as a guide to digital recording in home and project studios. The book presented useful recording techniques and cleverly wrought tips and tricks for working with the available technology. That technology included computers that came new with only 32MB of RAM, read-only CD drives, stand-alone hard disk recorders limited to four and eight tracks, and DAT decks as the only viable choice for quality mixdowns on a budget. The book deftly combined breezy good advice with warnings and work-arounds for the various limitations of any given system.

It's astonishing to consider how far the industry has come in just five years. Between the first edition of *Digital Home Recording* and this one, many technological shortcomings that hobbled home recordists since the dawn of Portastudios have simply evaporated. Maturing hardware and software design, faster chips, and ever-plummeting memory costs have dispatched these drawbacks in turn with each new upgrade and release. Home recording in the digital domain these days is a cinch, technologically. Inexpensive systems abound, and are all impressively powerful and easy to use.

In this second edition of *Digital Home Recording*, I have introduced such new technologies as USB—the one-stop communications protocol that obliterates serial, parallel, printer, and modem ports, and can carry multitrack 24-bit audio as well as MIDI and control information. I've kept to a minimum the discussions of CD-R/RW burners and their operation, which are commonplace in both computers and many stand-alone workstations. And I've presented in detail a host of other technologies that were not available just a short time ago and are now in full swing: FireWire interfaces, MP3 files, 24/96 resolution, streaming hard disk samplers, 5.1 surround sound, and VST plug-ins—terms not even mentioned in the first edition, because they simply didn't exist. Conversely, much more ink than seems necessary today was spilled on MIDI-only sequencers, device drivers, MiniDisc recorders, and DAT decks, so I've cut way back on those and other fading technologies. But that was all we had to work with back in the digital Stone Age of the late '90s.

As luck would have it, the hardware evolution has been exponential compared to the more linear growth of digital audio needs: Both computers and stand-alone systems have progressed so rapidly that now it's virtually impossible to purchase an underpowered system if it's less than a year old. Even a modest, semi-pro system for home use can comfortably handle a fairly heavy workload of digital recording tasks including multitrack audio and MIDI recording with plug-in effects and virtual instruments, stereo mastering, and CD burning. What's fascinating amidst all this change is just how true the advice still rings from the first book—and how much it is welcome in the face of such rapid progress.

The insights in the original text are timeless because they come from the best minds in the audio industry, distilled from the essays of Craig Anderton, Mitch Gallagher, Roger Nichols, Greg Rule, and the others who graced the pages of *Keyboard, EQ,* and *Music & Computers.* It's heartening to see that good sense, creativity, and guerrilla tactics still count for so much, regardless of technology's ever-evolving state. Fortunately for musicians and engineers, the laws of physics don't upgrade themselves nearly as often as RAM and hard disk requirements. It is in the universal truths of music, acoustics, aesthetics—and frequent dashes of humor—that our contributors reveal their best stuff.

I have preserved the writers' original words when they encourage us to find fresh and bold approaches to the technology at hand while knowing it cold and working within its limitations. But I've also brought focus to the issues that concern musicians armed with today's more-advanced systems. It seems we're safely out of the bad old days when you couldn't make a CD without spending a lot of money. In fact, home systems now have the capability of producing high-resolution audio where the record companies are still searching to find a commercially viable medium. Musicians and home recordists are ahead of the curve—at least for the moment.

But the technology curve is one that must be negotiated irrespective of your current position on its slippery slope. What's important is making sure the technology serves the art. Nothing should be too easy or too hard, based solely on the technology. It should all be hard, in a way, but easy to be hard—at least when it's about making the best music possible. I hope that, while your creative struggles might be hard-won victories, this book helps to make all your technological problems easily solvable no-brainers.

—Jon Chappell

Acknowledgments

Digital Home Recording is a collaborative effort on the part of many talented contributors, who all lent their insight and unique perspective to a topic that is fascinating though sometimes daunting. The authors of these articles and essays herein have a special gift for making technology accessible, and through their efforts, readers will be encouraged to go forth without fear and make great music while mastering their machines. My sincere thanks to all the journalists, engineers, and musicians whose thoughts, theories, and musings grace these pages. It wouldn't have been a book without you.

I'd like to extend special thanks to Richard Johnston and Matt Kelsey at Backbeat Books, who led the charge for this book, and who were accommodating, patient, and wise on the road to its production. Thanks also to Debbie Greenberg at *Keyboard* and Brian McConnon at Steinberg. I'd also like to send out a big, steaming heap o' gratitude to Craig Anderton, whose scary smarts and unflinching generosity have benefited me in more ways than I can begin to count.

This book is dedicated to the memory of Jay Kahn, a man who loved music, publishing, people, and life, and who continually serves as a source of inspiration to me and to all the folks at Backbeat Books.

—JC

About the Editor

Jon Chappell is an author, editor, writer, and publishing professional with 15 years in senior-level positions in prestigious music and pop culture publications. He started professional life as multi-style guitarist, transcriber and arranger, attending Carnegie-Mellon University where he studied with guitarist Carlos Barbosa-Lima, and then earning his master's degree in composition from DePaul University, where he also taught theory and ear training.

He has served as editor-in-chief of *Guitar* magazine, technical editor of *Guitar Shop* magazine, and musicologist for *Guitarra*, a classical magazine. He is founder and the first editor-in-chief of *Home Recording* magazine.

Jon has played and recorded with Pat Benatar, Judy Collins, Graham Nash, and Robert Cray, and has contributed numerous musical pieces to film and TV. Some of these include *Northern Exposure*, *Walker, Texas Ranger*, *All My Children*, and the feature film *Bleeding Hearts*, directed by actor-dancer Gregory Hines.

In 1991, he became associate music director of Cherry Lane Music where he transcribed, edited and arranged the music of Metallica, Guns N' Roses, Steve Vai, Bonnie Raitt, and Eddie Van Halen, among others. He has written 15 method books, which have sold in excess of 200,000 copies, and is the author of *Guitar for Dummies*, *Rock Guitar for Dummies*, and *The Recording Guitarist—A Guide for Home and Studio*.

The World of Digital Audio

Your mother thinks your home studio looks like the bridge of the starship *Enterprise*. You try to tell her, "No, Mom, it's really simple. See, the computer handles the MIDI sequencing and hard disk audio recording. That's a 40-gigabyte hard drive for the digital audio, and those points in the patchbay are the effects sends from the mixer, and this is how you enter Edit mode on the DAW, and. . . ." Her eyes wander. She mentions that you forgot to water the fern.

You should know better. It *is* simple—once you've spent years getting familiar with it all. But do you know how the technology that you use every day works? Or do you just scrunch your eyes shut, hit the power switch, and hope nothing blows up?

There's nothing wrong with just hooking up a few gadgets and concentrating on the music. That may even be more productive than getting lost in the digital ozone. However, there are important advantages to knowing a little about what's going on behind the front panel. Like getting the most out of your equipment. Like not wasting money buying things that don't meet your needs. And, possibly, impressing your friends by dropping technical jargon into casual conversations.

Most of us, even if we've been wallowing in electronic music technology for years, have a few blank cards in our fact files. If you'd like to test your expertise and maybe stretch it a little, read on. If you're new (or comparatively new) to the whole process of making music with digital hardware and software, we'll try to get you up to speed in some basic areas that may come in handy down the line. And if you're a whiz at computers but weak in the MIDI department, or vice-versa, this is your chance to become better rounded.

The Fundamentals of Sound

Getting the most out of any electronic music system requires a basic understanding of acoustics—the physics of sound. (For more in-depth coverage, investigate further at your local library or check "For Further Reading" at the back of the book.)

Sound consists of rapid variations in air pressure. A vibrating string creates these changes directly: Twang it, and it moves back and forth, pushing the air molecules first one way, then another. A speaker does much the same thing when driven by an electrical current: The speaker cone moves in and out, displacing a certain amount of air.

These waves of air pressure, or *sound waves*, travel through the air at about 1,000 feet per second (the speed of sound). In the conventional diagram of a sound wave (see Figure 1), high points indicate zones of greater pressure, while low points show zones of lesser pressure.

Our ears are most sensitive to sound waves that vibrate at more than 20 cycles per second and less than 20,000 cycles per second. A cycle typ-

Figure 1

Sound is composed of waves of compression and expansion. The conventional diagram of a sound wave represents zones of higher pressure (compression) as hills and zones of lower pressure (expansion) as valleys.

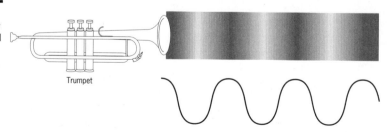

Trumpet

ically includes both the positive and negative part of a wave; "cycles per second" is abbreviated as Hertz (Hz), and measures the sound's frequency. A thousand cycles is called a *kilohertz*, or kHz for short. The range from 20Hz to 20kHz is commonly considered the range of human hearing, though older people, or people of any age who abuse their hearing, often suffer hearing loss in the upper range—say, above 8–10kHz.

Overtones. A plucked string doesn't simply vibrate as a unit, producing sound waves of one pure frequency. Instead, it vibrates in a complex way that includes vibrations that are mathematical multiples of the basic frequency. Essentially, the whole string is vibrating, the halves of the string are vibrating, the thirds of the string are vibrating, and so on. All of these vibrations occur in the same string at the same time; the tone that we perceive as coming from the plucked string includes vibrations of all these different frequencies.

The frequency of the whole string vibrating is called the *fundamental*. The higher frequencies at which the same string also vibrates are called its *overtones*. The fundamental and its overtones are related mathematically: If the fundamental is at 100Hz, for example, the overtones may fall at 200Hz, 300Hz, 400Hz, 500Hz, and so on (the exact frequencies depend on the string's overtone structure). Usually the higher overtones will be lower in volume than the lower overtones. You'll also hear the terms *harmonics* and *partials* used. Technically, the fundamental is the first partial, so the second partial is the first overtone. Any component of a sound, whether or not it has the mathematical relationship we've just described, is a partial. With sounds that exhibit this type of mathematical coherence, a harmonic is the same thing as a partial.

In different sound sources (violin, pipe organ, the human voice), the fundamental and various overtones are mixed in various proportions—some louder and some softer. It's the mix of overtones that gives each instrument sound its characteristic *timbre* (pronounced "TAM-br"), or sound quality.

Some acoustic instrument partials are "out of tune" with respect to the fundamental rather than vibrating at the frequencies predicted by mathematical theory. An extreme example is a church bell, whose fundamental and first overtone are usually separated by an interval of about a major sixth (from 100Hz to about 166Hz, for example). Partials that are not whole-number multiples of the fundamental are called *clangorous*, because they resemble the sound of a bell.

Fourier Analysis. A Frenchman named Fourier (pronounced "foor-yay") proposed a method of mathematical analysis to describe any sound, clangorous or not, in terms of its fundamental and overtones. Fourier analysis considers every sound as containing some number of *sine waves* that are vibrating at different frequencies. (A sine wave is a pure tone with no overtones.) Because few sounds in nature are static, in Fourier analysis each sine wave also changes in amplitude (loudness) over time.

The concept that a sound consists of many components at different frequencies is important to many processes involving electronic music. For instance, when using an equalizer (see "Effects Processors"), you boost or cut the amplitude of some frequency band—for example, 4kHz. This has an audible effect only if the original sound feeding the equalizer contains overtones around 4kHz. If most of its overtone energy is at 1kHz, boosting at 4kHz won't do much. Another example: Some synthesizer patches use a second oscillator tuned several octaves above the first (and usually set to a lower output level) to add a specific overtone to the timbre.

A synthesizer *filter* shapes a sound's overtone content (usually this is under the control of an *envelope generator*, which changes the overtone content over time). When a lowpass filter removes the higher overtones from the latter part of each note, it mimics the response of an acoustic instrument (especially a struck or plucked instrument like piano or guitar) in which physical sound energy dissipates gradually, starting with the upper overtones.

Analog Audio

Compared to the world of digital audio, the old-fashioned analog way seems intuitively obvious: Just plug in your instrument, crank the volume knob, and go. Nonetheless, how you hook up various devices can definitely influence your music's sound quality.

Impedance. Signal level is one of the most important issues we need to cover, but to understand it properly, we need to cover some basic audio principles such as impedance and decibels.

Ohms measure impedance, which generally stands for opposition, or resistance, to current flow in an electrical circuit. Most audio equipment has a very low output impedance so that the signal goes through the minimum possible resistance, thus producing the strongest possible signal. The input impedance, on the other hand, measures the resistance an incoming signal sees to ground. Here you want a relatively high impedance, so that as little of the signal as possible goes to ground, and the remaining signal can proceed directly to the next input stage. Figure 2 summarizes how input and output impedance affect the signal. Incidentally, gear designed for guitar, bass, and other instruments using passive pickups will have an extremely high input impedance to avoid loading down the pickups, whose output impedance is higher than most other gear.

High-impedance equipment usually has a ¼" phone plug. Feeding a high impedance output, such as a guitar, into a low impedance input, such as a mic input on a mixer, requires a transformer called a *direct box*. This lowers the signal to mic level and matches impedances. (Note that there are other types of direct boxes, such as devices that provide gain, add tone controls, use active circuitry instead of a transformer, etc.)

Decibels. A *decibel* (abbreviated dB) is one tenth of a unit called a *Bel* (named after Alexander Graham Bell), which was originally developed to measure the power of various signals in telephone systems. A decibel is not an absolute measurement like pounds or centimeters, but is a *ratio* between two numbers, one of which is a standard reference value. Without knowing what the reference is, the number is meaningless.

Most people think of decibels as a measure of volume, where 0dB is referenced as the threshold of hearing, and 130dB is called the threshold of pain because the sound is so loud it hurts. But there are different types of decibels, as indicated by a single-letter suffix (e.g., dBV, dBm, dBu, etc.), which reference the signal being measured to different standardized levels. For example, the dBm, which describes a signal's power or wattage, is referenced to 1 milliwatt of power. In audio equipment, 1 milliwatt equals 0.775 volts into a 600-ohm input impedance, and with the dBm scale, equals 0dBm.

Since not all audio gear is based on changes in power (or 600-ohm output and input impedances), another scale was invented based on *voltage*, the dBV. This is referenced to 1 volt, so that 0dBV = 1 volt. The dBu

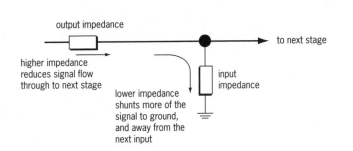

output impedance

to next stage

higher impedance
reduces signal flow
through to next stage

input
impedance

lower impedance
shunts more of the
signal to ground,
and away from the
next input

Figure 2

How impedance affects signal strength as it flows from one stage to the next scale (used to eliminate the 2.2dB difference between the dBV and dBm scales) determines voltage independent of impedance. It is simply referenced to 0.775 volts (so 0dBu = 0.775 volts, regardless of impedance).

Signal Levels. There are also more qualitative ways to define levels. Microphones put out a *mic-level* signal (around -60dBV). This low-level signal requires a preamp to boost it to *line level*. Passive guitar pickups generate signals that are stronger than mics but weaker than electronic devices such as synthesizers. Typically, synthesizer outputs and mixer inputs are line-level; this level is nominally -10dBV, though in fact synth outputs tend to hover around 0dBu. Professional devices quite often work with higher-level, +4dBm signals.

One ramification of using devices based on different nominal levels is that if you feed a +4dBm signal into an input designed for -10dBV signals, the +4dBm signal will be too strong, and will cause distortion unless the -10 dBV input includes a pad, switch, or knob that lowers the incoming signal's level before it reaches the rest of the circuitry. Going from a -10dBV output into a +4dBm input causes the opposite problem: The signal level is too low, and boosting it will likely increase any background noise.

For the most part, you shouldn't have to worry too much about the-

Figure 3

In an unbalanced cable, the inner "hot" conductor is surrounded by a grounded shield that fences out hum and interference (although shielding is not 100% effective).

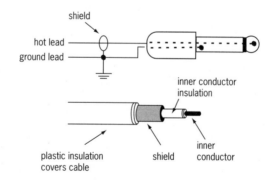

Figure 4

In a balanced line system, the hot and cold leads carry the same signal, but are out of phase with one another.

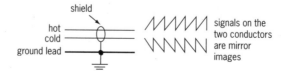

ory. You should be able to plug equipment with ¼" jacks into anything else that has ¼" jacks (with the exception of instruments that use passive pickups, as noted above). At most, a little tweaking of a mixer channel's input pad (also called a trim control) should be all that's needed.

Cables and Connectors. Pro-level +4dBm signals are often carried on three-conductor XLR cables, which are used in *balanced* audio systems. Balanced cables resist noise build-up much better than two-conductor *unbalanced* cables, the kind that have ¼" phone plugs or RCA plugs on the end. Figures 3 and 4 show the difference between the two. Some balanced cables do use ¼" plugs; in this case, the three conductors are wired to the tip, ring, and sleeve of a *stereo* plug. These "balanced TRS" connectors carry only one channel of audio, even though they use a "stereo" plug. (As you can probably guess, "TRS" stands for "tip-ring-sleeve.")

The reason balanced cables are less noisy is because the output signal going through the cable splits between two wires, a hot (+) signal and a "cold" or neutral (–) signal, which are reversed in phase. Both wires pick up noise as they travel down the cable, but on the receiving end, the phase-reversed signal is switched back in phase. So any noise is now in phase in one wire and out of phase in the other. Mixing these two back together causes the out-of-phase noise to cancel out the in-phase noise, and the signal is (at least in theory) noise-free (see Figure 5).

Even unbalanced connections normally use shielded cable, which

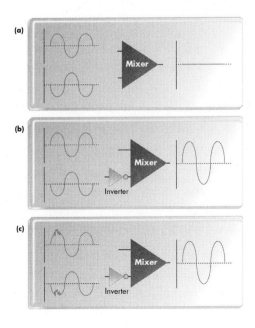

Figure 5

Signals with opposite polarity cancel when summed together (a). In a balanced audio system, two "hot" connectors carry identical audio signals—but the polarity of one signal is reversed as it is being transmitted. At the receiving end, the polarity is flipped again, and the two signals are added (b). Any interference that was introduced to the signal as it traveled down the cable is now "out of phase," and will be canceled out, leaving only the desired audio signal (c).

means that the thin metal strands that make the ground connection wrap around a layer of insulation surrounding the center "hot" wire. The shielding provides some protection against noise build-up. Unshielded lamp cord (also called "zip cord") is suitable *only* for audio connections between a power amp and speakers. Here the level is so high that noise buildup isn't likely to be a problem, but the ability to carry large amounts of current is crucial.

For the best audio performance, use the best cables and connectors you can afford, keep cable runs as short as possible, and avoid routing audio cables too close to power cables. An audio cable functions as a radio antenna; coiling a too-long cable magnifies the antenna effect. If you can't avoid placing audio cables in proximity to power cables, make sure they cross at an angle rather than run in parallel.

AC Plugs. What about power connectors? Most modern devices use three-prong, grounded plugs. Do not attempt to defeat the grounding by using three-to-two plug adapters. For best results, plug your entire music studio into a junction box that is hooked to a single outlet (assuming, of course, that it can handle the current your studio draws). This provides your entire studio with a common ground, minimizing the likelihood of ground loops, which are notorious sources of 60-cycle hum. If you're not sure whether the outlet you'll be using provides a true ground on its third prong, you can buy a tester at hardware stores for around $6. If your wall outlet doesn't provide a true ground, consult an electrician. Ungrounded electrical equipment is a safety hazard. (See Chapter 7, "Hums and Ground Loops," for more on grounding.)

Digital Audio

Digital audio is definitely a great leap forward for musicians wanting to make good recordings on a budget. The advantages of digital recording compared to analog (tape) recording include better potential signal-to-noise ratio (i.e., recordings with less "hiss"), cut-and-paste editing with no need to resort to a razor blade and tape splicing block, seamless integration between sequencers and audio recorders, and the ability to make perfect backup copies (clones). Among the disadvantages: Digital is less forgiving than analog tape of a too-hot input signal.

A/D and D/A Converters. When recording an analog signal (such as a microphone, guitar amp output, etc.) into a digital system, the signal first enters an analog-to-digital converter (ADC or A/D). This reads the voltage of the incoming analog signal, and converts it into the binary equivalent; in other words, the A/D converter expresses the voltage numerically as a series of ones and zeroes, which is the only language that computers understand.

When the digital data plays back, the ones and zeros pass through a digital-to-analog converter (DAC or D/A), which translates the numbers back into voltages. These voltages, which are essentially the same as those coming from the line output of a cassette deck or CD player, can proceed to an amplifier for monitoring.

Sampling Rate. The process of capturing the incoming signal's voltage is called sampling, and the number of times per second that the sampling process occurs is the sampling rate. Generally, a higher sampling rate more accurately represents high-frequency waveforms. A rate of 44,100 times per second, as used on consumer CDs, is called a 44.1kHz sampling rate. Other sampling rates commonly found on digital audio systems include 192kHz, 96kHz, 88kHz, 48kHz, 32kHz, 22.05kHz, and 11.025kHz. 96kHz is the ultra-hi-fi rate specified for DVD; 22.05kHz and 11.025kHz sound more like AM radio.

Resolution. Typically, each sample is stored as a 16-bit word—a string of 16 ones and zeroes. The number of bits corresponds to the number of discrete digital numbers available to represent the incoming analog voltages, which specifies the signal's resolution. For example, a one-bit piece of data can represent only two values—on and off. Two bits can indicate four possible values (both on, both off, 1st bit on and 2nd bit off, or 1st bit off and 2nd bit on). Four bits can give 16 values, five bits 32 values, and so on.

The bottom line is that more bits allow more accurate quantifying of specific voltages, just as increasing the number of lines per inch with video gives a higher-definition picture. And the more discrete voltages you can measure (65,536 in the case of a 16-bit recorder), the greater the system's dynamic range and signal-to-noise ratio. This means that the softs are softer, the louds are louder, and the numbers that represent the stored sound more accurately represent the original signal (see Figure 6).

For this reason, more and more gear is going to 24-bit resolution. While this requires storing 50% more data respectively than a 16-bit signal, the difference in sound quality is significantly better. (For more on high-resolution audio, see "Moving into the High-Resolution Era" below).

Quantization Noise and Aliasing. On paper, 16-bit "encoding" combined with a 44.1kHz sample rate equals high-fidelity, CD-quality audio. But in practice, other factors—particularly the hardware used in the system—affect the overall sonic performance. Not all 16-bit, 44.1kHz converters exhibit the same audio quality. The problem is not with digital audio per se, but with its communication with the analog world. Both analog-to-digital (A/D) and digital-to-analog (D/A) conversion can alter the sound, due to factors such as *quantization noise* and *aliasing*.

Quantization noise occurs due to differences between the digitized signal and the original analog signal. Aliasing occurs when a converter fails to grab both the positive and negative parts of a wave's cycle, resulting in an inaccurate representation of the original waveform (the converter records a lower frequency waveform instead). According to the *Nyquist Theorum*, the highest frequency you can record without aliasing is one half of the sampling rate. Therefore, if you record with a sampling rate of 22kHz, you can't capture a 12kHz frequency.

S/PDIF and AES/EBU. Two types of connectors are commonly used for stereo digital audio. The S/PDIF (Sony/Philips Digital Interface) format uses RCA (phono) or fiber-optic (TOSLINK) cables, while the AES/EBU (Audio Engineering Society/European Broadcast Union) format generally uses XLR cables. Both formats carry left and right stereo signals together on a single cable. If you're planning to add a DAT deck to your computer music system, for example, ideally you'd like both the DAT deck and your sound card to have S/PDIF, AES/EBU, or optical input and output jacks, as this will allow transferring your music to and from the DAT in digital form, without passing through an intervening

Figure 6

Sound is digitized by rapidly measuring its level and storing the measurements. Two primary factors affect digital sound quality: the frequency of the measurements (sampling rate) and their resolution (bit depth). At right, you can see the individual measurements. As we increase the sample rate, the sampled waveform more closely resembles the original. Similarly, the higher the bit depth, the more accurate the level measurements can be. An 8-bit converter will divide the level scale into 256 possible values, whereas a 16-bit one will allow 65,536.

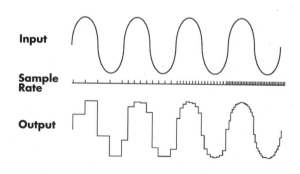

digital-to-analog and analog-to-digital conversion process. (This conversion process always degrades the audio, though with good converters the impact will be minimal.)

Moving into the High-Resolution Era

Although 16-bit, 44.1kHz audio was hailed as a sonic revolution—and it was—we always knew we could do better. Well, that time has come. High-resolution (HR) audio features higher bit resolutions (greater than 16 bits), along with sample rates higher than the usual 44.1 and 48kHz standards.

Granted, there aren't many commercial outlets yet for delivering high-resolution products to consumers, so there hasn't been that much incentive for engineers to upgrade their studios to the HR world. However, the situation is changing fast. DVD is now becoming a standard, and audio manufacturers have recently brought sonically mature, well-implemented HR technology to the marketplace. What could possibly be wrong with having more dynamic range, better frequency response, more "air," less drastic output filtering, and higher overall audio fidelity?

Nothing, but just remember there's no free lunch. Getting involved with high-resolution recording involves more than simply changing a program's default sampling rate from 44.1 to 96kHz.

24/96 and Beyond. Fortunately, there are many high-quality products now available at various price points. MOTU, Digidesign, Steinberg, and Apogee are just some of the companies offering great HR products. Most modern, pro-level digital audio workstations and digital audio MIDI sequencers offer at least 96kHz recording/editing/playback, with up to 24-bit resolution. TASCAM's DA-98HR can record and play back up to two channels at 192kHz, and four channels at 96kHz; it's a terrific option for archiving final HR mixes to tape. Digidesign Pro Tools/HD records multiple tracks of 192kHz, and several 48kHz hard disk recorders allow you to record 96kHz by splitting two 48kHz signals onto two separate tracks.

And, as with previous evolutions in the improvement of sound quality, you may need to upgrade your mic preamps, room, and other gear—any flaws become magnified when recorded at high resolution.

Who's Minding the Storage? Another major consideration is storage, because you have to capture (or retain) much more data at higher sample rates and resolutions (most programs specify reduced track counts with higher-resolution recording). Whereas 16-bit, 44.1kHz audio requires approximately 5MB per minute of mono storage, 24-bit, 96kHz requires more than three times that amount.

Not only does a lot of data have to be shoved through the computer's bus, but the hard drives used to record and play back audio need to be very fast in order to read and write more data simultaneously. Multiple 10,000 RPM, mega-GB hard drives will be the standard for most high-resolution multitrack applications.

Backup systems will also need to be much bigger to allow archiving of high-resolution audio. Twenty-five GB used to be considered a large amount of offline storage, but not anymore: You'll need tape drives that can hold at least 60GB of compressed data on one tape (available, at this writing, for just under $1,000), or high-capacity drives that can hold upwards of 200GB compressed.

Try It, You'll Like It. HR audio has arrived, and you're going to start working with it sooner than you might think. HR sounds better, and its fidelity makes long-term audio archiving a reality—time to offload those DATs, analog masters, and LPs to 192kHz digital!

So re-evaluate your system, both in terms of storage size and system stability. Even if you have to make do with fewer tracks, or cut back on the plug-ins, pick a project and try recording and mixing at high resolution. You'll hear new levels of detail, and enjoy better-sounding audio than the usual "CD-quality" audio we've been listening to all these years.

Digital Audio Recorder Overview

Digital audio recorders come in several different forms: multitrack tape decks, stand-alone hard disk recorders, portable MiniDisc multitrack recorders, and computer-based hard disk recorders. (Computer-based recorders are covered below in the section "Computers and Music.") DAT (digital audio tape) decks and CD recorders (the newest addition to digital audio recording) are two-track recorders used mostly for mixdown—tracks from multitrack recorders are combined onto these recorders to provide a final, two-track master suitable for mass-producing CDs and cassettes. They can also make backup, or archive, copies.

For more information on some popular multitrack digital recorders, see Chapter 2, "Digital Recording: What Do I Need?"

Multitrack Digital Tape Recorders. Multitrack digital tape decks currently come in two main families based on the Alesis ADAT and

TASCAM DA-88. The two use different tape formats (S-VHS and Hi-8, respectively), so tapes recorded on one can't play back on the other. Both systems provide eight audio tracks, but locking together multiple 8-track recorders expands the track count, eight tracks at a time. This explains why these machines are sometimes called *modular digital multitracks* (MDM).

Stand-Alone Hard Disk Recorders. These tapeless digital recorders store their audio on computer-type hard disks. They operate much like an ADAT or DA-88—or, for that matter, an analog multitrack—complete with front-panel level meters for each track, and rear-panel audio inputs and outputs.

The enormous advantage of tapeless recording is random access. Magnetic tape, either analog or digital, records sound linearly from beginning to end. For example, the sound at 1'00" is physically separated from the sound at 1'30" by a length of tape. Playing the two segments of audio back-to-back requires a razor blade and splicing block. (Actually, this primitive method of analog tape splicing can't be used with most digital tape, since it would disrupt codes that are recorded onto the tape and because most digital tape uses a rotating head that creates diagonal tracks across the tape.) In contrast, hard disk systems can "rewind" or "fast-forward" instantly from any point to any other. Most of them allow widely separated segments of audio data (or "tracks") to play back seamlessly, in any order. Stand-alone hard disk recorders can come with just the recorder (which operates like a tape deck) or with an onboard mixer, effects, and a CD burner (a workstation).

Portable Digital Multitrack (MiniDisc) Recorders. MiniDisc recorders resemble analog cassette-based four-track personal studios, yet boast superior sound quality. They use MD data discs for audio storage of four or eight tracks, depending on the model (see "MiniDisc Recorders" in Chapter 2).

DAT Decks. DATs are the most basic digital tape recorders. These machines offer two tracks of digital audio—more precisely, stereo digital audio. (Distinguishing between "2-track" and "stereo" is necessary because most DAT recorders do not allow recording of the left and right tracks independently; both tracks must be recorded at the same time.) The primary application for DAT in modern recording is creating a master tape. If you're happy with your recording setup and simply want a high-quality recorder that will allow creating a clean, quiet stereo master suitable for transferring to CD, DAT's the ticket.

There are other reasons for considering a DAT recorder: They can back up digital audio data, and the converters they contain can provide the audio in/out for hard disk recording systems. Their downside: They were never really designed as a "pro" medium, so DAT cassettes are relatively fragile.

DAT cassettes, which look like miniature VCR tapes, can record stereo audio with slightly higher fidelity than CDs (a 48kHz instead of 44.1kHz sampling rate). However, most musicians record at 44.1kHz, even with DAT, to avoid having to convert the sample rate from 48kHz to the 44.1kHz rate used by CDs (the sample rate conversion process can color the sound somewhat).

CD Recorders. CD recorders (also called CD-R drives or CD writers) used to cost tens of thousands of dollars, but in the past five years their prices have fallen dramatically, giving the home studio musician the ability to record and make one-at-a-time CDs without having to work with a mastering and duplicating facility. Rewritable CDs (CD-RWs) allow you to rewrite information that has previously been recorded. Some CD recording software also gives you the ability to create photo CDs and video CDs. See "CD Recorders" in Chapter 2.

MIDI

You can record digital audio and never touch a computer, but why limit yourself? The advent of MIDI in 1983 made it practical to hook up low-cost personal computers to synthesizers, and musicians' lives have never been the same since.

But first, here's a little history. By the early '80s, several manufacturers were building synthesizers that were controlled internally by digital messages. The messages told the built-in microprocessor which keys were being struck on the keyboard and which knobs were being turned; this data could even be recorded on the digital sequencers that were being built at the time. But each manufacturer had a different method of encoding the messages, so a Roland sequencer could only work with a Roland synth, a Sequential Circuits sequencer with a Sequential synth, and so on.

In a rare, and highly laudable, instance of industry-wide cooperation, many companies banded together to produce the Musical Instrument Digital Interface (MIDI), a universal form of communication that allowed synths and sequencers built by different manufacturers to talk to one another. Debuting in 1983, MIDI kicked off an unprecedented period of growth in the electronic music industry. Other factors, such as the declining cost of microprocessors, played key roles too, but MIDI was the glue that held it all together.

Originally, MIDI was designed to handle a fairly simple set of tasks. The initial idea was that when you played one MIDI synthesizer's keyboard and attached a cable from its MIDI out to another synthesizer's MIDI in, the second synth would receive messages from the first synth that told it which notes to play, thus layering the sounds of the two devices. The most basic messages are note-on and note-off; each MIDI note-on also includes a key velocity message, which tells the receiving device how hard the key is being struck. Other performance data, such as pitch-bends and modulation wheel moves, could also be transmitted as MIDI data. Timing synchronization between devices such as drum machines and sequencers was handled by MIDI clock messages (see Chapter 4 for more on synchronization).

Over the years, MIDI has been expanded to allow for more complex types of communication, but the original MIDI specification has never been abandoned. While MIDI instruments built in 1983 don't have some of the advanced functionality that has been grafted onto the MIDI spec, they still work with MIDI gear built today.

MIDI remains popular for sequencing, live control of synths (and samplers) from master keyboards, and studio control (typically, signal processors and mixers). It's also used for sending patch data from synths to storage devices, and synchronization via MIDI time code.

MIDI is not without limitations. Its bandwidth (31.25 kbaud) is just barely high enough to handle multitrack music performances without choking. The original implementation called for only 16 separate channels of music data on one cable, which seemed plenty at the time—but today, rigs that require 32 or more channels are quite common. (This requires the use of multiport MIDI interfaces for computers, as described later.) Most important, MIDI is a keyboard-oriented language, and doesn't work well to describe performances on instruments like electric violin. Alternatives and extensions have been proposed over the years and added to the spec, thus keeping it vital well over a decade and a half after its introduction. In any event, the huge installed base of MIDI devices makes it extremely unlikely that MIDI will become obsolete any time soon.

MIDI Interfaces and Operating Systems. Getting MIDI in and out of a computer requires a specialized piece of hardware called a MIDI interface. Except for Atari ST-series computers and the now-obsolete Yamaha C8, both of which had built-in MIDI jacks, the MIDI interface is a separate piece of hardware. Modern MIDI interfaces hook up to computers via the USB ports. Most sound cards have MIDI in/out capability, but require an adapter since MIDI jacks are slightly too wide to fit in a standard PC's rear-panel slot. The adapter usually has two or more MIDI jacks (or plugs) connecting to a DB-15 connector that plugs into a matching connector on the sound card. Some sound cards include this adapter, while other cards require purchasing the adapter as an accessory.

Note that more and more pro-level MIDI interfaces are *dual-platform*, meaning that they can work with both Windows and Mac computers. Also, these higher-end devices also provide more than one MIDI output and input. For example, there may be eight MIDI output jacks, allowing the device to address 128 separate MIDI channels (16 MIDI channels x 8 cables = 128 channels total). In many instances, these interfaces can even be stacked to provide more channels. Do you really need, for example, 256 MIDI channels? Probably not, but it means you can hook up a large system to your computer without having to do any re-patching.

In addition to the interface, computers need some sort of MIDI operating system to route data from the application (the sequencer or editor/librarian, for example) to and from the interface. In the PC, Windows MIDI drivers can be installed either from the Windows master diskettes/CD or from a disk provided by the interface manufacturer. On the Macintosh side, some music software uses Apple's cumbersome MIDI Manager system extension, but thankfully, this has been largely superseded by Opcode's OMS (Open MIDI System) and to a lesser extent, Mark of the Unicorn's FreeMIDI. These programs recognize your studio setup (the MIDI devices connected to your interface), and you can select the appropriate model names (K2600, VP-9000, etc.) from a menu instead of referring to them as something like "the device connected to cable A." The Name Manager in OMS also learns all of the patch names in your synths by retrieving them from OMS-compatible librarian documents. Thus when you choose a record track in a program like Digital Performer, you can choose device and sound assignments by name.

In addition to routing MIDI data, MIDI operating systems can provide real-time MIDI processing (e.g., keyboard splitting, delay, transposition, etc.) and also make information, such as the names of the patches currently being used on particular synthesizers, available to other MIDI applications.

Computers and Music

Computers can record and play back MIDI data, edit and print out music notation, customize and store synthesizer patches, and record, play back, and edit digital audio. We'll look at each application in turn.

Sequencers. Sequencers record the MIDI events that are generated as you play MIDI-compatible instruments, and play those events back into MIDI-compatible gear to re-create your performance. Because MIDI consists of data, not actual sound, the sound depends on what plays back the MIDI data. MIDI is conceptually like the holes in a player piano's paper roll; if you put the paper roll in a piano that's out of tune, or one in which certain strings are missing, the sound will be altered even though the paper roll doesn't change. Sequencers also allow editing of the MIDI data after it's been recorded, so you can fix bad notes, timing problems, etc.

When a sequencer sends commands to the receiving module in the form of MIDI messages, the sequencer doesn't care how (or even whether) the module responds. It could be playing notes, or turning light bulbs on and off.

Think of a sequencer as the musical equivalent of a word processor. Like a word processor, you can cut and paste blocks of data (in this case, MIDI notes rather than alphabetical characters (see Figure 7). You can alter the data in numerous ways, just the way you can change the wording of a sentence in a word processor, then save your work to disk.

A sequencer is more complex than the average word processor, however, because MIDI data has more dimensions than text. For each note in a sequence, the sequencer needs to store, and allow you to edit, at least the following note-related parameters:

- Pitch (also called the note number)
- Velocity (how hard you struck the key, which gives a value for dynamics)
- MIDI channel
- Start time
- Duration (note length)

MIDI sequencers also record and play back many types of events

Figure 7

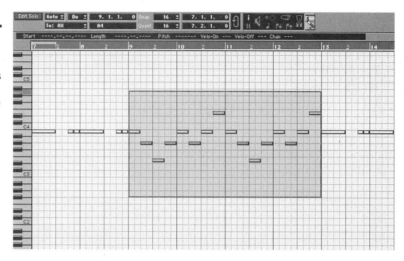

Clicking and dragging across a region (in this example, from measure 9, beat 1, to measure 13, beat 1) in Steinberg Cubase's Graphic Editor window highlights that area. It's now ready to be cut, copied, or otherwise processed.

other than notes. Pitch-bends, controller data (vibrato, timbral changes, etc.), and program changes to select different instrument sounds are the most common of these events (see Figures 8 and 9).

Like a multitrack tape deck, sequencers organize their music data into tracks. Each track will typically (though not necessarily) be dedicated to a single MIDI channel of notes, such as the piano or bass part. Tracks can be individually muted so that you can hear the rest of the music without the muted track. With punch-in recording, you can replace part of a single track—for instance, bars 9 through 11—and leave the rest of the music untouched.

One common sequencer editing process, quantization (sometimes called auto-correct), tightens up a performance's timing by shifting each note forward or backward slightly so that its start lines up with the nearest specified rhythmic value. The user defines the quantization "grid" to which notes will be adjusted, such as 16th or triplets.

In order to do this job, or any other related to rhythm, a sequencer must have an internal clock to keep track of the music's timing. The more precise the clock, the more accurately it will record and play back music. A sequencer clock's precision is measured in ppq (pulses per quarter-note). A basic sequencer that offers only 24 ppq of clock resolution isn't enough to represent the subtleties of a musician's performance. The clock resolutions on typical sequencers range from 240 to 960 ppq. However, note that finer resolutions may be irrelevant if the computer on which the sequencer is running has "loose" timing (generally caused by a slow processor, or multi-tasking operation). For more on quantization, see Chapter 4.

Many sequencers also contain software "mixers," where the mouse can control a screen full of virtual faders and buttons. These controllers send MIDI data that adjusts the volume, stereo panning, or other aspects of

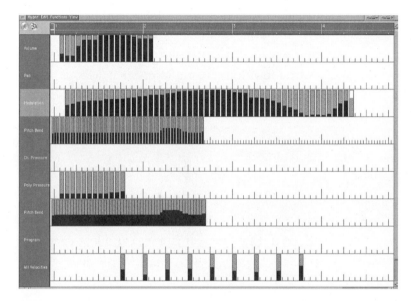

Figure 8

Emagic Logic Audio can show several strips of continuous controllers simultaneously in the Hyper Edit window. The strips can have their own background to make them easier to differentiate.

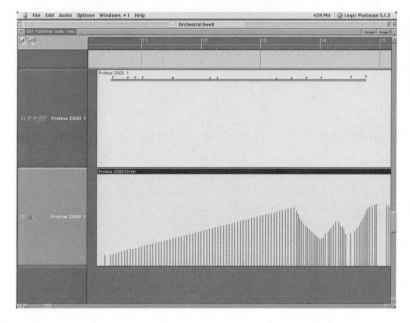

Figure 9

The Controller window in Logic currently set to display Controller #7 (MIDI volume). This curve is controlling the main volume for the selected channel above it.

the synth(s) being controlled by the MIDI messages (see Figure 10). Sequencers can also automate non-MIDI, audio tracks via MIDI-controlled volume faders. The fader inserts in an analog signal path; the fader level depends on an incoming MIDI controller value. Using different MIDI controllers, or sending data over different channels, allows automating multiple faders.

With sequencer software and a MIDI interface (or MIDI-savvy sound card), a computer can record and play back arrangements using anything from a single, multitimbral synthesizer (i.e., a synth capable of playing several sounds at once) all the way up to a fully loaded rack of synths. Sequencing a song allows building up layer upon layer of music, with the ability to edit and revise as you go along. Various types of graphic displays of the music data, from standard music notation to numeric lists of the recorded data, help streamline this editing process.

Many programs integrate MIDI and digital audio hard disk recording, so you can record MIDI and audio data in the same environment. Or, a sequencer can sync to digital tape or hard disk, and send data to MIDI instruments while the digital recording system handles the audio. But you can use just the MIDI functions if you like, or just the audio.

Figure 10

In the Mixer window of Cubase SX, you can set levels, change MIDI routing assignments, and add MIDI effects, like filter sweeps and arpeggiation.

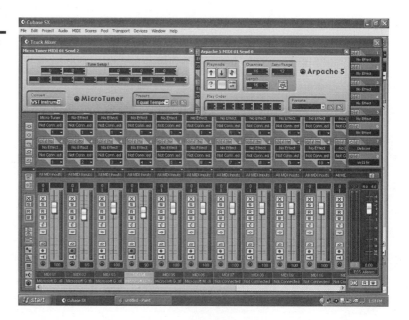

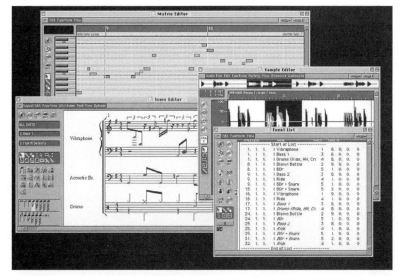

Figure 11
Emagic Logic Audio offers notation editing (left window), along with piano roll editing (upper window), and event list editing (foreground window). Each type of editing window has associated advantages and disadvantages: notation is the most familiar to many musicians, piano roll editing provides lots of information at a glance, and event list editing allows for extremely precise, detailed editing.

Notation Software. Many software sequencers offer some form of traditional scoring notation (see Figure 11), and almost all will transcribe as you play. You can edit the sequence by dragging notes around on the screen, and then print out the results. These notation utilities are fine for many purposes, including songwriter lead sheets (sheet music with melody, lyrics, and perhaps piano accompaniment).

Dedicated notation software, however, typically provides more convenience features, more specialized symbols, and more precise control over the page's appearance. Notation software, like Coda Finale, may also include some MIDI sequencing capabilities, and will allow you to enter note pitches by playing them on a MIDI keyboard (see Figure 12).

Editor/Librarians. An editor/librarian program stores the bank of patches (sound programs) from your synthesizer's internal memory onto a computer's storage medium (floppy disk, hard disk, etc.). You can generally combine patches from separate banks into a single new bank, and edit the patches themselves using the computer screen's large, detailed graphics rather than the synth's small LCD. If the synth has been popular enough to garner third-party support, you can buy banks of patches from sound developers on a CD-ROM (or download them from an online service) and transmit the data to your synth. A sophisticated editor/librarian includes some database features, allowing you to search for

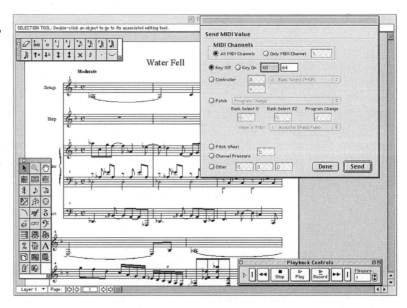

Figure 12

The screen shot of Coda Finale (Mac, PC) shows some of the features found in its score notation program. Musicians seeking a traditional notation interface can enter music in a number of ways, and have it displayed on a staff. Finale boasts publication-quality output and professional page-layout flexibility and power. Furthermore, there's interaction between the graphic elements and the MIDI commands. For example, adding an accent on a note sends a MIDI command to increase that note's velocity relative to other, unaccented notes.

patches by category or keyword. For instance, you could ask the program to find all bass patches with "fretless" as a keyword.

Sequencer/Recorders. All of the programs mentioned earlier combine sequencing with digital audio recording. Programs like Mark of the Unicorn Digital Performer, Cakewalk SONAR, Steinberg Cubase and Nuendo, Digidesign Pro Tools and Emagic Logic Audio treat audio and MIDI data similarly, allowing you to assemble a song that includes both synthesizer parts and acoustic tracks in a single integrated environment. Other audio recording software (like BIAS Peak and TC Works Spark) may record and play back only stereo audio, but still allow you to edit and process the results with great versatility and precision. Professional software often has 16 tracks or more (see Figure 13), and the number of tracks is limited only by the speed of the processor, and the RAM.

You can also use the sync output from an external multitrack tape recorder to drive a MIDI sequencer program, which is another way to synchronize audio and MIDI in older, non-hard-disk-based systems. However, since these decks typically have eight audio outputs, you'll need a mixer that has a sufficient number of inputs. Another option is to run a hard disk recorder *concurrently* with a MIDI sequencer. In other words, two programs run simultaneously within the computer, and are synchronized to a common timing signal (on the Mac, this is usually generated by OMS, a MIDI-oriented operating system extension). This allows you to use the MIDI aspect of, say, Logic Audio with the audio recording features of Pro Tools.

Sound Cards. Audio recording software requires a computer with analog-to-digital (A/D) and digital-to-analog (D/A) converters, typically in the form of a plug-in card. Without such converters, there is no convenient way to get the audio in and out of the computer. Note that not all converters offer the same sound quality. Pro recordists use cards with higher-quality converters designed specifically for pro audio.

If all you need is stereo recording, the built-in digital audio converters on the new Macs are adequate. Depending on the software, a Mac can play back four or more channels of sound, but the audio will be mixed to two channels (in other words, to stereo) before being sent to

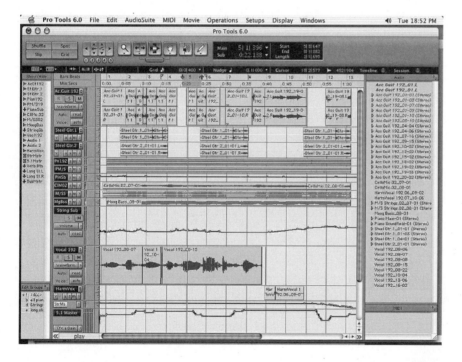

Figure 13

This screen shot is the main window of Digidesign Pro Tools, a professional-level multitrack digital audio recorder and MIDI sequencer that allows you to work with digital audio and MIDI data in the same environment.

the hardware output jacks. However, there are sound cards for both Windows and Mac machines that offer more than two channels of simultaneous audio recording and playback. See "Choosing a Sound Card" in Chapter 2 for more information on sound cards.

Effects Plug-Ins. Perhaps the biggest boon to computer-based digital recording—aside from the developments in higher resolution at cheaper and cheaper rates—is the incredible growth in the plug-in industry. Plug-ins are discrete audio applications that extend the functionality of a host program. Host programs include the high-end digital audio recording/MIDI sequencing packages such as SONAR, Cubase, Nuendo, Digital Performer, Logic Audio, Pro Tools, plus any audio-only recorder/editors (such as BIAS Peak, Sonic Foundry Sound Forge, and TC Works Spark). A plug-in effect might provide, for example, guitar distortion effects within a hard disk recording program that otherwise offers only basic processing, such as tone and dynamics control. Plug-ins often replace effects that used to be done with external outboard gear, such as compression, expansion, reverb, delay, EQ, gating, noise reduction, vocoding, spectrum analysis, surround sound, pitch correction, analog tape simulation, tube emulation, and a lot more.

VST Formats. The first aspect when contemplating a plug-in is to consider its format. Since plug-ins can operate only within a host application, their format dictates in which application or applications they'll work. There are currently eight plug-in formats: AudioSuite, DirectX, MAS, Mixtreme, Premiere, RTAS, TDM, and VST. The most applicable for pro work are DirectX, MAS, Mixtreme, RTAS, TDM, and VST, because they work in real time (as opposed to working *destructively*, as *file-based* operations), and because they fit popular pro-level applications. (Automation works with realtime plug-ins as well.) TDM plug-ins are the most popular of the DSP hardware plug-ins, but require special Digidesign-made hardware to work. VST plug-ins are the most popular of the native (computer-based) versions, because they work in both the Mac OS and Windows operating systems and in several popular programs (Logic Audio, Cubase, Peak, Spark, etc.). The table below shows how and where the eight plug-in formats work.

Adding versatility (and possible confusion) to the compatibility issue of plug-ins are *shells* or *wrappers* that allow plug-ins of one format to work in an application designed for another. For example, Cycling '74 Pluggo and Audio Ease VST Wrapper allow VST plug-ins to work in MOTU's MAS plug-in environment, benefiting Digital Performer users who want to take advantage of the highly popular and established VST format. Pluggo also supports Digidesign's RTAS plug-in format.

Plug-ins are so popular that it was worth some manufacturers' effort to create stand-alone products from them, meaning no host application is necessary to run them (see the section "The Softsynth Go-Between" below). And some manufacturers, notably Waves, release their plug-in bundles in both TDM and multiple host-based formats, including VST, RTAS, AudioSuite, DirectX, Premiere, and MAS.

Virtual Synths and Samplers. It seems more and more tasks are being turned over to computers. First was recording (MIDI and audio), then signal processing (thanks to plug-ins), and now, synthesis and sampling.

Although computer-based synthesis and sampling isn't new, the advent of Steinberg's cross-platform VST 2.0 (Virtual Studio Technology) specification lets these instruments become part of a sequencing/digital recording environment. A virtual instrument can act like a MIDI track with respect to recording and note editing, but is more like digital audio when it comes to plug-in processing, automation, and mixing.

Purists have traditionally questioned whether software synthesis can sound as good as "the real thing." In the early days the answer was no, but today's software synths are in some ways superior to the devices they replace. Not only do they offer excellent sound quality, they are stable, automatable (allowing real-time, expressive gestures for your synths—opening and closing the filter, changing envelope decay times, bending

PLUG-IN FORMATS

FORMAT (MANUFACTURER)	APPLICATION (HOST PLATFORM)	NATIVE or DSP HARDWARE	REALTIME or FILE-BASED
Premiere (Adobe)	multiple applications (Mac)	native	file-based
AudioSuite (Digidesign)	Digidesign Pro Tools (Mac/Win)	native	file-based
RTAS (Digidesign)	Digidesign Pro Tools LE (Mac/Win)	native	realtime
TDM (Digidesign)	multiple applications (Mac/Win)	DSP hardware	realtime
MAS (MOTU)	MOTU Digital Performer, AudioDesk (Mac)	native	realtime
DirectX (Microsoft)	multiple applications (Win)	native	realtime
Mixtreme (Soundscape)	multiple applications (Win)	DSP hardware	realtime
VST (Steinberg)	multiple applications (Mac/Win)	native	realtime

pitch, whatever) devices that eliminate MIDI timing problems (delay etc.) on playback.

VST is officially endorsed not just by Steinberg but by other major software houses, such as Emagic, TC Works and BIAS. (VST instruments can be used within other systems, like Cakewalk and MOTU, thanks to shells or wrappers—inexpensive programs that allow VST to work in other environments). VST is truly a global standard, and its acceptance—while always strong—has strengthened with time.

How VST Instruments Work. MIDI + digital audio programs generally include a software mixer. Its inputs typically come from digital audio tracks. A VST instrument models sound in software, and is equivalent to a digital audio track: it shows up in the software mixer like other tracks, and can be processed (plug-ins, mixer EQ, etc.).

However, although the end result seems like digital audio, a VST instrument is driven by data from a MIDI track. This makes it easy to quantize notes, add modulation, and use other MIDI-based processing (arpeggiation, transposition, and the like).

VST instruments have several advantages over outboard gear:
• Patch data is saved as part of the sequence, which recalls all settings.
• Low cost compared to hardware equivalents.
• Centralized, on-screen environment.
• Patch cords exist only in software.

The disadvantages are:
• Loads down the host processor (however, hardware DSP-based solutions for running VST devices without loading the processor are just starting to become available).
• Lacks the hardware controls of "the real thing."
• Some feel that the original, non-emulated instruments have more "presence."

Audio Processing. Because the VST instrument outputs digital audio, as this signal goes through your program's mixer, you can add plug-ins, or use any processing the program itself offers (dynamics, EQ, etc.). But as you add more instruments and plug-ins, at some point your machine will start to choke...the question is when. The faster and more memory-laden the computer, the more instruments, voices, and processes you can run. An 850MHz, 256MB RAM, Windows 98SE, Q Performance Systems computer can run Cubase 5.1, eight instruments (the maximum allowed—1 instance of LM9, 3 instances of Neon, 2 Native Instruments B4, and 2 Native Instruments Prophet-52), and several audio plug-ins, while the VST Performance meter cruises along at around 40%.

However, an easy workaround is to render the VST output to audio, which then plays back as an audio track. This frees up the VST resources, as audio tracks require less processing power than a VST instrument.

The Softsynth Go-Between. Plug-in instruments make a great enhancement to an audio sequencer, but how about incorporating stand-alone software instruments—ones that don't run inside a host application, but are independent? If you plan to use a stand-alone software synth in conjunction with a MIDI/audio sequencer, the sequencer and synth must support one of two "go-between" methods for transferring audio data to and from the two applications. One method involves using one of two software protocols—ReWire from Propellerhead Software, or Virtual Input Plug-In (VIP) from Mark of the Unicorn—and the other is a Digidesign plug-in called DirectConnect (Mac only). All three allow you to "pipe in" the audio outputs of a synth into the mixer channels or audio tracks within compatible sequencer/recorders.

ReWire and VIP. ReWire and VIP let you route up to 64 channels of audio into a sequencer in real time. In addition, ReWire allows for synchronized transport control and playback of step sequences from such compatible programs as Propellerhead's ReBirth and Koblo's Gamma 9000.

DirectConnect. Like ReWire and VIP, Digidesign's DirectConnect plug-in lets you stream up to 32 channels of audio into Pro Tools and Pro Tools LE or other programs that support Mix hardware. However, DirectConnect doesn't provide for synchronization between two applications. Instead, timing and playback control information for stand-alone synths is handled by OMS.

Every program handles ReWire streaming a little differently, but it basically works like this: The audio outputs of a software synth (or sampler for that matter) show up as audio input choices in your sequencer's recording/mixing environment. Typically you'd assign the synth's outputs to a mono or stereo auxiliary track. Depending on the synth, you'll have the choice of main stereo outputs and up to 16 individual outputs. As with plug-in synths, you can use insert effect plug-ins to process the outputs of stand-alone synths. To play a ReWire compatible synth using a MIDI keyboard, you have to select the synth as the "destination" instrument for a MIDI track and record-enable it.

With DirectConnect, synth outputs are selected from insert slots on mono and stereo auxiliary tracks. To play a DirectConnect synth you'd assign it to a record-enabled MIDI track just like you would to play a ReWire synth.

Most sequencers let you recall patches from stand-alone synths by name using ReWire or DirectConnect; you just won't be able to edit the patches within the sequencer. If you want to adjust the characteristics of the filter on a stand-alone synth patch, you have to do so using the synth's own editing software. To eliminate this sort of jockeying between two programs, we're starting to see stand-alone synths such as BitHeadz Retro AS-1 becoming available as plug-ins.

Data Storage. Recorded audio is stored on a computer's hard disk (either the internal disk or an external disk). If you do the math (2 bytes x 2 channels x 44,100 x 60 seconds), one minute of stereo audio sampled in a 16-bit format at 44.1kHz takes up more than 10MB (megabytes) of hard disk space. That's one reason why tapeless recording is not cheap. However, as hard drive prices (especially cartridge-based, removable types) have plummeted, it has become a more attractive option.

Hard Drives. Hard disk drives are sometimes internal—i.e., mounted inside the computer or sampler—and sometimes external. The most common way of linking external hard drives to the host device is with a SCSI or USB cable. SCSI (the Small Computer Systems Interface, pronounced "scuzzy") is a communications protocol that allows up to eight devices, including hard drives and CD-ROM drives, to share data. SCSI connections are not quite as simple or trouble-free as MIDI connections or USB. Cables must be short, cannot be plugged or unplugged while power is on, and use several different connector types (bring on the adapters!). Newer Macs and Windows machines typically require a SCSI adapter card, such as those made by Adaptec. SCSI cards are fairly common for Windows machines, so your nearby computer store is likely to have a decent selection, as well as someone who can help you choose the right type for your application. FireWire (official name IEEE 1394 protocol) is another way for a hard drive to connect externally to a computer, and while not quite as fast as SCSI, FireWire is fast enough to offload data from your internal hard drive (which you can use as your primary, "capturing" drive for recording).

Drives used for digital audio require a fast access time (better than 15 ms, although that's sluggish if you expect to get lots of tracks), high rotational speed (7200 rpm is typical), and "A/V" operation. Hard disks periodically calibrate themselves, which you don't want to have happen while recording digital audio or a CD. A/V types postpone calibration to periods of inactivity. In any event, the faster the drive, the better the performance; interestingly, bigger drives are often faster than smaller-capacity drives.

Computer hard disks come in sizes from 10 gigabytes (billions of bytes, abbreviated GB) up to 80GB and more. At present hard drives are rapidly growing in capacity and speed (in fact, it's getting difficult to buy a drive smaller than 20GB), and prices continue to drop.

Removable-Media Drives. Removable-media drives are also upping their speed and capacity. Early drives featured 44 or 88MB of storage; 100MB and 250MB disks (e.g., the Iomega ZIP format) are now commonplace, and removable hard drives (that go in and out of a machine via a caddy or a special holder) are becoming the norm (see Figure 14).

Recording to removable cartridges is doable, but in general, these are best for backing up audio. It's more common to record audio to a traditional hard drive, then back up the data to a removable drive. Other removable backup options include magneto-optical drives (which, while slower than fixed hard drives, are very robust and can store up to 4.6GB of data) and special DAT cassette decks (these store 2.4GB and more

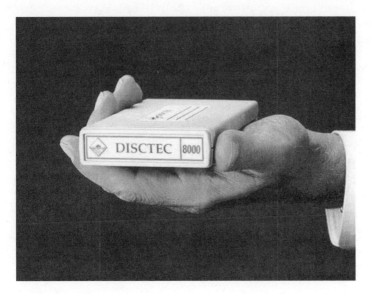

Figure 14

Removable hard disks are an ideal way to store digital audio files, which are often too big to fit on conventional removable media, like Zip disks. The Disctec 8000 fits in the palm of your hand, yet can hold from 2 to 20 GB of data. It slides easily into and out of a special holder in the computer's drive bay.

with data compression; ordinary DAT recorders can error-correct digital audio without perceptible signal degradation, but they're not reliable for computer files because individual bytes can become corrupted). However, backing up to DAT is quite slow.

Recordable CDs. Recordable CDs are another option, as the prices of both CD recording hardware and blank CDs have declined dramatically in recent years. CD-recordable media have a storage capacity of 74 minutes. Rewritable CDs (CD-RWs) are commonplace, and are more environmentally friendly than the non-reusable, "write-once" types (though they're a bit more expensive).

Synthesizers

Classic analog synthesizers use discrete analog components (transistors, diodes, capacitors, etc.) to create devices called *oscillators*. These generate simple, periodic electrical waveforms, such as sawtooth, triangle, and square waves (so named because of their shape when viewed on an oscilloscope; see Figure 15).

The oscillator's signal (or a mix of multiple oscillators) then goes through a *voltage-controlled filter* (VCF), which modifies the oscillator's basic timbre by changing its harmonic structure. Like most filters, this changes frequency response in a selectable, predictable way. The key filter parameter, *cutoff frequency*, determines which frequencies are boosted or attenuated, as opposed to passing through the filter unaltered.

The filtered signal then proceeds though a *voltage-controlled amplifier* (VCA), which determines the loudness contour (dynamics).

Figure 15

A few cycles of classic synthesizer waveforms

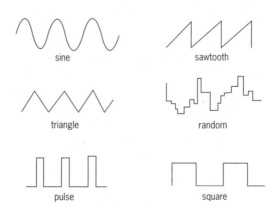

sine

sawtooth

triangle

random

pulse

square

Both the VCF and VCA are controlled by modules called *envelope generators*, which shape the overall sound dynamically by changing the VCF cutoff frequency and VCA gain over the course of a note. With the help of the envelope generators, the raw buzz of an oscillator can swell and fade away slowly like a string orchestra, start and stop abruptly like an organ, or start quickly and fade out smoothly like a plucked guitar string.

Today, most synthesizers create sound digitally, but many of them still use the same concepts to shape sound. Instead of producing a simple periodic waveform, digital oscillators typically play back a digitally sampled recording of an actual sound, such as a note played on trumpet or bass guitar. This is called *sample playback* synthesis. Before reaching the output, the sample still passes through a digital filter, which shapes the tone, and through an amplifier stage, which applies an amplitude envelope to each note. You'll see lots of bells and whistles grafted onto the sample playback process, but the basics don't change much from one instrument to another.

Sample playback is common in both $100 sound cards and $5,000 synthesizers, but many factors influence differences in sound quality between low-end instruments and expensive ones. The amount of memory available for samples (measured in megabytes of ROM) has much to do with the samples' variety and quality. The sample rate at which the samples were originally recorded, and the rate at which they're played back, affects the synth's high-frequency response. (Pro instruments typically have a 44.1kHz sample playback rate, the same rate as CD recordings, or higher.) More expensive instruments generally have better digital filters as well.

Transposition is an important part of sampling technology. To make a long story very short, a sample is recorded at one pitch—let's say a trumpet note at Middle C. Rather than record a separate sample for every key, which takes up a great deal of memory, playing notes above and below Middle C triggers the same sample. However, the keyboard digitally retunes the sample "on the fly" to a higher or lower pitch. Usually, a sample can survive being tuned up or down by a couple of half-steps without any drastic effect on the sound quality, but greater transpositions can introduce unwanted sonic artifacts. A sample that has been pitch-shifted too far down can sound grainy or dull; shifting too far up can sound thin and toylike. Then again, sometimes this is what you want, but it's fatal when trying to emulate orchestral instruments.

To make a synth "trumpet" (or any other instrument) sound more realistic across a wide range of the keyboard, samples are taken at multiple pitches (this is called multisampling). These samples are then "mapped" to a keyboard so that each of them has to play only a narrow range of keys. For example, an instrument might be sampled every three or four semitones.

It's quite difficult to create a seamless timbral match when transitioning from one sample to another, even if the samples are of the same instrument, played by the same player, into the same microphone. This is especially true when one of the samples is being transposed upward (say, from Middle C to the F above it) and another downward (say, from the C an octave higher down to F#). The point on the keyboard at which one sample meets another is called a multisample split point. It takes considerable effort to avoid an undesirable jump in sound quality between one sample and the next. The number of samples in a multisample, the care with which they are matched, the lengths of the individual samples (longer is better), the creative use of filtering to "mellow out" pitches that are transposed upward, and the care with which the samples are looped are among the factors that affect the sound quality.

Other types of digital synthesis are not based on sample playback, but instead create complex, musically interesting timbres using mathematical formulas rather than recordings of "real" instruments. One familiar example is FM (frequency modulation) synthesis. Although FM has gotten a bad name because a simple form of it is used in inexpensive sound cards, in more powerful FM instruments it's capable of creating sounds that are both musically pleasing and more responsive to the player's musical gestures than sample playback. A newer technology, called physical modeling, goes much further than FM in generating expressive, responsive tones; it creates a computer model of an instrument's sound, and "plugs in" different numbers into these models to create the various tones.

Some electronic keyboard instruments only play preset sounds, while others are user-programmable. Synthesizer programming is the process of giving the sound-generating circuitry instructions about what it's supposed to do when you play a note. Programmable synths do this by allowing you to edit the values of certain parameters that influence sound quality, such as vibrato speed, filter cutoff frequency, oscillator tuning, attack time, and so on. Programmable synthesizers have a block of RAM (user memory) set aside for storing new sound programs, which may consist of hundreds of possible parameters.

Incidentally, sound programs are sometimes called patches rather than programs because 30 years ago, analog synthesizers used actual patch cords for connecting the oscillators, filters, and VCAs to one another.

Tone Modules. Once you can send note-on and note-off messages down a MIDI cable, there's no reason to put a set of keys on every sound generator. In fact, you can save a lot of money by buying one MIDI instrument with a keyboard, or for that matter a MIDI guitar or percussion controller (see "Alternate Controllers," below), and then adding to your rig by hooking up tone modules. (On the other hand, for live playing, you might want to have several keyboards handy.) A tone module typically has everything that a keyboard synthesizer has, except the keyboard, and makes sound only in response to incoming MIDI messages. (See Figure 16 for an example of a tone module.) As we explain a few more key concepts in this section, remember that these apply equally to synths and tone modules.

Most current tone modules are multitimbral, meaning that a single module can respond on several MIDI channels at once—usually on all 16 channels. Each channel will usually produce a different sound—perhaps piano on channel 1, strings on channel 2, bass on channel 3, and so on. Each multitimbral part can play polyphonically—that is, play chords, up to the polyphonic voice limit of the module.

This is an important concept to grasp: Each tone module has a limit to how many voices (i.e., how many notes) it can play at once, which is called polyphony. Many modules provide 32-note polyphony or even more, but some of the richer, more interesting synth patches "layer" two

Figure 16

Ever seen an orchestra without bows, reeds, and valves? E-MU's Proteus 1000 module contains stereo digital samples (recordings) of individual instrument sounds, but with no visible means to play them. Connect the module to a keyboard's MIDI Out jack and you can play a virtual orchestra as well as synths and drums. This unit features 64-voice polyphony, over a thousand presets, four layers per preset, an expansion slot, playback on 16 MIDI channels, and stereo effects.

or more voices per note. If you're using patches in which each note requires two voices, a "32-note polyphonic" module will only produce 16 notes simultaneously. If you try to play more notes than this, either the excess note-on messages will have no effect, or they will cause some notes that are still sounding to drop out. This phenomenon, sometimes called note stealing, can be especially troublesome when a single tone module plays back a complex musical arrangement.

Most tone modules come equipped with some sort of onboard effects processor (see "Effects Processors," below). This can add reverb, chorusing, and other sonic enhancements. You will probably be able to set the effect send level separately for each of the multitimbral parts. For example, you might want lots of reverb on the piano but only a little on the bass, and both reverb and chorus on the strings. Many tone modules have only one effects processor, so the available processor(s) must be shared by all of the multitimbral parts. However, more sophisticated modules allow individual processing for specific parts.

If you're using the module to play only one sound—that is, not playing multitimbrally—you should be able to obtain a richer, fuller sound by using the effects settings that have been programmed into the individual patch. But individual patches that were programmed with spectacular effects may sound a lot less wonderful when used in a multitimbral setup that utilizes more generic effects. Conversely, if you use the module's copy utility to copy the great effect in the string patch to your multitimbral setup, the bass, piano, and drums may sound quite odd because they have to share the string effect. Since the module has only a limited number of hardware effects processors, it's often not possible to use several patches in the same multitimbral setup and have each patch retain its original effects.

A tone module's operating system is the onboard software that reads and responds to the front-panel buttons and displays messages in the LCD or other display. Operating systems are sometimes upgraded by manufacturers to provide enhancements or fix software bugs. The upgrade will usually be in the form of a chip that plugs into a socket on the circuit board, although some older samplers load their operating system from a floppy at the start of each session. If you're not familiar with how to install a chip, have it done by an authorized service center. While replacing a chip is easy, if you accidentally break off one of the chip's pins, plug it in backwards, or fry it with a static electricity discharge, the chip can't be fixed.

Alternate Controllers. As mentioned before, MIDI was developed as a language for controlling electronic keyboard instruments. However, not everyone wanted to abandon performance techniques perfected over years of practice on guitars, drums, and wind instruments in order to be able to make noise with MIDI tone modules. Not only that, but the traditional black-and-white keyboard is just plain lousy at certain types of expressive musical nuances. To address these two problems, a number of alternative MIDI controllers have been developed (see Figure 17).

Alternate controllers actually predate MIDI: The Lyricon wind synthesizer, for example, used a saxophone-type interface to actuate an analog synthesizer. Robert Moog also produced ribbon and drum controllers.

MIDI has made it practical for manufacturers of alternate controllers to do what they do best—build a sensitive performance interface—while taking advantage of existing tone-generator technology. For example, percussion controllers can hook up to any drum machine or sampler. More visionary alternate controllers like the Buchla Thunder (touch pads) and Buchla Lightning (infrared wands) have also appeared from time to time; guitar, Chapman Stick, violin, voice, and many other MIDI controllers are available (and achieve varying degrees of success, both in terms of commerciality and ability to translate performance gestures to MIDI).

Another option for players of traditional instruments is the pitch-to-MIDI converter. This translates a monophonic musical line, such as you might produce by singing or playing sax into a microphone, into a stream of MIDI data. Pitch-to-MIDI conversion technology is not perfect, but works surprisingly well, especially if you're using it as an input into a sequencer, where you can later clean up any glitches that the converter might introduce.

Figure 17

MIDI lets you separate the controlling instrument from the sound generator. This wind controller provides an alternative to the traditional piano-style keyboard. The strength of the player's breath can be tied to the volume of the notes.

MIDI Master Keyboards. MIDI master keyboards look like a keyboard synthesizer, but they only transmit MIDI data and make no sound by themselves. Small, lightweight master keyboards are especially useful with computer sound card music setups; some models are even battery powered.

Why not buy a master keyboard that also makes sound—in other words, a synthesizer—thus saving money by getting both keys and a sound generator at the same time? That's a valid question. However, to meet a particular price point, a synth might skimp a bit on keyboard features, whereas a dedicated master keyboard is optimized for playing "feel" and flexibility. It may have a better mechanical action—many have 88 keys that are weighted to simulate a piano action—as well as a bank of programmable buttons and sliders that can send out any MIDI message. You may also be able to program the keyboard to split into as many as eight separate zones, each transmitting on its own MIDI channel. This allows up to eight different sounds to play at once, or be layered with one another for a fuller sound.

Drum Machines. For a few short years between the advent of affordable microprocessors and MIDI's birth, drum machines were a vital part of pop music. They included both a selection of drum sounds (either synthesized simulations or actual digital recordings) and a sequencer for recording drum beats—often called patterns—and stringing the patterns together into songs. In place of a keyboard, a drum machine offers a bank of pads to which you can assign various drum sounds (see Figure 18). In recent years, all but the least expensive drum machines have had

Figure 18

A drum machine is a synthesizer that's been optimized for playing back percussion sounds. The 16 large buttons on this Akai MPC4000 can each play a different sound, which are typically drum samples (but programmable as other sounds, or even loops). Drum machines also include pattern-based sequencers that allow you to build drum beats by overdubbing new sounds on a looping track.

velocity-sensitive pads. Hit them harder and the sound gets louder, just as it does on a real drum.

MIDI sequencing has cut into the drum machine's turf pretty heavily. Most musicians prefer to record an entire sequence (drum parts and other parts) in a single sequencer. You'll still see dedicated percussion tone modules now and then, but they tend not to have built-in sequencing.

Another variation on the theme is the "groove box," which combines drum-machine-style pads with sampling and full-featured MIDI sequencing. Many players swear by these because of their fast, efficient interface which makes it easy to lay down grooves quickly.

One advantage of drum machines is that striking their pads with your fingers is more like drumming than entering a drum part on a keyboard. Some machines also have features like dedicated hi-hat open/close sliders, or the ability to add types of performance nuances that can't easily be duplicated by a MIDI sequencer. As a result, many rap and dance music artists use drum machines for their real-time features.

General MIDI

General MIDI is where synthesizers, MIDI, and consumer electronics meet. As MIDI technology began to appear in consumer-oriented products such as computer sound cards and digital pianos, a problem surfaced. Each manufacturer used its own method of storing patches in memory. Remember, MIDI doesn't specify actual sounds; it only transmits data. A MIDI program change message with a value of 29 might call up a flute program on one synth, a combo organ on a second synth, and a drum kit on a third. Especially when sharing Standard MIDI Files (see below) among MIDI equipment, getting the music to sound as the composer or arranger intended was difficult or impossible without detailed notes that specify which instruments should correspond to which program changes.

General MIDI (GM) addresses this problem, and some related ones. GM is not a change in MIDI data format; rather, it's a list of basic features required by any synth that wants to claim GM compatibility (see "The General MIDI Rulebook" sidebar). First and foremost, GM provides a list of 128 standard sound programs. Program 37, for instance, is always a slap electric bass sound. An arranger who wants to be sure that a GM playback synth plays a slap electric bass for a particular track can simply insert a program change message with a value of 37 at the beginning of the track.

THE GENERAL MIDI RULEBOOK

In order to conform to GM System Level 1, a sound source must:

• Respond to messages on all 16 MIDI channels.

• Be 24-voice polyphonic, with dynamic allocation (polyphony can be 16-voice for pitched instruments, 8-voice for drums). This means that the synthesizer must be able to play 24 simultaneous voices (notes), and automatically reassign voices to play new notes whenever required by the musical input from MIDI.

• Have drums and percussion sounds assigned to MIDI channel 10 (offering at least 47 specified instruments mapped to specific keys).

• Have a minimum of 128 tones and sound effects set out according to GM categories and program change locations (see the GM tone map, page 40).

• Implement the following MIDI controllers: 1 (mod wheel), 6 and 38 (data entry), 7 (volume), 10 (pan, i.e., stereo position), 11 (expression), 64 (sustain pedal), 100 and 101 (master tuning), 121 (reset all controllers), and 123 (all notes off).

• Respond to MIDI velocity, pitch-bend, and aftertouch.

• Pitch its instruments so that Middle C corresponds to MIDI note number 60.

GM tones: instruments & program numbers. Punching up the program numbers shown on page 40 on a GM module will call up the corresponding sounds (except on MIDI channel 10, which is dedicated to playing drum sounds). If your instrument or sequencer numbers programs from 0 to 127 instead of 1 to 128, subtract 1 from each value shown.

GM has some additional requirements. A GM instrument must provide at least 24 notes of polyphony, respond on all 16 MIDI channels at once, and its drum kit (which is always assigned to channel 10) must be laid out with a specific note-number assignment—kick drum on low C (MIDI note #48), snare drum on D, and so on.

Note that GM does not impose an upper end on an instrument's capabilities. For example, it can have 96-note polyphony and 512 programs, and still qualify as a GM instrument. GM provides only a minimum standard for instrument performance. Both Roland and Yamaha have proposed supersets to GM. Roland's GS instruments and Yamaha's XG instruments comply with the GM spec, but they offer an added palette of features that are available to other synth manufacturers, should they wish to use them, and to developers of SMFs (Standard MIDI Files), who can put GS and/or XG data into their sequences to enhance the quality of the music (see "General Plus" sidebar).

Problems with GM. General MIDI was intended to solve problems, not create them. However, some GM definitions are rather fuzzy. Consider polyphony: What is a voice? GM says that an instrument must have a minimum of 24 voices. This sounds fine until you realize that some manufacturers refer, perfectly legitimately, to a voice as an instrument's simplest, individual sound-producing generator. In theory, an instrument can be 24-voice, but in practice, since all its sounds may use two or three "voices," it may only be 12-voice or even 8-voice polyphonic. Fortunately, the current trend is towards 64-voice or greater polyphony, so no matter how these instruments slice up their memory, they should be able to generate 24 bona fide voices. When buying an older GM module, check to see how the device handles polyphony.

Though GM was a big step toward standardization, some complained that it didn't go far enough. Suppose a GM file is created while playing through one GM synth, then played back on a different GM synth. Quality can suffer because of a mismatch in balance between sounds— the violin sound on synth A might be way louder than the violin sound on synth B, for example. So if you compose a piano/violin duet on synth A and play it back on synth B, the violin part could become practically inaudible. This kind of problem shouldn't happen, but it does.

The root of the inconsistency is an incomplete definition in the General MIDI standard. When GM was defined, only the names of the required sounds were specified, not how they sounded. That was a necessary compromise at the time, but it's now a major problem.

A limitation of GM is that 128 instrumental sounds and 47 percussion sounds aren't enough for many applications. If GM is your entire sonic world and a desired sound is not available, you have to settle for an approximation from within the GM set. Some manufacturers have tried to improve matters by creating compatible extensions to GM that provide hundreds of additional sounds. But even though the Roland GS and Yamaha XG systems try to maintain backward compatibility, a MIDI file that is optimized for these extended sets doesn't sound as good when played back on the standard GM instrument set. Furthermore, no General MIDI extension has been adopted as a standard by the industry as a whole.

No manufacturer is deliberately going to substitute a bassoon tone where the electric piano is supposed to be, but sound is subjective. Nowhere is the disparity more noticeable than on violin tones. A violin can be played sweetly and gently, or bowed fiercely. Not only will this produce vastly different sounds, but different attacks, different decays, and even different tunings. GM specifies that program 41 is a violin, and one violin is all you get.

GENERAL PLUS

Although General MIDI provides a degree of standardization to MIDI tone modules, many people feel it doesn't go far enough. Here are highlights of two other standards that build on GM.

Roland GS

While Roland was careful to make GS fully compatible with the GM standard, this enhanced format—adopted so far only by Roland and several sound card manufacturers such as CrystaLake Multimedia and Orchid Technology—offers additional sounds that are selected by using MIDI program changes in conjunction with MIDI Bank Select commands.

NRPNs (MIDI Non-Registered Parameter Numbers) are harnessed to give users an element of sound-programming control over synthesis parameters such as filter cutoff frequency.

A special SFX (sound effects) set is also offered.

Yamaha XG

The XG format expands on GS as well as GM, requiring a minimum of 32-voice polyphony, three separately controllable effects processors, plus over a dozen more MIDI-controllable synthesis parameters (such as attack time, brightness, etc.). NRPNs are also supported. While GM is limited to one bank of 128 sounds, XG defines over 100 banks of 128. There are several dedicated effects banks, which should please the gaming crowd.

GENERAL MIDI TONE MAP

Piano
1. Acoustic grand piano
2. Bright acoustic piano
3. Electric grand piano
4. Honky-tonk piano
5. Electric piano 1
6. Electric piano 2
7. Harpsichord
8. Clavi

Chromatic Percussion
9. Celesta
10. Glockenspiel
11. Music box
12. Vibraphone
13. Marimba
14. Xylophone
15. Tubular bells
16. Dulcimer

Organ
17. Drawbar organ
18. Percussive organ
19. Rock organ
20. Church organ
21. Reed organ
22. Accordion
23. Harmonica
24. Tango accordion

Guitar
25. Acoustic nylon guitar
26. Acoustic steel string guitar
27. Electric guitar (jazz)
28. Electric guitar (clean)
29. Electric guitar (muted)
30. Overdriven guitar
31. Distortion guitar
32. Guitar harmonics

Bass
33. Acoustic bass
34. Electric bass (fingered)
35. Electric bass (picked)
36. Fretless bass
37. Slap bass 1
38. Slap bass 2
39. Synth bass 1
40. Synth bass 2

Strings
41. Violin
42. Viola
43. Cello
44. Contrabass
45. Tremolo strings
46. Pizzicato strings
47. Orchestral harp
48. Timpani

Ensemble
49. String ensemble 1
50. String ensemble 2
51. Synth strings 1
52. Synth strings 2

53. Choir aahs
54. Vocal oohs
55. Synth voice
56. Orchestra hit

Brass

57. Trumpet
58. Trombone
59. Tuba
60. Muted trumpet
61. French horn
62. Brass section
63. Synth brass 1
64. Synth brass 2

Reed

65. Soprano sax
66. Alto sax
67. Tenor sax
68. Baritone sax
69. Oboe
70. English horn
71. Bassoon
72. Clarinet

Pipe

73. Piccolo
74. Flute
75. Recorder
76. Pan flute
77. Blown bottle
78. Shakuhachi

79. Whistle
80. Ocarina

Lead Synth

81. Lead 1 (square wave)
82. Lead 2 (sawtooth wave)
83. Lead 3 (synth calliope)
84. Lead 4 (chiff)
85. Lead 5 (charang)
86. Lead 6 (voice)
87. Lead 7 (sawtooth wave in fifths)
88. Lead 8 (bass + lead)

Synth Pad

89. Pad 1 (New Age, fantasia)
90. Pad 2 (warm)
91. Pad 3 (polysynth)
92. Pad 4 (space choir)
93. Pad 5 (bowed glass)
94. Pad 6 (metallic)
95. Pad 7 (halo)
96. Pad 8 (sweep)

Synth Effects

97. FX1 (ice rain)
98. FX2 (soundtrack)
99. FX3 (crystal)
100. FX4 (atmosphere)
101. FX5 (brightness)
102. FX6 (goblin)

103. FX7 (echoes)
104. FX8 (sci-fi)
105. Sitar
106. Banjo
107. Shamisen
108. Koto
109. Kalimba
110. Bagpipe
111. Fiddle
112. Shanai

Percussive

113. Tinkle bell
114. Agogo
115. Steel drum
116. Wood block
117. Taiko
118. Melodic tom
119. Synth drum
120. Reverse cymbal

Sound Effects

121. Guitar fret noise
122. Breath noise
123. Seashore
124. Bird tweet
125. Telephone
126. Helicopter
127. Applause
128. Gunshot

This can be disastrous, as a violin part written for and played back on one module could sound completely different on another. Composers working in GM can either avoid such unpredictable sounds, or design sequences tailor-made for a particular GM instrument.

Another problem concerns how individual GM sounds respond to controller messages. GM proclaims that instruments should respond to a list of controllers such as volume, mod wheel, aftertouch, etc., but it does not specify _how_ it should respond. On one module, a mod wheel message might introduce vibrato (a slow pitch oscillation), while on another, it could introduce panning effects that cause the sound to spin crazily between the speakers. This difference in response can even occur between two sounds in the same module. And even if the mod wheel introduced vibrato on both of the two modules (or sounds), General MIDI says nothing about the vibrato's rate or depth. The results could still be very different.

For these reasons, many professionals choose Roland's Sound Canvas as a standard of comparison and base their sequences on what will sound good when played back through this module.

Standard MIDI Files. The Standard MIDI File (SMF) allows the sharing of data between different models of sequencers, even those running on different computers. Each sequencer uses its own format for saving sequence data to disk, and it would be rare for a sequencer created by one manufacturer to be able to read files created by another manufacturer's software. Most sequencers, however, will also store and load their sequences as SMFs. Some types of data (e.g., lyric or notation info) that are peculiar to an individual sequencer will be lost when the sequence is stored as an SMF, but all musical data remains intact.

SMFs can be transferred between sequencers and between the Mac and PC platforms, and between a computer and a stand-alone sequencer. Many online services also offer SMFs, and an entire cottage industry of commercial music in SMF format, like Band-in-a-Box, have sprung up.

Even stand-alone and built-in sequencers that format their disks according to their own schemes will usually read SMFs off of MS-DOS disks. (Handy hint: If you need to transfer files between two sequencers and neither of them will format disks in MS-DOS format, you can probably solve the problem by buying a box of preformatted disks at your neighborhood computer store. If they're both Macintosh sequencers, of course, this isn't necessary.)

Samplers

Instruments called samplers have become a vital ingredient in contemporary music-making. The concept behind sampling is simple: Plug in a microphone (or the line-level output from a mixer, CD player, VCR, DAT, etc.), record any sound, and then play it back from a MIDI keyboard. With a sampler, you can make audio collages that draw from a wide variety of sources—old movies (better get copyright clearance, though), your friends' conversation, the roar of a passing freight train—you name it.

Many computer sound cards support basic sampling, and now software is available to play individual digital recordings (samples) in response to MIDI commands (in such programs as Bitheadz Unity DS-1, TASCAM GigaStudio, IK Multimedia SampleTanks, and Steinberg HALion). A dedicated sampler, however, is optimized for MIDI operation.

Digital sampling was first introduced as a way of triggering recordings of real sounds (violin, timpani, or dog barks) from a keyboard. In other words, samplers began as a modern electronic version of '60s tape-playback keyboards like the Mellotron. Today, they're still used for this purpose. If your sampler is equipped with a SCSI port, you can hook up a CD-ROM drive and quickly load material from a variety of discs recorded by professional sound developers. If you have a CD filled with high-quality orchestral samples, and if you understand classical orchestration, you can almost fool knowledgeable listeners into believing they're hearing the real thing. In fact, samplers routinely "sweeten" the true orchestras heard on major movie soundtracks.

Sound developers typically sell material for samplers in both audio CD and CD-ROM format. You can record samples from an audio CD using the sampler's analog sampling input. CD-ROMs are more expensive (as are the SCSI-equipped samplers that can connect to CD-ROM drives) because they include both the audio samples themselves and program data for setting up the sampler to play the samples. Finally, some computer programs (such as Steinberg WaveLab) can import samples from an audio CD loaded into the computer's CD-ROM drive. This requires a CD-ROM drive, and you still have to figure out how to get the samples into the sampler—usually via SCSI.

The main advantage of a sampler over a typical sample-playback synthesizer is that the samples in a sampler play back from RAM (random access memory) rather than ROM (read-only memory). Because of this, you can load a different string orchestra for every recording session, customize the samples as required, or even plug in a microphone and make samples of noises that no synthesizer designer ever imagined. Once the sample is in the sampler, you can play it backwards, or perform edits like cutting single words out of a spoken sentence, then pasting them back together in a different order.

By sampling a beat from a record and *looping* it (that is, setting a one- or two-bar segment to play over and over), even musicians with limited technical ability can quickly put together a rhythm track. To release a song that you create by this method, you have to get permission from whomever owns the record(s) that you sampled from (unless you enjoy being sued). If you're doing it strictly for fun, though, you can sample whatever you like.

Hip-hop and techno artists often get their beat loops from the sampling CDs mentioned earlier. These contain no complete songs, only dozens or hundreds of rhythm loops. Using such disks, you can mix and match beats to create your own song arrangements.

Like synthesizers, samplers are generally equipped with filters and envelopes for shaping the raw sampled sound. Many also include DSP algorithms with which you can process the samples in various ways. Typical DSP applications include *time-stretching*, which changes a sample's length without altering the pitch (and hopefully, without altering the timbre too much), and normalization, which boosts a quietly recorded sample's level so that it is as loud as possible without distorting.

Effects Processors

Electronic sound that comes straight from a synthesizer can be pretty sterile. Even an acoustic instrument track, such as guitar or conga drums, can sound naked when you listen to it just the way the microphone picked it up. The purpose of effects devices is to enhance these sounds. When effects are used subtly, the listener tends not to notice that they're being used at all; the result is merely that the sound is more natural, which helps the track "sit better" in the mix. More drastic use of effects can enrich a sound in spectacular ways, or even transform it beyond recognition.

Some synths and samplers have built-in effects processors. Free-standing processors generally come in a standard 19" rackmount configuration, and typically patch into a mixer's effects send and return jacks. In this setup, the effects processor's contribution to the overall sound returns to the mixer and blends with the rest of the mix. Less expensive effects are available as *stompboxes* (floor units with built-in footswitches) that patch between a guitar and amp.

In years past, effects devices often used analog circuits or even mechanical parts, such as the metal springs in a spring reverb. These days, except for some stompboxes, most effects are digital and use real-time DSP (digital signal processing—a fancy term for effects). DSP is not a guarantee of high quality: A low-quality digital reverb still sounds cheap compared to a high-end digital reverb. But overall, the trend is toward far better sound quality and greater power for the price. The multieffects processor, which can produce several types of effects at once, is often a good choice for smaller studios.

The most common effect is reverb. Reverb simulates the echoing wash of sound in a concert hall, gymnasium, tiled room, or cathedral. It's important to make a distinction between reverb, which is a more or less smooth ambience, and delay, an effect that produces individual, distinct repetitions of a sound. Just to keep things confusing, both reverb and delay are sometimes called "echo."

Chorusing, flanging, and phasing are effects that add a rich rolling or whooshing quality to the sound. Stereo chorusing also enhances the sound spatially by spreading it across the stereo field. Although there's some overlap between the concepts, phasing (also called phase-shifting) is usually a more focused effect that is most prominent in the upper overtones of the sound, making it sound whispery or ocean-like.

Probably the most "natural" effects processing is _equalization_ (EQ). An equalizer boosts or cuts selected frequencies in the audio spectrum. The usual applications are to help a track "cut through" better in a mix, reduce "boominess" in the low end, or prevent instruments in a mix from mushing together into an indistinguishable audio mess by cutting response for some instruments at frequencies that interfere with other instruments.

Equalizers designed for serious signal processing come in two main varieties—_graphic_ and _parametric_. A graphic equalizer typically has a number of fixed frequency bands, each adjusted by its own front-panel cut/boost slider. A parametric usually has fewer bands of boost/cut, but offers greater control over each band by including a variable width, or _Q_, control that determines how broad the affected range is.

Dynamic effects alter the loudness characteristics of a signal by restricting or expanding the available dynamic range. (Some companies use the term "dynamic effects" to refer to effects devices whose processing parameters can be controlled in real time via MIDI. While that's an important application, it's not what we're talking about here.) The most common dynamic effects, compression and limiting, can tame signals that have a few loud peaks sticking out above a generally lower level. Compressing the peaks allows boosting of the overall level, because the signal has a more even dynamic level. Compression is often used to bring out the quieter bits of a sound, but it's important to remember that compression can alter a sound's tone color. See Chapter 4 for more on compression.

Other categories of effects include distortion, audio enhancers, noise-gating, and vocoding.

Mixers

If you have more instrument outputs than amplifier inputs, you'll need a mixer (also called a board or console; in England, it's called a desk). Mixers are indispensable in recording. They may look intimidating because of the sheer number of knobs and sliders spread across their face, but they're fairly simple to understand, because the controls for each individual channel are basically the same as those for all of the other channels—learn one channel and you've learned them all. The smallest mixers have as few as four or eight channels, while the largest have 96 channels or even more. To the right of the channel controls, a mixer will usually have a set of *master* controls, and perhaps some *sub-mix* controls. The submix section is a separate output group that provides an additional mix to the main mix.

Let's start by looking at the channels (see Figure 19).

A channel has some sort of input jack. This links directly to an *input trim* knob, the first stage in the channel's signal path. The trim control can turn down a signal that's too loud, or boost one that's too soft, to ensure that the rest of the channel circuitry receives a signal that's at the right level for clean performance—loud enough to be above any noise, but not so loud as to cause distortion. (Sometimes the console will provide only a button to reduce the level by a fixed amount; this is called a

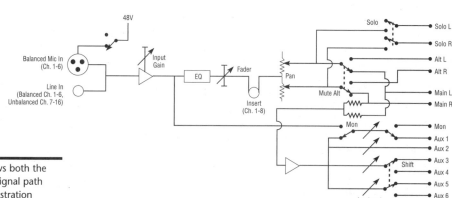

Figure 19

This diagram shows both the schematic of the signal path (right) and the illustration (above) of one channel of a 16-channel mixer. The signal enters at the left, gets processed by the EQ, faders, and whatever's plugged into the insert jack, then exits at the right.

pad.) After setting the trim properly, you use the channel's main *fader* (the slider or knob conveniently located nearest the bottom edge of the mixer) to set how loud the channel's output will be in the mix.

Faders are also called *attenuators*, because they attenuate (diminish) the loudness. Setting the fader at the bottom of its throw gives infinite attenuation, because no sound gets through.

Above the channel fader you'll most likely find a *panpot*, which positions the channel's signal anywhere in the stereo field between the left and right speakers, and perhaps a pair of buttons for *muting* and *soloing* the channel. The mute button removes the channel from the mix without having to change the channel fader, which may already be set at the precise level called for by the song's mix. Solo allows you to hear only that channel.

Most mixers offer some EQ for each channel. The usual layout for semi-pro mixers provides low and high shelving EQ from a pair of knobs labeled "bass" and "treble," and one *semi-parametric* midrange band. The low and high EQ are called "shelving" because a graph of their response curve looks vaguely like a drawing of a shelf (see Figure 20). With a treble shelf, the EQ boosts or cuts any portion of the signal above a factory-preset frequency (such as 10kHz). Similarly, for bass, the EQ affects any portion of the signal below a preset frequency, such as 100Hz. Some shelving EQs even let you adjust the shelf frequency.

The semi-parametric midrange band has two controls: frequency and boost/cut. A fully parametric band (see Figure 21) can adjust not only the center frequency and the amount of cut or boost, but also the *width* of the affected frequency band.

Each channel will also have from two to six *auxiliary* sends (also called *effects* sends). These knobs determine how much of the channel's sound gets sent to a separate output jack that patches to an effects processor's input. Several channels' signals can all be sent to a single effect's send jack. The effects processor's output then patches into the mixer's *aux return* jacks. The master section usually includes knobs for turning the effects returns up or down. When overdubbing, aux sends can also create a separate headphone mix that the musicians can monitor. For example, a bass player might want a drums-heavy mix in order to best lock in with the beat.

A mixer designed for use with a multitrack tape deck will usually have a *tape/line* switch for each channel. This switch allows selecting whether the channel input comes from the line input jack or one of the tape

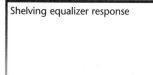

Figure 20

Shelving equalizer response

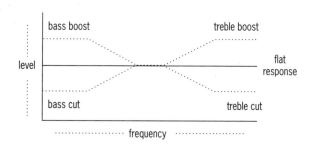

Figure 21

A parametric equalizer allows independent control over frequency, level, boost/cut, and bandwidth

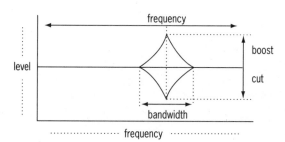

recorder's outputs. During initial tracking (the process of recording the song), the tape/line switches will be in the line position. During overdubbing or mixdown, they will be switched to the tape position, and the faders will be used for mixing the song from the multitrack tape deck to a stereo mixdown deck.

Each channel may also have an *insert* jack. The insert is often a ¼" stereo tip-ring-sleeve jack. If no plug is in the jack, the jack is "invisible" to the channel. Inserting a plug interrupts the signal passing through the channel: the channel signal is "sent" from the tip connector, and whatever signal "returns" on the ring connector passes on through the rest of the mixer. An insert allows patching an effects processor "in-line" with a single channel without using up an effects send and return.

Once all the channels are mixed, they proceed to the *master* section. This will have, at the very least, level controls for the left and right outputs. It may also have effects return-level controls, separate output levels for headphone outs, and perhaps the output level controls for a submix.

Mixers commonly have two or more *VU meters*, which graphically show the levels for various signals ("VU" stands for "volume unit"). The VU meters may be the old-fashioned, mechanical type, with needles on a gauge, or they may have multiple LEDs. LED meters often use different colors, such as green for normal, yellow for strong signals, and red for signals that are about to clip. A single pair of meters may be switchable to show the levels at several different points in the signal path, or each channel and output bus may have its own dedicated meter.

Mixers are easy to outgrow. You'll need at least twice as many inputs as recorder tracks, and more if you use a lot of virtual MIDI tracks (i.e., MIDI instruments driven by a sequencer synced to a multitrack recorder) or do live recording with multiple mics. Note that MIDI-controllable automated mixdown accessories can help create more professional mixes, as you only have to get a mixing move right once—the automation remembers it.

Monitors

Compared to the complexities of synthesizers and computers, a speaker/amplifier system seems like a no-brainer: Turn it up, turn it down, end of story. But, in fact, there are some important considerations in choosing a monitoring setup.

Using a consumer-type stereo for studio monitoring is probably a bad idea, because consumer gear is often "juiced" to sound better. Both the lows and the highs are boosted, which means you won't get an accurate picture of what's being recorded to disk or tape. On the other hand, once you've crafted a rough mix it's a good idea to play it on as many different systems as possible, including boom boxes and car stereos. If it sounds good on a bad system, it will probably sound great on a great system. For years, pro studios with $5,000 speakers have also been equipped with cheap monitor systems to simulate the sound of an AM car radio or television set.

When shopping for speakers, take your own CD to the store. Because you know exactly what the source material is supposed to sound like, it will be easier to evaluate any coloration caused by the speakers and amp.

Most of the speaker enclosures you'll run into have both a *woofer*, which is a large speaker to reproduce the low frequencies, and a *tweeter* to handle the highs. This is a *two-way* monitoring system; a three-way system has a third speaker to handle the midrange frequencies. Two-way and three-way enclosures use *crossover networks* to separate the lows from the highs, so that each speaker can efficiently do what it does best. Note that three-way systems are not inherently better than two-way systems; the value of either approach depends on the design engineer's skill and the materials used.

For the most accurate representation of the sound, keep the speakers away from the walls and floor, since these surfaces tend to magnify the bass. Mount the speakers about one meter (three to four feet) from the position where your head will be, and about one meter apart, so that the speakers and your head form the points of an equilateral triangle. Mounting the speakers at this close distance will also help minimize any coloration that may be caused by the room—often a problem in home studios. Since high frequencies in particular are somewhat *directional*, point the speakers directly at the listening position. You can sometimes place the monitors on their sides, with the tweeters to the outside, to widen the field slightly (tweeters, because they handle the high frequencies, are more directional than woofers).

Should you include a subwoofer in your system? That depends on the type of music you're mixing, and on the size of your main speakers. The bigger the speaker, the better the bass. If you're trying to do a dance mix through 4" speakers (or worse, headphones), you may keep cranking the bass until it's way too hot for a larger sound system. On the other hand, if you're using a subwoofer, you may be tempted to pull back on the bass frequencies, and end up with a mix that's bass-shy.

While shopping for *passive* speakers (speakers that require a power amp), you may also want to upgrade your amp. If your amp's not powerful enough (100 watts per channel is recommended), it can be driven into distortion trying to keep up with the strong bass frequencies produced by electronic instruments. *Powered* monitors have the amplification system built in (see Figure 22). Manufacturers of these speakers claim they provide better stereo imaging as there is no crosstalk between the amp's left and right channels (as each speaker has its own amp). Also, while these speakers are heavier, you don't have to leave room for a separate amp.

It's vital that your speakers be wired in the correct polarity, with the + and - connectors hooked up the same way on both speakers. (This is only an issue with speakers that connect with actual bare-wire strands, not ¼" or XLR jacks.) If one speaker is wired backwards, the two speakers will be out of phase, and the stereo image will be ruined: Sounds that you pan to the center of the field won't appear to come from the center, but from the two sides. Also, phase cancellation will cause some frequencies to disappear.

Near-Field Monitors. A near-field monitor is a loudspeaker system designed specifically to be listened to in the near field—at an ideal listening distance of about one meter. They are smaller and produce less volume than large studio monitors, and are designed to operate in imperfect acoustic surroundings (home studios). Near-fields are by far the most popular type of monitors being sold, and you can find a good pair to suit any budget or small-studio needs.

When shopping for speakers, find a pair with a flat frequency response. Speaker frequency response is usually stated in the manufacturer's brochure, and it looks something like "20Hz–20kHz +1/-3dB." The plus-or-minus numbers tell you how much the speakers deviate from a flat frequency response. Ideally, the number should be as small as possible: +/-1dB is considered excellent.

Figure 22

The Mackie HR824 is a popular powered near-field monitor for commercial and project studios.

2

Digital Recording: What Do I Need?

Know Before You Go

Setting up a digital home studio isn't something that most of us do all at once. Maybe you start out by plugging your synthesizer into the aux inputs on your stereo. Then you splurge on a MiniDisc or cassette-based multitrack recorder, and a microphone. A year later you've added a rackmount sampler and a reverb. Another six months go by and you now have a computer with a sequencer program, the stereo has been replaced by a power amp and some monitor speakers, and you're eyeing that ad for a discount DAT deck. About this time, your significant other looks at the tangle of wires and gear in the corner of the living room and says, "Isn't it about time you built a space for that stuff out in the basement/closet/garage?"

Looks like you're a home studio owner.

FIVE RULES FOR MUSIC EQUIPMENT SUCCESS

Rule 1: In music, the three most important factors are sound, sound, and sound. If you don't like the sound, you won't be happy with the instrument or recorder, no matter what the salesperson is trying to tell you about its features.

Rule 2: For software, the three most important factors are compatibility, technical support, and compatibility. Compatibility means not only will this software run on your computer, but it will also work with all of the other software and hardware it's supposed to work with. Be skeptical of all claims. Where possible, try installing any software and verifying that it runs before you buy it.

Rule 3: There are no dumb questions. If you don't understand how something works, ask. If the explanation you get doesn't make sense, ask more questions.

Rule 4: Shop around. Never believe a salesperson who tells you you'll get a special deal if you buy today. That's a sales tactic. Keep looking until you're sure about what you want: chances are, that same great deal will still be available next week. Of course, this doesn't apply to used gear. If it's one of a kind, when it's gone it's gone. Shop around and compare even when you're broke; that way when you do have some bucks, you'll know whether or not you're looking at a bargain.

Rule 5: Don't worry about having the latest and greatest of everything. Put your energy into making wonderful music with what you have. Sometimes the greatest musical moments come from pushing equipment past the edge because you have to.

Home studios offer some wonderful advantages for musicians. You have the freedom to record what you want, when you want. You can do as many takes as you want without running up a bill. You can learn the allied arts of recording and arranging at your own pace, without having anybody lecture you about what's right and wrong.

All the same, working in a home studio is not guaranteed to be trouble free. Home studio owners wear a lot of hats: You have to be the engineer, arranger, and producer as well as the performer. When something goes wrong, it's up to you to fix it, and headaches caused by hardware and software problems will definitely sap your creative energy. Working alone, you may not have the benefit of feedback from anybody else, which can make the artistic, technological, and financial decisions a lot tougher. This chapter and the ones following are geared toward helping you wear your different hats with confidence. This chapter will help you decide what to put into your studio.

Develop Your Resources. Despite the wealth of information packed into this book, it can't cover everything. Check out the music sections in bookstores or libraries for more information on areas in which you're interested. Your local community college may offer courses in electronic music technology, and an Internet search can yield a lot of information. Several magazines contain articles on recording as well as reviews that can help you decide which gear is best for you. Go online for articles, group discussions, and downloadable manufacturer demos.

Other musicians can be valuable resources. If you get to know musicians who have home studios, and share information with them, you'll both come out ahead. (By working together on recording projects, you can learn even more.) And it never hurts to develop a relationship with a salesperson at a nearby music store, or at several stores. By asking questions of several people, you should be able to get a well-rounded picture of the current technology. Needless to say, after taking up their valuable time, you should return the favor by making your purchases at their store rather than shopping elsewhere for the lowest price.

The Vision Thing. In planning your home studio, think seriously about your musical needs and goals. Are you looking to have a little fun? Write songs and pass them around to your friends? Is a self-produced CD the goal? Or are you aiming at a record deal and a career? Knowing how far you want to go will help you keep your equipment lust in line with reality.

And not only how far, but in what direction. What style of music will you be playing? For hip-hop and techno, you'll probably want a computer-based sampler and Sonic Foundry ACID. A hardware sampler may also be a high priority. Try to find one that already has the maximum possible amount of memory, as an extra half-meg of sample memory can sometimes make or break a tune, and some units (especially secondhand ones) cannot easily be upgraded with currently available RAM. You may want to budget for sampler peripherals as well—a program for sample editing, and an extra hard drive for file storage.

For New Age recordings, high-quality reverbs may be more important, to say nothing of excellent microphones and mic preamps for recording acoustic instruments. If you plan to record experimental improvisations, a good recording workstation is probably a higher priority than a powerful sequencer, and an alternate MIDI controller (or a pile of miscellaneous percussion toys) may be preferable to a master keyboard.

What will be the format of choice for what you produce? For finished pop music demos and self-produced CDs, you'll need a CD recorder. If you buy a rewritable (instead of write-once) CD recorder, remember that CD-RW discs are not suitable for playing back on standard CD players. Check whether the unit can record standard CD-Rs as well.

If you're planning to distribute your music online, make sure you have

an MP3 encoder with plenty of features. Test your mixes on a portable
MP3 player too, and not just your computer-based system.

What instruments will you be recording, and what special requirements do they have? For example, if you're recording a vocalist who is
less than perfect and requires multiple takes, being able to cut and paste
virtual-track vocals on a hard disk recording system will greatly ease the
task of assembling an impressive performance. If you plan to record
ensembles, how many microphones will you need? If the ensemble will
be playing along with pre-recorded material, a headphone preamp with
independent volume knobs is probably a must. When live musicians get
into the act, the size of your room—or the number of rooms you can
string cable to and from—may become an issue as well.

When budgeting for your studio, don't forget to allow more money
than you think you'll need. Accessories such as blank CDs, connectors,
cables, insurance, and so on, can definitely take a bite out of your bank
account.

Hardware Follies. Going out and spending your lottery winnings on
23 pieces of equipment all at once is guaranteed to produce frustration,
wasted effort, and panic. Building up a studio over an extended period
of time is not only financially more practical; it's also the best way to
master the myriad techniques required by the various pieces of gear.
MIDI, for example, is not a terribly complex technology, but when on
top of MIDI you start delving into synthesizer programming, sampling,
audio mixing, and composing and arranging all at the same time—oh,
yeah, and also getting equipment from eight or ten manufacturers to
work together smoothly—you'll have your hands full. Setting yourself
up with an "instant studio" is quite likely to be a waste of money, too.
After you've worked for a while with one or two synthesizers or samplers, you'll have a much clearer idea of what features are important to
you and what bases your existing equipment fails to cover. When it
comes to specific equipment choices, versatility is a key ingredient. Your
first effects processor (software-based or not) should probably be a multieffects that can offer many different options; it shouldn't be dedicated
to a single function, such as reverb.

Choosing the wrong equipment is a common mistake—planning
your purchases wisely isn't easy. This may sound obvious, but don't make
a decision on buying a new piece until you can audition it. If you're not
sure about whether you really need something, ask if you can rent it.
(Some stores will even lend gear out "on approval," so you can listen to

it for a few days in your own studio and return it if its sonic performance isn't up to your standards.) Renting can also be viable if you need
an item for a special project.

Getting rid of "obsolete" equipment can also be a mistake. There are
times when you'll be tempted to trade in or sell older gear for something
more immediately useful, but you may find that the money gained is
less important in the long run than the loss in musical power.

Thinking you always have to have the latest and greatest can be
another trap. In the real world, cutting-edge technologies quite often
don't work yet or aren't adopted as a standard. The relevant variable is
how much time and effort you're willing to devote to getting your system up and running.

And beware of the one-piece-does-everything system. While this can
really simplify the music-making process, these types of systems have
limitations. Check if there are ways to interface with other pieces of gear
if needed, and remember that with an all-in-one box, if it goes down
you're out of business until it's fixed.

Synths and Sensibility. A single workstation-type synthesizer (keyboard, sound programs, sequencer, and built-in effects) can be a great
resource, at least if you're into styles of music that involve traditional elements like melody and chords. However, any workstation—even a new
one—is probably not a good choice for somebody who wants to do
hardcore industrial or techno, because the sound set is not likely to be
right for the next new style. For that, you may need to look more closely at groove boxes or a computer-based system and a raft of sample,
loop, and groove CDs.

You might also want to avoid instruments that produce only one
particular type of sound, no matter how popular, unless you want to
specialize in playing (as opposed to recording) and plan to focus on
that particular sound. Versatility is important for your introduction to
synthesis.

Your first synth should be multitimbral. Buy used gear if you want to
save some major money (except for certain high-priced, vintage synths).
Used equipment, if it's in good condition and comes with a manual, is
often an ideal place to start. If compatibility with older gear and files is
an issue, don't make assumptions: Ask specific questions before you buy.
In the rush to get a sexy new product out the door, manufacturers sometimes overlook the fact that their gear will be used in a studio with hardware and software that is still performing perfectly well after five years

of steady use. This applies especially to waveform editing software and editor/librarians. A new synth may not be supported by any of the universal editor/librarian packages for six months to a year—or ever, if the synth isn't a success.

Used Computers. With a newer PC, a standard sound card and bundled software will give you access to both MIDI sequencing and digital audio recording. However, it's easy to forget that many musicians did just fine with a Mac Plus or even a Commodore-64. There are perfectly good MIDI sequencers that will run on an Atari ST, Amiga, Mac Plus, or a PC-XT with an early version of DOS, all of which can be picked up for next to nothing. The trick will be to find suitable software, since much of it was sold by companies that no longer exist. (Networking with other musicians and trolling the online auction sites will help here.) However, use old software only if it's not copy-protected. You don't want to risk losing your creative work if your only copy of the program becomes corrupted.

As a final thought, if your tracks don't sound good with budget gear, evaluate your skills as a recordist and arranger before plunking down thousands of dollars on new gear. Many hits have been cut on equipment that would now be considered laughably obsolete.

Digital Audio Recorders

For multitrack recording, your choices have never been greater. However, you can also bet that in the future, your choices will be greater still. The audio industry evolves at a breakneck pace; today's state-of-the-art gear is tomorrow's dinosaur.

What accounts for this dizzying rate of change? Digital technology—the same technology that spawned the personal computer revolution. In this highly competitive field, companies that don't come out with something newer, faster, and better every few months risk losing it all in the high-tech sweepstakes. The huge sales numbers associated with the personal computer market allow for economies of scale that keep pushing technology forward. As musicians, because our machines are based on the same "raw materials" used by computers, we benefit every time the technology moves up a notch: for example, when the price of memory decreases, we get more storage in our samplers. When hard drives decrease in price, it becomes less expensive to do digital audio (it wasn't more than ten or fifteen years ago that $2,000 was considered a great price for a 1GB, rackmount hard drive).

As a result, in some ways this section will be out of date before the ink is dry on this page. In fact, it will be out of date before it even reaches the printer! Not to worry; this is not intended as the definitive guide to what's available but a reference for the specs and features of different types of gear. Besides, this information is accurate; the problem is that newer gear and updates can't be included. But you can safely assume that the gear of the future will cost less, do more, and deliver higher quality than what's available today.

So with those caveats out of the way, let's look at some real-world products currently available.

Multitrack Tape Recorders

Digital multitrack tape machines broke open the budget digital recording market in the early '90s. The two main types are the Alesis ADAT and TASCAM DA-88. TASCAM also makes a scaled-down version of the DA-88, the DA-38, and an upscale version, the DA-98. Sony made a DA-88 format machine, and Fostex and Panasonic have made ADAT-compatible machines. There are several different types of ADATs available at various price points and with various features.

Alesis ADAT. The basic ADAT is an 8-track recorder that digitally records audio as 16-bit data on S-VHS tape. It operates exactly like an analog tape recorder, with hardware controls for play, rewind, fast forward, punch-in/out, etc. It also has some features you'd normally find on professional multitrack recorders, such as selectable input monitoring, auto locate, and varispeed control.

In addition to analog ins and outs, the ADAT also features a digital I/O in the form of a fiber-optic cable (nicknamed "Lightpipe"). This can digitally transfer eight tracks of data from one ADAT to another, as well as send data back and forth to compatible computer recording/editing systems, digital mixers (such as the Yamaha 02R), and synthesizers.

Up to 16 ADATs can link together to provide more tracks, with each one daisy-chained to the next via a single cable that carries sync code and transport commands. (You don't need to dedicate an audio track to SMPTE time code to synchronize multiple machines.)

The ADAT's recording medium, S-VHS tape, is cheap and reliable. An S-VHS cassette costs under $15 and offers a total recording time of up to 62 minutes, depending on what tape length (ST60–ST180) you use. Digital tape is cleaner and quieter than analog tape, and it doesn't suffer from the ill effects of generation loss when bouncing tracks or making copies.

ADAT Options. The original ADAT, which is no longer in production, was fairly basic. The unit had both -10dBV and +4dBm analog inputs and outputs, making it easy to interface in both pro and semi-pro environments. The +4dBm I/O was via an ELCO connector; if you had a +4dBm mixing console, you needed to buy or make a special cable. Although the ADAT's native sampling rate was 48kHz, you could use variable speed to shift it down to 44.1kHz—a crude, but useable, workaround. For convenience when using multiple ADATs, the BRC (short for "Big Remote Control") served as a master synchronizer, selector, and time code generator/receiver.

The ADAT-XT, also out of production, updated the original ADAT with additional front-panel controls, a sturdier transport, and other extras. It was fully compatible with the original. The shuttle speed was four times faster, and several of the BRC functions were included. A 44.1/48kHz sample rate selector was added so that no manual pitch-changing was necessary. In a controversial move, all $\frac{1}{4}$" audio connectors were replaced with RCA phono jacks. The XT also had better converters: 18-bit, 128x oversampling A/D converters, and 20-bit, 8x oversampling D/A converters. (For information on buying a used ADAT, see sidebar, page 80.)

The latest ADATs have all been upgraded from 16- to 20-bit operation. The current family includes the entry-level LX20, which functionally resembles the ADAT XT but with fewer frills (for example, the analog I/O is -10 unbalanced only). The XT20 (see Figure 1) replaced the XT, and is similar with the exception of 20-bit audio. The top-of-the-line M20 is now out of production, but was designed as an expensive, pro-level machine designed for continuous use in recording and post-production applications. It includes a variety of bells and whistles, including extremely sophisticated sync options.

TASCAM DA-88. The TASCAM DA-88 (see Figure 2), while never selling in as great quantities as the ADAT, became a favorite of the post-production crowd and essentially took over that niche. Like the ADAT, you can lock multiple units together to expand the number of tracks. The machine differs from the Alesis unit primarily in that it uses Hi-8 8mm cassette tapes rather than S-VHS tapes. The two formats are thoroughly incompatible, like VHS and Beta. Think about whether you'll need to play your tapes on someone else's machine, either at a friend's house or in a major studio. If so, you'll likely want to go with the S-VHS format, as there's a large installed user base of ADATs. Hi-8 tapes are

Figure 1

The Alesis ADAT (the XT20 model is shown here), which records on S-VHS tapes, revolutionized home recording.

Figure 2

The TASCAM DA-88 digital 8-track recorder, which uses Hi-8 videocassettes, played a significant role in post-production home recording.

slightly more expensive than regular 8mm tape, yet they are reliable and easier to store than S-VHS tapes. One cassette can provide up to 1 hour and 48 minutes of recording time, making the DA-88 ideal for live recording.

TASCAM-family machines also have a way to transfer eight tracks of digital audio data from one machine to another, called the "TDIF" protocol. This doesn't use fiber optics, but rather, standard wire cables. Although TDIF is not as common as the ADAT Optical Interface, TDIF interface cards for digital mixers exist, and several converters allow you to convert TDIF to ADAT formats, and vice-versa.

TASCAM DA-38 and DA-98. The DA-38 also uses Hi-8 8mm recording cassettes. This lower-priced unit is specifically geared toward musicians, with an easy-to-use interface. Like the DA-88, you get 1 hour and 48 minutes recording time on a single 120-minute tape. The unit features 18-bit A/D and 20-bit D/A converters with Delta-Sigma oversampling. Options include a MIDI machine control interface (MMC-38), remote control (RC-808/848), and IF-88AE AES/EBU

Figure 3

The Roland VS series was the leader in the stand-alone workstation paradigm. Pictured here is Roland's flagship, the VS-2480.

digital interface. The DA-98 is the highest-end digital tape machine TASCAM makes, with numerous features of interest to the post-production market, and very robust operation.

Stand-Alone Hard Disk Recorders

Disk-based systems beat digital tape for editing. You can undo, cut, copy, paste, move and sometimes even perform digital signal processing, such as EQ or time compression/expansion. The weak link for this technology used to be storage; once you've generated all that data, you need to save it somewhere (generally to hard disks, removable cartridge drives, or recordable CDs). But the price of hard disk storage has gone steadily down and now rivals or surpasses tape-based storage.

Many hard disk recorders (both stand-alone and computer-based) feature a playlist option, which allows you to string together snippets (regions) of audio data into a continuous piece of music. You can, for example, define your song's verse as one region, the chorus as another, the breakdown as another, and so on. You can then construct a song arrangement simply by entering the regions into the playlist in the desired order. You can create and edit as many playlists as desired using the same audio data, and (usually) these edits are nondestructive, resulting in no loss of the original data.

Hard disk recorders need ports to connect to external backup devices, and so you should note which type of ports—SCSI, FireWire, USBV, or Ethernet—comes with a given recorder. Offloading data quickly and reliably is essential for serious work. Alternately, many machines produce data compatible with the Alesis ADAT digital tape recorder, via fiber-optic connectors, or TASCAM's TDIF protocol. You can transfer audio in either format to another machine that's equipped with a suitable interface or converter.

Digital Audio Workstations

Some hard disk recorders are built into a complete system with transport, digital mixer (sometimes with automation), equalization, effects, and even a CD burner. The goal is to create a "studio in a box," and this goal succeeds to a remarkable degree. In fact, some CDs have been cut solely on these workstations. The Roland VS series (see Figure 3), the Korg D-1600, the Fostex VF-160, the Akai DPS-16, and the Yamaha AW series (see Figure 4) all feature fully integrated mixers, onboard dig-

Figure 4

Yamaha stunned the music world with two innovations in its AW4416: onboard CD burning and motorized faders. The AW4416's mixer is based on Yamaha's well-regarded 02R.

Figure 5

The Mackie HDR24/96 is a high-quality hard disk recorder that features sophisticated editing capabilities along with its 24/96 resolution.

ital effects processors, multitrack record and playback, and the ability to master and burn CDs within the same environment.

Rackmountable HD Recorders

Rackmountable hard disk recorders usually offer some editing features via the front panel instead of employing traditional knobs and sliders. You enter commands with push buttons and view the results on an LCD. While not as fully featured as the stand-alone workstation, the rackmountable recorder is more modular; it functions like a tape deck. You can upgrade your mixer without having to change the recording mechanism. In many ways, these units are like MDMs, but using a hard disk—and all the benefits of random access technology—instead of the slower, linear, and decidedly clunkier tape format. Mackie has produced several models of hard disk recorders in rackmountable form, their flagship being the HDR24/96 (see Figure 5).

MiniDisc Recorders

These also take the studio-in-a-box approach, with an integrated mixer and MiniDisc-based multitrack recorder (see Figure 6). MDs are not the preferred choice for work on major albums, jingles, or film scores due to their less-than-professional sound quality—all MDs use data compression to fit more data into a limited amount of storage. Remarkably, though, this influences the sound far less than you might think. Also, the data compression software (called ATRAC) is continually being

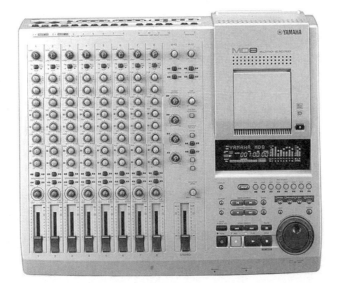

Figure 6

Yamaha's MD8 is the only MiniDisc recorder to feature eight tracks of recording and playback.

refined, so the latest generation is vastly smoother than earlier efforts. Unfortunately, units cannot be upgraded easily.

Points in the MD's favor are clear when compared to cassette multitracks, their nearest rival in price and performance: MiniDiscs lack the motor and cartridge noise of cassette machines, produce a sound quality that is vastly superior to cassette-based multitracks, and boast an extremely sturdy optical recording medium. Like cassettes, they are also portable and easy to use. They are good for semi-pro work, multimedia music, or demos.

CD Recorders

There are two types of CD recorders. The stand-alone type works just like a tape deck, where you plug in the analog or digital outputs of your mixer and burn a CD in real time. The second kind works by copying a group of static audio files to produce a CD that will play back in a conventional audio CD player, or can contain data (in the form of WAV and AIFF files). Most musicians use the second kind, because so much work is done on the computer (mixing, mastering, song sequencing) that to simply burn a CD as the last step in production is the most convenient. CD burning software is so prevalent (with programs from

Figure 7

Roxio makes a whole series of burning solutions for the Mac and PC. Here, their Toast Lite program makes CD assembly and burning drag-and-drop simple.

Roxio, Steinberg, and Digidesign, to name a few), inexpensive and simple to use that it's no more an effort to drag and drop files onto a Zip disk icon than it is to burn a CD (see Figure 7). Plus, CD burners for computers are much cheaper (as of this writing, about $129 for an internal drive, and under $200 for an external drive).

Nevertheless, if you like the stand-alone prospect for producing CDs—where your CD recorder acts just like your favorite tape decks of yore, and you don't ever need to go near a computer—you can get inexpensive units from HHB and TASCAM (see Figure 8) for as little as under $500, or opt for the higher-end Alesis MasterLink ML-9600 (see Figure 9), which offers a host of special processing and mastering features in addition to the ability to burn CDs in standard as well as high-resolution modes.

Media

Just as with drives, while there are lots of brands of blank CD-Rs on the market (every drive vendor has its house brand), there's only a handful of manufacturers. That short list includes Mitsui Toatsu, Ricoh, Taiyo

Yuden, TDK, and Verbatim (a division of Mitsubishi); all other brands are actually made by one of those companies. Kodak is also considered a manufacturer, but it seems their discs are actually made by Verbatim— though they're not the same as either of that company's discs.

There are three basic types of discs, distinguished by the kind of dye they use. Ricoh, Taiyo Yuden, TDK, and Verbatim's regular discs use cyanine, and are often called "green" discs from the color of their bottom, dye-side layer. Kodak Info Guard and Mitsui Toatsu discs use pthalocyanine, and are often called "gold" discs. (This green-gold business can be confusing, as CD-Rs in general are also called gold discs, since the top side is always gold rather than the silver of a regular CD, and the Verbatim discs are no greener than Kodak's and Mitsui Toatsu's.) Verbatim's new Data Life Plus discs use a different technology, with a bluish metal azo dye on a silver rather than gold substrate.

If you're curious about the technology, you can find more info in the

Figure 8

The TASCAM CD-RW700 is a stand-alone CD recorder, for people who don't want to record on a computer.

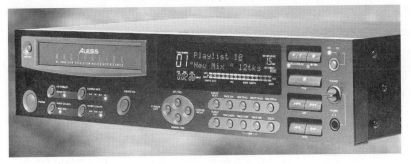

Figure 9

The Alesis MasterLink 9600 is a high-end CD recorder with mastering features and high-resolution audio capabilities.

comp.publish.cdrom newsgroup and on the Web at www.cd-info.com. However, all you really need to know is that there's some controversy about the relative merits of the various types. In a nutshell, manufacturers of gold discs say they'll last longer, up to 100 years; manufacturers of green discs say they last plenty long, 70 years easy; and Verbatim says its blue discs will be dancing on the others' graves. The manufacturers and others have done accelerated aging experiments to try to support these claims, but the truth is that no one really knows how long the media will last, except that they won't last as long as regular CDs.

Which discs are compatible with your drive is a lot more important than any abstract technological comparison.

Putting It All Together. It's quite a challenge to get all this hardware and software to work in concert to produce perfect CDs every time—in fact, it's pretty much guaranteed that you'll ruin at least a few discs before you perfect the process.

Take your CD-R vendor's advice, and use only recommended discs and software—or, better yet, take your CD-R software vendor's advice and buy a recommended drive. Always make sure the software is able to write in disc-at-once mode.

Recording with Computers

The desktop studio resembles the integrated studio but squeezes several functions—hard-disk-based recording and editing, customizable on-screen mixing, processing, even routing and software plug-ins (signal processors and virtual instruments)—into a personal computer.

Requirements and Cautions

If you buy a new or slightly used computer (less than a year old), you should be in good shape to record a project of modest power needs (eight tracks of audio, eight MIDI tracks, just a few plug-ins). The newer your computer, the better chance you have that it will handle more powerful tasks "out of the box," but you can always upgrade an older computer to perform almost as well as a brand new one. Here are some considerations to be aware of when selecting a computer for recording.

Processor Speed. Although you generally want the fastest possible processor speed, the computer in question may not be completely optimized for the higher processor speeds in terms of system bus speed, architecture, cache design, and speed tolerance. Anything faster than 200MHz may be running too fast for software optimized for Mac 68030 and 68040 machines. However, the faster your machine, the more tracks you can record. A 386 may only allow two tracks at a 22kHz sampling rate, while a 100MHz Pentium might play back 12 stereo tracks at 44.1kHz. But these days, processor speeds are in the gigabyte range, so you don't have to worry whether your new computer will be fast enough for computer recording. It will be. At least till you start producing really processor-intensive music with multiple tracks and scads of plug-ins.

Playback Capability. Make sure you get a full-duplex board (for a PC), which allows you to monitor previously recorded tracks while you record new tracks.

Hard Drives. A 6GB internal hard drive is sufficient for digital audio projects, but you should really get a 30GB or more ultra-fast external drive, as large internal drives use up lots of time to search, index, run disk utilities, and/or defragment. To keep prices down, installed internal hard drives are usually slower than specialty external hard drives optimized for audio and video work. Also, keeping your audio on the same drive as your system really exercises the hard disk, as it has to run around picking up not just audio but system data. A separate drive dedicated to audio/video work is a worthwhile investment.

Not all hard drives are fast enough to record and play back digital audio. The key specs to look for, in addition to capacity, are *data throughput* and *seek time.* Data throughput relates to the speed at which you can continuously pull bytes off the disk. As long as you have a new, fast CPU, the hard drive data throughput is typically the limiting factor in determining how much data a given system can process at a time. If your computer has an older CPU, however, its speed will also limit the number of audio tracks you can play back simultaneously.

In a nutshell, if your hard disk can source a lot of data in a small amount of time, you can play back several audio tracks at once. If not, your final mix may be limited to a small number of audio tracks, and you will have to be creative to work around this limitation. Before buying a drive, check with the manufacturer of the recording software you plan to use to find out the recommended throughput. (The manufacturer will probably recommend specific drives that they have tested and know will work.)

Average seek time measures how fast (on average) a hard drive can find any given piece of data on the disk, no matter where it is reading currently. Remember, hard drives have moving parts, and we haven't conquered the limitations of physics yet. If you try to play back a number of audio files that are scattered all over the disk, the drive heads will have to jump around constantly in order to access the required data. The shorter the seek time, the less time the drive will waste on mechanical activity, and the more time it will spend transferring real data. A fast seek time is the usual distinguishing factor for an audio/video drive. Typical recommended values are around 10–12 milliseconds, but slower drives are out there, so beware. Also, be careful to differentiate between average and maximum seek times. The average figure may appear impressive, but if the seek times periodically get much slower, you're in trouble. A maximum seek time specification lets you know the worst-case performance.

Another factor that can impact hard drive usability is *thermal recalibration*. If the drive sometimes interrupts its data output to perform thermal recalibration, the audio can glitch. The best way to avoid this is to query the recording software's manufacturer for a list of recommended drives.

System RAM. The old saying that you cannot be too rich, too thin, or have too much RAM still holds true. Nothing optimizes computer usage, especially with digital audio or graphics tasks, as much as maximum system RAM. Virtual Memory and RAM Doubler help up to a point, but you really need at least 128MB of physical RAM for audio. It may be cheaper to buy less RAM with the machine and add RAM from less expensive mail-order or online sources after sale.

What does more RAM do for you? Here are some benefits:

- In most cases, more RAM increases your operating speed. It does this in many machines via memory access interleaving. This can mean up to a 20% speed boost on some machines.
- Having enough physical RAM to run everything you use on your computer also increases speed. Forcing a computer to go back and forth to the hard drive while performing millions of computations slows down performance. Sufficient RAM also cuts down on the use of virtual memory schemes, where the computer substitutes hard disk space for inadequate amounts of installed physical RAM.
- Sufficient RAM also allows opening up various RAM caches that speed up processor "scratch padding," operating system assisted applications (such as Speed Doubler, which needs as much as 2MB), and CD-ROM pre-caching of repetitive data.
- Application size can be increased to optimize usage, and the likelihood is decreased that the application speed will suffer due to insufficient

memory situations. If a RAM substitute such as RAM Doubler is used, it will not compensate for the physical RAM needed for actual audio and video manipulations. With adequate amounts of physical RAM, however, RAM programs do work much more effectively.

- Audio and video applications will have enough room to run in RAM or in RAM disks, and to manipulate (edit) large audio and video files.

So how much RAM is enough? The minimum RAM that should be in any Pentium or Power PC computer used for recording is 128MB. More memory is better, and there are many Macs running Pro Tools or similar audio recording software that have 2GB of RAM installed. Finally, buy your RAM only from reputable local or mail-order suppliers, and install it yourself only with careful and adequate static electricity protection and knowledge of your PC or Mac! You don't want to blow up your motherboard by trying to save a few pennies.

Choosing Software

MIDI plus Digital Audio. Several Mac and PC programs integrate MIDI sequencing with hard disk recording (these require capable systems with sufficient RAM and a fast hard drive). Almost all entry-level PC programs allow two tracks of digital audio and often more. For the Mac, many sequencers now take advantage of Apple's Sound Manager to record digital audio with no external hardware. Mix the sequenced sounds along with the digital audio into your final two-track master, and you have a master tape.

The software often includes mixer functions. MIDI messages can change the mix and stereo position of the sequenced tracks, as well as the digital audio tracks. So, you may need only a very simple hardware mixer to combine the MIDI sound generator outputs with the sound card's digital audio. If you use internal sounds, you may not need a mixer at all, since the sound card output will contain the final stereo output signal.

Software runs from $99 to $1,000, and an appropriate computer for around $1,000 to $3,500. A low-end sound card costs $200; a few hundred dollars more gets really good sounds and a music industry pedigree (e.g., E-mu/Ensoniq, Roland, Yamaha). However, the general cautions about hard disk recording—a big hard drive, RAM, and a backup system—still apply.

To find the right program for your studio, start surfing the web and looking for demo versions. These often do everything the regular programs do except some crucial function, such as saving data. Make sure you have at least the minimum hardware/system software necessary to run the program. (For a comprehensive comparison of digital audio recorders and their features, see *Music Technology Buyer's Guide,* from the publishers of *Keyboard* and *EQ*.)

Getting by with Less. Those with limited budgets can capture acoustic instruments on digital tape, bounce them over to a two-track computer-based digital audio editor for editing, then bounce back to tape for inexpensive, non-volatile storage. If you're using a small hard disk, you can then erase the disk, record more tracks, and bounce these over to tape. In a way, the tape recorder serves as a multi-purpose peripheral for the computer that provides A/D and D/A conversion as well as mass storage.

Note that MIDI tracks must all play back in real time. With tape, you can overdub the same instrument over and over on different tracks; with MIDI, if you're using instruments with lots of outputs, you need more mixer inputs.

Incidentally, MIDI isn't just for notes. A sequencer can sync to tape during mixdown to provide automated mixing and signal processing, or change presets on a guitar multieffects while you record. And if using a computer seems like overkill, many keyboard "workstations" include an onboard sequencer. This can drive not only onboard sounds but often external equipment like signal processing and automated mixdown gear. A setup consisting of a MiniDisc recorder and a keyboard "workstation" synchronized to tape can be a price/performance winner.

A few final considerations:

- Choose something that's comfortable for you. If you hate computers, a hard disk system might not be right, so digital tape would be a better choice. However, if you already have a great computer, then adding studio peripherals could be a very cost-effective option.
- Look for expandability. You'll always want more tracks, more power, more inputs and more editing features.

Choosing a Sound Card

Nearly all PCs sold today include either a pre-installed sound card (see Figure 10), or the equivalent circuitry built into the motherboard. AV and Power Macs have built-in audio capabilities, although not a MIDI synth. Professionals usually supplement the Mac's built-in sound with additional, high-quality audio interfaces. In any event, even though virtually all sound cards advertise "CD-quality sound," in reality there's a wide range of quality.

PC sound cards are available in three basic configurations. The most common type for consumers is the *audio-plus-synthesizer* version, which contains both a MIDI synth and the ability to record and play back digital audio. Examples include the Creative Technology SoundBlaster family and the Ensoniq Soundscape. Sound card synthesizers are *multi-timbral*—up to 16 different instruments can play simultaneously. (This is because MIDI supports 16 channels.) Most of today's sound card synthesizers have at least 24 voices of polyphony, but some have as many as 64 and more. More voices let you develop fuller musical arrangements and allow "layering" of sounds without having to worry about notes being cut off due to not having sufficient voices.

The second type of card, the *sampling* sound card, is generally more flexible. It lets you load in your own sounds by storing audio files (samples) in the card's RAM. Typically, these cards also include a synth and digital audio recording/playback capabilities.

The third type of sound card, the *audio interface*, is a high-end product optimized for recording digital audio to the computer's hard drive. It will likely support multiple channels of audio and not include a synthesizer.

Installing Sound Cards. Connecting a sound card to a computer involves plugging the card into an expansion slot in the motherboard. Older Macs use the NuBus slot protocol, and older PCs use ISA bus-standard slots. Newer models, Mac and PC alike, use the faster PCI bus protocol that provides better throughput.

Figure 10

A typical sound card for audio recording will have stereo analog in and out plus digital I/O (here in the form of an optical link on the right). This card, from Audiotrack, also has a headphone out (left).

The universality of the PCI bus has encouraged the development of *cross-platform* applications, which work on both Macs and PCs. Often all that's needed to coax a piece of hardware into working on one platform or the other is a different set of *drivers*—small software routines that handle communications between the card and the computer.

When you buy a computer, the salesperson will usually know how many slots a particular model has, but be sure to ask whether they're vacant or not. Sometimes the slot count includes slots that are already occupied (by the video monitor card, for instance).

Unless you're planning to record to the internal hard drive, you'll probably need another slot for a SCSI adapter card. Some sound cards include onboard SCSI connectors, which can save you money as well as a slot.

IDE vs. SCSI. The original standard for PC disk drives was called IDE. Your PC's internal hard drive, floppy, and CD-ROM are probably IDE devices. IDE can be a slower data bus than the original SCSI (now called SCSI-1); the newer SCSI-2 format is faster yet. Macintosh computers have a SCSI connector on the rear panel, but PCs don't, so you'll probably want a SCSI card. SCSI-2 is backward compatible with SCSI-1—all you need is the right connector cable.

For digital audio applications, which can require quite a lot of data throughput, software manufacturers tend to recommend SCSI rather than IDE. To a large extent, SCSI peripherals are also compatible with both Mac and Windows systems.

IRQs & DMAs. To install hardware in a PC, you generally have to configure each card with the proper IRQ (interrupt request) number. Each hardware device in the computer requires its own unique IRQ so that the CPU can communicate with it. If two devices share an IRQ, typically one of them will fail to work, and your computer may even lock up (however, sometimes it is possible for two devices to share an IRQ if one of them is disabled). Some cards also require DMA (direct memory access) settings.

Until recently, setting these numbers meant physically moving jumpers or DIP switches on the circuit board, as described (hopefully!) in the manual. A jumper is a tiny, horseshoe-shaped piece of plastic with a conductive metal liner. It's best handled with fingernails or needlenose pliers (and tends to fly out of your grip, especially when you're working over a shag carpet).

It's important to keep a list of which devices in your system use each of the IRQs and DMAs. If you consult the list before installing a new card, you're less likely to have to pop open the case, pull out the board, and reconfigure it.

Board Handling. Even a small static discharge, such as one you can easily produce by shuffling your feet across a rug, can fry delicate electronic components.

Before touching any board, ground yourself by touching the PC's metal chassis. Some people recommend leaving the PC plugged in (but switched off) while you install boards, as the power cable's ground connection will help protect against static discharge. If you're clumsy about dropping little screws, though, it's probably wise to unplug the computer, since you don't want one rolling around and doing something like shorting out the AC line.

After you ground yourself on the chassis, don't shuffle your feet on the rug and pick up a fresh charge. Handle the board by its backplate, or by holding edges where there aren't any components or metal traces. Don't touch the gold edge connectors along the card's bottom, and don't touch the exposed components. Insert the board with firm, even pressure (*never* force it), and make sure that it's seated correctly before you power up again.

Also, keep the silvery envelope in which the board was packed. This is made of conductive plastic that provides protection to the board during handling and shipping. You may need to pull the board sometime—and for some weird reason, most computer stores don't stock these envelopes.

Ins and Outs. Inexpensive sound cards typically provide two line-level audio inputs (for stereo), two line-level outputs, and one or two microphone-level inputs. The line-level connectors transfer sound from cassette decks, electronic keyboards, or other standard analog audio devices. Since microphones generate a very low audio level, the mic input goes through a preamplifier on the sound card. Some sound cards also provide amplified speaker outputs, but you'll almost always get better audio quality by using the line-level output to feed a "real" power amp, because the onboard amplifiers are usually a cheap consumer convenience and can easily pick up the considerable electrical noise inside the computer.

Digital-Only Sound Cards. Higher-end sound cards offer digital audio inputs and outputs. These special connectors let you patch the sound card directly to compatible devices such as select CD players and

DAT decks. Using these connections gives you the best possible sound, because analog/digital conversion occurs away from the noisy computer. The main limitation with digital-only cards is that this remains an analog world, so you still need to convert digital signals back into analog again before you can hear them.

One common approach is to use the converters in a DAT machine. You feed the analog signal into the DAT, put it into record mode, and patch the DAT's digital out to the sound card's digital in. During playback, you patch the sound card's digital out to the DAT's digital in, and monitor from the DAT's audio output. Unfortunately, you usually can't use both a DAT's A/D and D/A converters simultaneously; you can do

SOUND CARD FEATURES CHECKLIST

Here's a summary of the most desirable features to look for when shopping for a sound card. Remember to check with the sound card manufacturer to see if your computer system is compatible. And if you plan to use third-party software, be sure to ask that manufacturer which cards they recommend.

Synthesizer Specs
- General MIDI (GM) compatibility (additional GS or XG compatibility if possible)
- 24-note polyphony (more is better)
- At least 2MB of wavetable ROM or RAM (more is usually better; RAM is also highly desirable)
- Effects processing (the more effects sends, the better; real-time control is useful)
- Programmable sounds
- Resonant filter
- Fat Seal (certifies consistent GM playback)
- MPU-401-compatible MIDI interface in hardware
- Daughterboard upgradeability

Digital Audio Specs
- 16-bit (or greater) resolution
- 44.1kHz sampling rate (additional rates are helpful)
- Full-duplex recording and playback (the more channels, the better)
- 20Hz–20kHz frequency response, with as little deviation (the "±XdB" spec) as possible
- 85dB (or greater) signal-to-noise ratio

Connectors
- The more, the better!
- Avoid ⅛" miniphone jacks if possible. ¼", RCA, or (best of all) a breakout box/cable or digital interface are all better options
- For high-end setups, get balanced connectors. Word clock and SMPTE support, which simplify interfacing with other devices in the studio, are also recommended

A/D while the DAT is in record mode and D/A while in play mode, but not both. For stereo-only applications, like two-track editing, this isn't much of a limitation—if you need to hear what's being recorded, monitor the analog signal going into the converters.

Another approach is to use outboard A/D and D/A converters. While this is the most expensive solution, it's also the most flexible. As the quality of D/A converters improves, you can upgrade the external box without changing your sound card. Outboard converters are currently a growth industry. The quality of conversion can make a profound difference in sound quality, and many people are finding out that using outboard converters instead of the ones included in their DAT deck or sound card can result in a substantial sonic improvement. Generally, the most noticeable changes are better stereo imaging, a lower noise floor, and more transparent sound.

Multichannel Interfaces. Most cards internally mix all of their audio sources down to one stereo signal during recording and playback. Pricier cards support software that accommodates multiple inputs and outputs, which lets you edit and process the audio more easily. The two de facto multichannel digital audio standards are the ADAT Optical Interface (also known as the "ADAT Lightpipe," so called because it uses a fiber-optic cable) and TASCAM's TDIF format, which uses wires and D-connectors. These interfaces can transfer eight tracks at a time from Alesis and TASCAM 8-track digital multitrack tape recorders, respectively, or devices (like digital mixers) that support them. You may want to look for a card that offers these interfaces as options, as you may need them later. In particular, the ADAT Optical Interface is being incorporated into more and more gear, including mixers, synthesizers, and stand-alone hard disk recorders.

Other Sound Card Considerations

Full Duplex. Look for a card with full-duplex capability, which means it can play back tracks while simultaneously recording new ones.

Wavetable Synthesis. Older sound cards used two-operator FM synthesis, which was inexpensive and sounded, well, inexpensive. (This is not to be confused with the four- and six-operator FM synthesis used in pro synthesizers.) Newer sound cards use an improved synthesis technology called *wavetable synthesis.* (If they don't have wavetable synthesis built in, they can often be upgraded by attaching a small circuit board called a *daughterboard.*) Wavetable synthesis can produce very realistic sounds because it plays back sampled real-life instruments and sounds. The main drawback to wavetable synthesis is that the samples are typically small, as they are stored in RAM or ROM memory rather than on disk. In general, the bigger the wavetable ROM, the better-sounding the sound card. Look for a wavetable size of at least 2MB.

Noise Specs. The *signal-to-noise ratio,* which indicates how much noise a card generates, is an important—but unfortunately, often meaningless—spec. There are many ways to measure this spec to make a card look better: for example, if a card has both analog and digital ins, the manufacturer will quote the spec for the digital I/O. Noise specs can also be unweighted (the total amount of noise) or weighted (which measures only the noise in the audible spectrum). Some companies even measure sound card noise with the card outside the computer to minimize interference. Given all this, look for the biggest number possible. 85dB is quite acceptable, especially if it's a "real world" spec. Well-designed cards can even push that to 95–105dB (but expect to pay more).

Frequency Response. A good sound card will cover the frequency response range from at least 20Hz to 20kHz. Even more importantly, the response curve should be *flat,* meaning that all frequencies are treated equally; there won't be any undue emphasis or loss at certain frequencies or frequency ranges. A variation of ±1dB or less is considered excellent.

Effects. Another desirable feature is realtime *signal-processing effects,* which can add an air of professionalism to any mix. Look for these on both the digital audio and synth specs of the card. 3D processing, which creates ultra-wide stereo imaging, is also becoming available.

Effects Sends. Finally, look for cards with multiple *effects sends,* which will let you apply different amounts of processing to different tracks or synth parts. While this is a pro- rather than consumer-oriented feature, it is important for interfacing with other hardware in your studio.

Interfaces and Control Surfaces

One of the most exciting developments in digital recording is witnessing what "cool boxes" get invented. Never mind all this stuff about increased hard-drive capacities and more transistors on ever-thinner chips; give us a cool-looking box! Several manufacturers have heard this cry and have answered with front-end interfaces, control surfaces, and audio mixers. And some combine all three aspects into a single unit. As digital recording moves further and further into the realm of software, we humans—with our itchy, idle fingers—find we want to control the

Figure 11

The TASCAM US-428 is a USB audio interface, control surface, and audio mixer that is compatible with a number of digital audio + MIDI sequencer programs.

software via tactile means. Let's take a look at some recent innovations in the cool box department.

USB Interfaces. USB (Universal Serial Bus) replaced the clunkier multi-pin serial protocol that connected printers, modems, and older MIDI interfaces to your computer. But beyond its small profile and ability to "hot swap" (plugging and unplugging cables while the computer is still on) USB brings another advantage: it carries up to four channels of digital audio reliably. This means that you don't necessarily need a sound card to get digital audio into your computer. M-Audio and Edirol are two companies that make a range of USB audio converters in a variety of configurations and price points.

If you had control-surface capabilities and mixer functions to a box that converts a mic or instrument to digital audio, and outputs it onto a USB cable, you can have a portable DAW controller and computer interface in one. TASCAM's US-428 (see Figure 11) and US-224, Event Electronics' EZbus, and Digidesign's Mbox represent the new crop of multi-function front-end USB boxes. The Mbox not only converts analog signals into digital ones, it includes two high-quality Focusrite preamps with phantom power. The EZbus, SAC-2K, US-428, and US-224 act as a stand-alone mixer as well as control surface for controlling faders, pans, EQ, bus levels, mute and solo switches, and transport controls for popular software recorders and other software packages.

Figure 12

The front and back panel of the Mark of the Unicorn 896, a multi-channel 96kHz FireWire interface with built-in mic pre-amps and extensive digital and analog I/O options

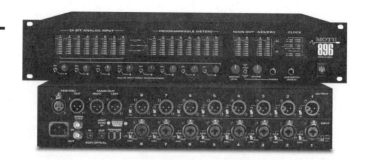

FireWire. When developers decided the protocol named IEEE 1394 wasn't sexy-sounding enough, the name FireWire was adopted, and musicians sat up and took notice. FireWire is way faster than USB, and so can carry a lot more digital audio over its data stream. While USB is considered a convenient limited-purpose protocol for audio, FireWire is regarded as professional, because it can move multi-channel signals as well as TDIF and Lightpipe formats. With a FireWire-equipped interface and computer, you don't need to use a sound card to get digital audio into your computer. And that means you don't need a PCI slot (which only come on behemoth "tower" configurations). The MOTU 828 was one of the first FireWire devices designed to convert analog signals to digital ones, and move them over FireWire. MOTU has since come out with an 896 (see Figure 12), and Digidesign joined the FireWire fray with their Digi 002, which has a full-featured control surface, complete with motorized faders.

FireWire and USB have blown wide open the gates of portable recording, because now you can use fully professional devices like MOTU's 828 and 896 with laptop computers. Laptop recording is also possible with PCMCIA cards and breakout boxes, such as the Digigram VXPocket, Layla 24 Laptop and Mona Laptop by Echo, the HDSP Cardbus series by RME, and the Nuendo AudioLink 96 Mobile by Steinberg. But USB and FireWire allow you to keep just one interface for use with both your desktop and laptop systems.

BUYING A USED ADAT

Some caveats and tips on buying a used Alesis digital multitrack recorder.

Recognizing the Variations

The earliest ADATs are easy to recognize: the ADAT logo on the upper right is blue-black and silk-screened onto the faceplate. (The Fostex RD-8 is essentially an Original Formula ADAT with built-in SMPTE time code.) In May 1994, Alesis went to a silver plastic logo that was glued onto the faceplate. These machines delineate the transition from firmware version 3.06 to 4.0, although older machines could be upgraded to version 4.0 performance. This upgrade gave users extended features, including increased record/playback times (from 40 minutes to over 60 minutes).

To check the firmware version, hold the SET LOCATE key and press FAST FORWARD. The current firmware level appears on the LCD. All ADATs, no matter how old, could be upgraded to the most current firmware (version 4.03) before Alesis ceased production of its Original Formula in November 1995.

Kicking the Tires

Once you've located some likely candidates you can narrow your choices by following this advice:

Consider the overall appearance. The original ADAT chassis is constructed from sheet metal onto which the transport is mounted. Severe mechanical damage to the external case and/or a warped front panel is cause for closer scrutiny and may possibly be a disqualifying factor. (The XT uses a die-cast chassis that is extremely resistant to "warp factors.") Most ADAT top and bottom panels get scratched from being swapped in and out of racks. It ain't pretty, but it doesn't affect performance.

Check the mileage by pressing SET LOCATE and STOP. The number on the alphanumeric display indicates how many hours the tape has been in contact with the rotary heads. Thus, "0060" means sixty hours of contact, while "4234" indicates over four thousand hours. Expect to pay more for machines showing fewer hours. Be sure to ask the ADAT's previous owner about its maintenance records.

Who Is Selling?

There are at least three categories of ADAT user:

1. People who have been using their original ADATs heavily and are switching to newer versions for their increased wind and lock-up speeds (and in the case of the latest ADATs, 20-bit audio converters).

2. People who need the ADAT for compatibility with the outside world, but do most of their work via MIDI and hard disk.

3. People who thought they would use the ADAT more but never got around to it.

User #1 is likely to have lots of head hours, but the machine should have up-to-date firmware and hardware. User #2 will have less time on the drum; the machine should look pretty good and be up to the latest firmware, but may need routine maintenance. User #3 will have minimal head hours, but the machine should be checked by Alesis and/or a qualified tech for firmware, circuit board revisions, the type of head, and related peripherals. A machine running version 3.04 firmware (for example) may behave well alone, but may not be a good team player when asked to lock up with other machines. Multiple machines should all be running the same software version for best results.

The bottom line? An ADAT that's been on a schedule of regular preventive maintenance should chug along quite nicely. From all sellers, ask for the Operator's Manual (it's worth having), the

LRC (Little Remote Control), optical and sync cables (if possible), and copies of maintenance receipts (if available).

First and Second Opinion

If the seller will pop the cover, check the area around the rubber tire (between the two reel tables) for shedding. Check the pinch roller to see if it looks "glazed" and be sure the capstan is clean and shiny, not encrusted with tape oxide remnants. If necessary, use a cloth *dampened*, not saturated, with low-moisture alcohol to clean the capstan. Avoid excessive saturation because alcohol will dissolve the lubricant in the capstan bearing. For cleaning rubber parts, use Athan ATH-500-CS or a water-based cleaner, such as Windex.

Before your purchase, contact Alesis technical support for the nearest service centers in your area. Compare service charges and turnaround times. Get a serial number and confirm the unit's age with Alesis. (This may also weed out possible "hot" boxes, which you definitely want to avoid.) The primary ADAT intermittent problem is due to a dirty Mode switch. If there are no service records for the past year and a half, get on the good foot by having the switch and all rubber parts (including belts) replaced.

Eyes on the Prize

Here are a couple of basic tests to determine transport condition:

Remove the ADAT's top cover and load a tape. Once the tape is wrapped around the drum (called the Engaged mode), check basic transport functions such as play, fast forward, and rewind. Watch the tape as it moves around the guides and through the capstan and pinch roller. (You should eventually get familiar with what "normal" tape motion looks like.) Tape movement should be smooth, and there should be no slack during fast wind or spillage during stop.

For example, press Rewind in the middle of a tape and watch the take-up side. Look for slack as the machine gets up to speed. Now press Stop (check for no slack or loops), then press Stop again. The tape should disengage from the head drum assembly. Press Fast Forward (the tape is still disengaged from the head) and look for smooth travel from the supply to the take-up reel. Try these exercises at the beginning, middle, and end of the tape, looking for consistent performance at each location.

Note: If the supply and take-up reels do not come to a complete stop, the brake solenoids are either out of adjustment or have failed. If tape continues to be pulled out of the cassette shell in Stop mode, the pinch roller may not be sufficiently clearing the capstan. A minor adjustment could be all that's required, but an intermittent problem is more likely Mode-switch related.

Avoiding Moans and Groans

Loud mechanical sounds during fast forward or rewind are minor problems that can be resolved by lubricating the impedance and tachometer rollers, or by replacing the tachometer belt.

If you notice problems toward the end of a reel, suspect either supply tension, take-up tension, or pinch-roller pressure. Fast forward to about 35:00 minutes and save that as Locate 1. Fast forward to about 38:00 minutes and press Set Locate 2. Use the Auto 2 <\>> 1 and Auto Play features to continuously run this loop. The tape should be formatted, signal should have been recorded on all tracks, and you should also punch in on each track during the loop. (A portable CD player can be your source and any mixer or amp with a headphone output can be used for monitoring.)

If the error display decimal LED (located in the counter) lights up after repeated loops, either performance is marginal, damage is being done to the tape, or the tape itself is at fault. There should be no analog distortion when the machine is in Input mode, or digital noise at the punch-in/out points. If the machine passes these tests, it is in good working order as a "soloist." Next, you need to see how well it works with other ADATs.

Team Player Performance Test

This last ADAT test is for system compatibility—how the machine gets along with others. For consistent lock-ups, it is important that each machine get to the locate point at the same time, otherwise a slacker will hold up the rest of the system. When the ADAT is in unthreaded, Fast-Wind mode, the tape counter relies on information received from a reel-table tachometer. (In threaded Fast-Wind modes, it is able to accurately read timecode information from tape.) Any major difference between tachometer "predictions" and tape-accurate code will cause sluggish lock-ups. To test for compatibility (this test does not apply to the Alesis XT):

1. Format two new tapes, of the same length, brand and batch.

2. Label one "Master" and the other "Slave."

3. Connect only two machines at a time using an officially sanctioned Alesis sync cable.

4. Power up the last machine first.

5. Insert tapes into the respective machines.

6. Press Locate Zero on the Master. (The slave should follow.)

7. In Unthreaded mode (press Stop twice), Fast Forward to 10 minutes and stop.

8. In Threaded/Engaged mode, each machine should be within 20 seconds of actual tape time.

9. Set Locate 1 at 10 minutes, then FF in Unthreaded mode to 40 minutes.

10. Stopped units should be within 30 seconds of actual tape time.

11. Set Locate 2 at 40 minutes, then Locate Zero in Unthreaded mode.

12. There should be 15 seconds or less difference.

13. For machines within spec, make the fastest/least-hours machine the last unit in the chain.

14. The best medicine for out-of-spec machines is to schedule maintenance for "the team." Take all the machines to one technician (at the same time) so the performance can be optimized.

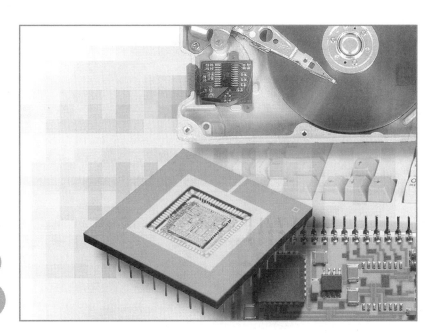

3

Studio Setup
and Maintenance

Studio Setups

Most home studios weren't built in a day. Traditionally, home studio owners collect equipment over the years, adding new pieces and replacing old ones according to current needs and available finances. So don't be afraid to start small. Today's equipment is remarkably powerful; you don't need a million-dollar control room to turn out a high-quality product as long as you have a few simple tools and a healthy dose of talent. Here are four digital home studio setups, ranging from the simple to the complex.

System One: Just the Basics

When you're just getting started, it's important to maximize the price/performance ratio of your gear purchases. You also need to be realistic about what you'll be able to accomplish in your studio, as well as its sonic quality.

Our first digital home studio setup is designed primarily for song-writers and composers who need to create demos of their ideas. It provides the basic tools for writing the music, recording it, and creating a stereo CD master. This is a good system for people just starting out, as the financial commitment is minimal.

At the heart of the system is the music-creation tool. For keyboardists, that means a synthesizer with a built-in sequencer. If you later find you need more voices, add a sound module. In a basic setup, a General MIDI module would be a good choice, as this type of unit covers lots of sonic ground. Augmenting it with a drum machine or drum sound module would be a logical next step, even if the keyboard has a good complement of drums sounds. You can get back some extra polyphony for synth sounds if you delegate the percussion tasks to a dedicated drum machine.

Another way to get more voices is to record keyboard parts to your multitrack deck. For basic demos, digital MiniDisc- or hard-disk-based multitrack recorders are excellent (if you're on a really tight budget, cassette-based multitracks are even less expensive, albeit less capable). Not only will they allow you to overdub multiple parts, they provide the means to add vocals, guitar, and other non-MIDI keyboard sounds to your production. Another advantage is their built-in mixers, so you can plug your instrument directly into the same device that records the sounds. These "personal studios" even have effects sends and returns, so you can easily route your signals through an external effects device.

One limitation of MiniDisc recorders is the ATRAC data compression they employ, and the coloration that results from *bouncing* tracks (i.e., combining the signals from several tracks into a new track, so you can record new sounds in place of the tracks you bounced). This coloration becomes particularly noticeable with multiple bounces, although the latest generation of ATRAC sounds much better than earlier versions. See "Data Storage" in Chapter 1 for more on ATRAC.

Though your synth may have built-in effects, you'll likely want to invest in an external effects device for processing vocals and other non-keyboard sounds. If you have a hard-disk or computer-based system, you can also use the built-in effects or plug-ins to expand a program's capabilities.

Regarding vocals, unless you have an electromagnetically charged larynx, you'll need a microphone to capture your vocals on tape. Considering that this mic will be the primary conveyor of your vocal talents, as well as the main connection between acoustic instruments and your recording deck, stretch your budget a bit and go for quality. If you can afford only one mic, it should be general-purpose enough to cover duties from vocals to electric guitars. In the lower price ranges, that means choosing a *dynamic* (versus *condenser*) microphone, such as the ever-popular Shure SM58 or its near-twin, the SM57. Both can withstand high sound pressure levels (important for amplified instruments and drums), yet they're clean enough to reproduce subtleties in a lead vocal.

Unless your finances dictate buying an inexpensive, high-impedance mic, purchase a low-impedance microphone. The only concern is that most low-impedance mics have XLR connectors, which may not work with your recorder's inputs. One solution is a low-to-high impedance transformer (about $20), available at electronic shops (such as Radio Shack) and most music stores. Don't simply use an XLR-to-¼" adapter; the transformer is an essential part of the electronic conversion process. However, not all transformers sound the same, and you get what you pay for. An audiophile-quality transformer could easily run $50–$100. Fortunately, these days most mixers and recorders include at least a few balanced mic inputs, so the need to add a transformer could be moot.

Then there's the monitor system—the amp and speakers or powered speakers you'll be using in your studio. For this basic setup, where expense is a prime factor, consider using your home stereo (providing it's

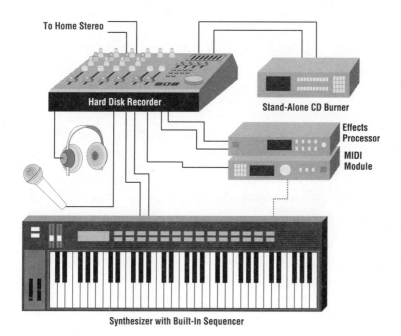

To Home Stereo

Hard Disk Recorder

Stand-Alone CD Burner

Effects Processor

MIDI Module

Synthesizer with Built-In Sequencer

Figure 1

System One contains everything you need to make good-sounding songwriter demos or sketch out compositions. Musical parts are created on the synth's onboard sequencer; the MIDI module provides extra voices and expanded timbral possibilities. Vocals and acoustic instruments go directly to the multitrack. There's no need for an extra mixer in this setup, as the one built into the recorder is more than adequate both for recording and for final mixdown to the stereo cassette deck. Monitoring is provided courtesy of your stereo system—just keep the volume down a bit so your speakers have half a chance of surviving.

at least a step or two above a boom box). Simply plug your recorder's master stereo outputs into the stereo's tape or aux input, and plug your instrument(s) into the recorder.

The biggest problem you'll face using a home stereo is determining whether it's a reliable sonic reference point, so that music you create in your studio will sound the same when played on other systems. See "Monitoring Tips" in Chapter 5 for advice on getting the most out of monitors.

One other caution when monitoring with a home stereo: Watch the volume! Keyboard instruments can produce transient signals that most home stereo speakers aren't equipped to handle. (High-energy transients are usually eliminated from CDs and tapes during the mastering process.) Unless you want to replace your speakers on a regular basis, play it safe, and monitor at reasonable levels.

The last component of your basic system is the mixdown deck. If you opt for a hard-disk system, try to get one that has a built-in CD burner, or you'll need an external device to mix to, such as a stand-alone CD recorder or a computer with a built-in or external CD-R/CD-RW drive. Of course, you still mix down to DAT for your master, and burn CDs as a separate step.

Finally, don't forget assorted cables, adapters, stands, power strips, and similar accessories (see Figure 1).

System Two: Movin' on Up
When you need improved sonics and enhanced capabilities, you'll be faced with a dilemma—whether to add to your existing system or replace the weak links. Unfortunately, there are no easy answers; weigh each purchase on its own merits. Here are some upgrade paths to consider, and what they can do for you.

The biggest weakness in System One is the lack of quality monitoring. If you want your work to sound good on systems other than the one in your studio, return the stereo to the living room and buy a good power amp and set of near-field studio reference monitors, or better yet, skip the amp and buy powered monitors. See "Monitors" in Chapter 1 for some tips on choosing the right monitor. Don't buy strictly on price or dealer recommendation. No speaker is perfectly accurate, and each has a distinctive sound. All things being equal (e.g., accurate frequency response and similar price range), choose the one that sounds best to your ears.

To create complex arrangements, you'll need more synth voices and audio tracks. If your keyboard is showing its age, consider moving up to a higher-end pro instrument with more polyphony (32 or more voices), built-in effects, better keyboard "feel," and a relatively sophisticated sequencer. Alternately, try pairing a stand-alone sequencer with a less expensive keyboard. Another option is to add a MIDI sound module.

Depending on how far you want to expand your sonic palette, consider adding a sampler. Generally speaking, samplers aren't a particularly good choice when you have only one instrument, as their memory constraints usually make them less than ideal for multitimbral operation (high-priced pro models are an exception; we'll save those for a bigger system). Samplers are, however, wonderful as a secondary sound source, as they let you customize your sound in lots of ways. As an added bonus,

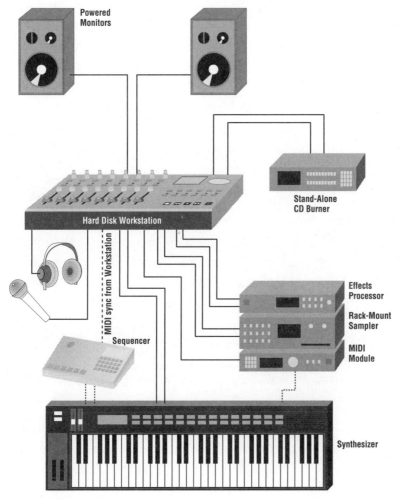

Figure 2

Upgrading from a basic setup to System Two isn't as expensive as you might think, provided you do things one step at a time. Logical paths to follow: Swap the home stereo for near-field monitors. Upgrade your multitrack. Add a rackmount sampler for timbral expansion and sound customization. And enhance your MIDI editing capabilities (or at least make your life easier) by getting a more sophisticated, stand-alone sequencer.

you can record background vocals into your sampler, and easily create thick double- or triple-tracked parts simply by layering a sample with a slightly detuned or delayed copy of itself.

Even though you've added synth voices, you don't necessarily have to record them. Synth parts can be "virtual" tracks—played live by the sequencer—right up to, and including, the final mixdown. Fortunately, MiniDisc-based multitrack recorders generate MIDI sync, so you can synchronize your sequenced sounds to parts (such as vocals) recorded on your MiniDisc recorder. See "Synchronization" in Chapter 4 for more information.

If your recorder has only four tracks, upgrade to a digital multitrack tape recorder (e.g., Alesis ADAT or TASCAM DA-88), or a hard disk recorder/workstation such as the TASCAM 788 (8 tracks), Fostex VF-160, BOSS BR-1180CD, or Yamaha AW16G. You can expand the digital tape system to 128 tracks (16 machines running synchronously), so there's plenty of room to grow; however, these types of machines require a separate mixer. Self-contained hard disk recorders are not as expandable, as they generally include a mixer, preamp, and effects. Either option has tradeoffs. Digital tape's modularity makes it easy to upgrade a piece at a time. Self-contained hard disk workstations are very convenient, but what you have is what you get, any upgrades notwithstanding (see Figure 2).

System Three: Getting Real

Better get ready to start spending some cash, as the next leap forward involves a few substantial investments, including a mixer, a computer, and/or a pro-level digital multitrack recorder. We'll also look at expanding our collection of synths, mics, and effects modules.

First up: the computer, which gives you access to powerful sequencing programs and comprehensive editor/librarians for your synths. You'll also be able to load software for digital audio editing, multitrack recording, and CD recording.

With prices plummeting in the IBM-compatible world, don't buy anything less than a fast Pentium. Any new computer will have enough RAM and hard disk capacity to get you started, but it's a good idea to buy extra RAM right at the outset (stock computers don't have enough RAM for serious music-making), and go for a larger hard drive, if the option exists and your budget allows.

The machine should also have plenty of full-sized slots (PCI types), or a FireWire port, for expansion. USB comes standard on all computers, so remember to check out music-based peripherals for USB, particularly MIDI and audio interfaces. Go for the biggest monitor you can afford—music software takes up substantial screen real estate, and you can never have too much viewing area. Systems are available at a wide variety of prices; shop the mail-order catalogs for some guidelines. (Consider buying locally, however, as you may get better service and faster support.) Try to get a computer with a DVD burner, as these will allow you not only to create DVDs, but store about seven times more data than on a conventional CD-ROM (4.7GB vs. 660).

PC and Mac sequencing software comes in all flavors. First-timers

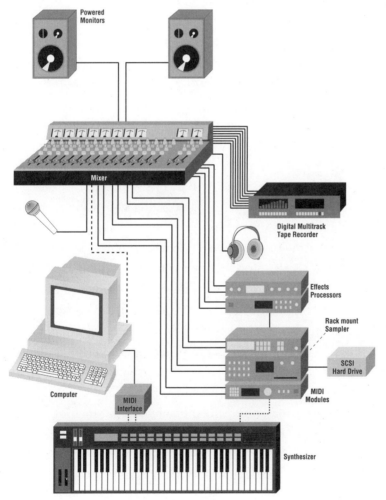

Powered Monitors

Mixer

Digital Multitrack Tape Recorder

Effects Processors

Rack mount Sampler

SCSI Hard Drive

MIDI Modules

Computer

MIDI Interface

Synthesizer

Figure 3

Be sure you're on good terms with your banker before you start entertaining the idea of making System Three your very own. Several major purchases are involved, including a computer for sequencing and editor/librarian chores, sequencing/recording software, CD burning, and a full-fledged mixer. You'll also need a MIDI interface. And an external SCSI or USB hard drive for sample storage. And a good microphone. If you keep adding—hard disk recording software, a digital multitrack tape recorder, compressors, exciters, microphones, and other assorted goodies—before you know it, you're the proud owner (or ower) of System Four. The digital tape recorder can record your tracks; however, if your computer is powerful enough and (preferably) has a sound card or interface with multiple inputs and outputs, you can dispense with the multitrack machine and record multiple tracks directly into the computer. But an 8-track digital tape recorder makes for a nice mixdown machine for six-channel surround projects.

should consider an entry-level or lite version of a sequencer (don't be put off by the term; most are very powerful, like Pro Tools LE and even Pro Tools Free). Most manufacturers let you upgrade from the entry-level version of their programs to the pro version for a reasonable charge, so don't feel that you'll be missing out on the good stuff if you don't dive in immediately at the upper level.

For your Mac or PC to communicate with your synths, you'll need a MIDI interface. If you want to simplify your life, several General MIDI modules have built-in MIDI interfaces, so you can take care of your polyphony and interface needs with one box.

Having a good sequencing setup isn't very useful without some MIDI modules to play back those sequences. When you move beyond Systems One and Two, you'll likely want to increase the scope of your sonic palette by looking for style- or timbre-specific sound modules.

Samplers also play an important role in expanding System Three. If you go for a used model, make sure the sampler is loaded with at least 8MB of RAM (preferably 16MB or more), and that you have a large hard disk or removable media drive available for storing sample data.

For effects processing, you could move up to a programmable multi-effects unit. Also consider adding a compressor, which can keep dynamics under control (particularly when recording vocals, bass, and guitar).

With a suitably powerful computer, you can record directly to hard disk using a digital audio card or a USB or FireWire interface that plugs into your computer. See Chapter 2, "Recording with Computers," for more on recording hardware and software.

Now is also the time to add a good condenser mic to your collection for cleaner, richer vocals, more defined acoustic guitar sounds, and a general quality boost, particularly with acoustic instruments. Most condenser mics require phantom power, so either buy a dedicated power supply, or make sure your mixer can provide phantom power.

As for mixers, you'll want at least a general-purpose (recording/PA) type with 16 input channels, built-in mic preamps, phantom power, six aux sends, four stereo aux returns, three-band EQ with sweepable midrange, and very good audio specs. Having an automation upgrade available doesn't hurt either. The next step up is a dedicated recording mixer that features tape returns and assignable subgroups (see Figure 3).

Since you've upped the equipment ante, take steps to protect it. Uninterruptible power supplies, line conditioners, surge protectors, and a decent insurance policy are all in order.

System Four: Playin' in the Big Leagues

With the additions described next (all of which are considered "pro level") and enough talent, you should be able to produce CD-quality recordings, suitable for release to the rest of the world. Just hope that one of those releases is a hit—you'll need it to pay for all this gear.

First, let's look at recording media. You may want to expand to a digital setup, or go for a pro-level hard disk recording system. The latter requires some type of audio interface (even with the Mac—its internal converters are no match for pro-level components), a PCI card, or FireWire (if you're using a FireWire interface) that links the computer to the outside and performs all of the DSP functions, and software to record and edit the audio data.

For any disk-based recording system, you need as fast and big a hard disk as possible—6GB is a minimum. Check with the manufacturer of the software you plan to use for recommended models.

One advantage of hard disk recording is that you can often use a single software program to record and edit digital audio data along with MIDI sequence data. Several companies offer these types of combined programs, including Cakewalk SONAR, Digidesign Pro Tools, Emagic Logic Audio, MOTU Digital Performer, Steinberg Cubase and Steinberg Nuendo. While we're talking software, operators of large MIDI systems usually can benefit from a "universal" editor/librarian, and if you plan to generate lead sheets, a notation program, like Sibelius or Finale, wouldn't hurt either.

For backup, you'll need a dedicated hard disk drive for audio (removable IDE drives in caddies are a good choice), magneto-optical cartridge drive, tape drive, or recordable CD capable of recording data (not just audio).

If you have an ADAT, several companies offer interfaces so you can transfer ADAT tracks to and from hard disk recording software (there are also interfaces for the DA-88, although these tend to be less common). This means you can record on tape, edit in the computer, and mix to either tape or the computer—pretty cool.

A good high-end sampler, or synth with a sampling option, is an essential part of any pro setup; you can even devote an entire computer to just sampling (outfitted with, say, TASCAM GigaStudio), and pipe that into your main work-environment computer. You may also find it easier to control your MIDI rig from a master keyboard. And you will need a multiport MIDI interface to drive more than 16 or 32 channels at a time, and some way to synchronize your sequencer to SMPTE time code (this is usually built into high-end interfaces).

It's probably a good idea to upgrade the effects, too. For software-based systems, simply add some effects plug-ins. If your studio is more hardware-oriented, some specialty processors (tube parametric EQ, aural exciter, etc.) are a good choice.

More gear also means you'll need more inputs, so think about adding a patch bay and possibly an additional *line mixer* to submix all your keyboards or percussion modules to your main mixer. And while you're at it, upgrade your mic collection (to include both large- and small-diaphragm condensers, as well as dynamics) and monitoring system.

Maintenance

The most important part of maintenance is preventative maintenance. Just like going in to the doctor for a flu shot before the season hits, you can prevent a lot of the problems that crop up in the studio by performing some day-to-day tasks that minimize the potential for catastrophes.

Maintaining Digital Multitrack Tape Recorders

Although we take them for granted, DAT machines, TASCAM DA-88s, ADATs, and their kin are pretty sophisticated pieces of equipment. It takes a lot of precision to align those hair-thin tracks across a moving tape with heads rotating faster than the tires on a Subaru at 60 miles per hour. In this environment, "cleanliness is next to godliness."

Regular cleaning of your DAT (or other helical scan) machine is a must. If you wait until the "CLEAN" warning comes on or for the error LED to start flashing, then it is probably too late. The heads will have become so clogged with oxide that no amount of cleaning will repair them, and you will have to spend a lot of money to replace the head drum. A once-a-week bout with the cleaning DAT (or 8mm or VHS) tape will save you a lot of misery in the end. Please remember that the cleaning tape should only be used for about 15 seconds, and should not be rewound. By not rewinding the cleaning tape, you ensure that a new, fresh section of cleaning tape contacts the heads during the cleaning cycle. The TASCAM and Sony machines know when you have inserted a cleaning tape and go through the process automatically.

Basic Maintenance Tips

- Fast-wind all tapes end to end before formatting
- Clean the heads after formatting
- Wind tapes to either end and remove from machine when not in use
- Know how to query the machine's total head hours
- Have a maintenance schedule and stick to it, or . . .
- You know it's maintenance time if the machine eats a tape, freezes up, and displays error messages.
- Get a humidity gauge
- Don't smoke

DAT machines are pretty forgiving, but weather extremes can make your digital eight-track more temperamental than usual. Too little air moisture increases static electricity. Too much moisture makes the tape stick to the heads.

Pick up a temperature/humidity gauge and take note of the changes from day to day. Try to regulate the humidity and don't forget to change the filter in the air handler. Vacuuming is also highly recommended (be sure to change that filter, too), while smoking is not.

DA-88 Cleaning. The TASCAM/Sony digital 8-track deck has fan cooling. The fan draws air into the machine across the electronics, which is good, but it can also suck dust in through the mechanism's

DIGITAL TAPE MACHINE HIDDEN FEATURES

Machine	1st Key Stroke	2nd Key Stroke	3rd Key Stroke	Function
ADAT	Set Locate & Stop			Drum "On" Time
ADAT	Set Locate & FF			Software Version
ADAT-XT	Set Locate & Stop			Drum "On" Time
DA-88	*Stop & Play			Total Drum Time
DA-88	*Stop & FF			Fast Wind Time
DA-88	*FF, Stop & Play	**Stop	Remote	Bar graph for tracks 1 & 2 will indicate errors for A & B heads when in "Play"

*The DA-88 requires the user to press these keys on Power-Up.

**Press STOP immediately after the machine is powered. The alpha-numeric display should indicate "test" mode. If so, proceed to the next keystroke.

tape-access "port." Use the high-velocity vacuum cleaner nozzle attachment and a ½-inch artist's brush to remove the stuff that collects in this area.

ADAT Maintenance. All ADATs, regardless of brand name, are made by Alesis. Some transports are noisier than others, particularly in fast-wind modes. The two culprits in the ADAT mechanism are white plastic rollers (see Figure 4).

Noisy rollers should be replaced, but a little lubricant will shut 'em right up. Both must first be removed before lube can be applied. (Power down and unplug before removing the cover.) A white plastic cap is pressure fit over the metal shaft on which the Impedance Roller spins. Use a flat-blade screwdriver as a wedge to lift the cap. Then, *gently* squeeze the cap with a serrated-jaw long-nosed pliers, alternating clockwise and counter-clockwise while *gently* pulling (see Figure 5).

Let the metal shaft enter a tube of Lubriplate (MCM, Tel: 800-543-4330, part number 20-1325) so that a light coating is left behind. Replace the roller and gently slip on the cap until there is minimal vertical play in the roller. Clean the roller with a lint-free cloth dampened with 99-percent alcohol.

To access the magnetic roller, it is necessary to power the machine and coax it to lower the tape loading "elevator." This can be done via software controls.

• Press Record 1 and Record 7 while powering up.

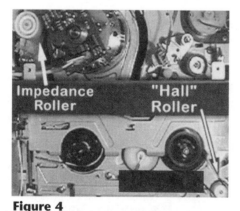

Figure 4

Figure 5

- The front panel should display "ProG."
- Press Pitch Up until the display indicates "CAP."
- Press Auto Play to extinguish the decimal point.
- Press Pitch Down to lower the elevator.

On some transports, the tape sensing latches will keep the elevator from moving; in that case, take the machine to a qualified service center.

Transport Problems. All tape machines suffer from transport-related problems. The electronics are nearly always very stable. The keys to reliable transport operation are the "Mode" and "Load" switches. These are sensors that report transport status to the system control circuitry. Dirty and worn switches generate misinformation, a.k.a. error messages and eaten or jammed tapes. If this happens to you, don't let it happen more than twice. It's time for service.

Scheduling Maintenance. Schedule maintenance every 250 hours (see table below for specific information). This is a typical schedule for the video transports used in digital tape machines. All digital 8-track decks have built-in counters that accumulate the time tape is on the heads. There are no buttons labeled "Total Head Hours." In all cases, a combination of magic buttons must be pressed to gain access to the digital netherworld.

ADAT MAINTENANCE SCHEDULE

Much like changing your car's oil every 3,000 miles, regular ADAT maintenance helps to avoid costly problems later on. Even if you think your ADAT is performing normally, hold the SET LOCATE button and then press STOP to check the head-on hours.

Every 250 Head-On Hours: The ADAT's tape path and idler wheel should be professionally cleaned.

Every 500 Head-On Hours: In addition to the above, check the tape tension and pinch roller; a service center should put the ADAT through its built-in self-test routine.

Every 1,000 Head-On Hours: In addition to the above, re-align the ADAT's tape path, check the motor, and perform tests to evaluate the performance of the ADAT's digital and sync interfaces, as well as the unit's audio quality.

Every 3,000 Head-On Hours: This is the time for a transport overhaul. In addition to the above, examine the headstack and motor, and several parts should be replaced.

Hard Disk Maintenance

Hard drives have no user-serviceable parts. However, a little preventive maintenance can help extend the life of your hard drive and possibly prevent a crash.

Preventive Maintenance

- Pay attention to early warning signs. If you hear a nasty noise when the drive is rotating, immediately back up everything! The noise probably indicates that the lubrication on the ball bearings that allow the platter to spin has broken down or dried up. Fans (replacement cost about $15) use cheaper bearings and are even more prone to this type of failure.
- Heat is the enemy. Make sure the fan/filter combination provides unobstructed air flow to prevent platter motor failure.
- To keep from losing the heads and the disk surface, avoid high impact shocks to the drive, especially while it is moving.
- Avoid having the power go off while the drive is operating (yet another argument for an uninterruptible power supply).
- Become a librarian. Since your hard drive will fail someday, always make copies of important files either on floppies, backup tapes, a second hard or MO drive, or a recordable CD. Regular backup is vital!
- Use disk diagnostic tools (such as Norton Utilities, or the Scandisk utility included in Windows) to test your hard drive's surface and data integrity. Do this at least once a week, or whenever an accident occurs that may affect hard drive data (e.g., the power goes out while the computer is shutting down).
- Reformat your disk periodically (but beware of copy-protected software; see below).
- Your software wants to write files to a contiguous chunk of memory. However, after repeated saves and erasures of files, it becomes harder and harder to find big chunks of memory. For example, suppose you fill up a 500MB hard drive with five 100MB files. Now you delete the second file and fourth files. Even though there are now 200MB free, if you want to save a 200MB file to disk, it will fill up the first available 100MB, then jump over to the next available 100MB and continue saving there. This creates two file fragments instead of one contiguous file. You can imagine that a drive with hundreds of files accumulated over months or years will be even more fragmented.

Fragmentation degrades disk performance because the head has to search around to find and store information. Use a defragmenting program, and periodically reformat your audio hard disk. To reformat, back up all data to another storage medium, fully erase the data from the drive, reformat the drive using appropriate software (e.g., Disk Tools from the Mac's system disks), then copy back the saved data. If you are not conversant with proper backup procedures, products such as Norton Utilities will save you much grief.

- There is still much copy-protected software for the Mac; these programs are generally "installed" on your hard drive, which sprays little invisible files around your system. Never defragment, optimize, or reformat a hard drive without deinstalling any copy-protected programs unless the manual specifically states that this is allowed. Otherwise, you will lose the install. Optimize only after de-installing the program(s).

Newer copy protection schemes "authorize" the hard drive, and as long as the program runs on that hard drive, you're safe—even if the hard drive is defragmented. However, if you have any doubt whatsoever whether you'll lose an install by defragmenting, de-install first.

Studio AC Protection

A chain is only as good as its weakest link, and all your gear has one link in common: the AC supply (see Figure 6). A clean, constant supply of juice reduces stress on components, cuts noise, and can minimize mysterious power-caused glitches and crashes that sometimes plague microprocessor-controlled gear. Here are some ways to clean up your AC.

- Surge/Spike Suppressors. A serious voltage spike (e.g., from a motor kicking in on the same line) can induce a glitch in microprocessor-based gear, and even cause physical damage. A spike or surge suppressor comes in two types: *Common-mode* and *transverse-mode*. A good suppressor offers both types of protection.
- Isolation Transformers. This kind of transformer isolates the gear from

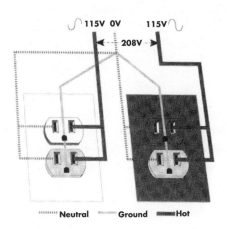

Figure 6

How electricity feeds the typical home studio

CONNECTIONS/WIRING

Cables, cords, wires—call 'em what you will, the typical home studio is filled with these long and narrow things that make no noise at all (you hope). Figuring out how everything hooks together can be pretty daunting for the newcomer.

Think of your studio's wiring not as a hopeless tangle, but as several independent networks for audio, MIDI, power, synchronization, and the computer. Here are some helpful pointers on dealing with all this.

- When rewiring or adding a new component to the system, deal with one network at a time.

- In general, power down the system before plugging and unplugging anything except MIDI cables (for audio cables, it's not necessary to power down, but you do need to turn your monitor levels all the way off). This is especially true with computer connections; you can fry a motherboard by trying to change SCSI connections without shutting down.

- Keep all audio cable runs as short as possible and away from power cables. Where the two types must cross, run them at right angles, not in parallel.

- Use color-coded cables, or tape paper labels to the ends of each cable, before plugging them into the system. This will make it far easier to troubleshoot the problem when (as inevitably happens) one of your synths refuses to make a sound.

- For cable runs of more than a couple of feet, twist-ties are an easy way to group cables into snakes and keep the rack and floor neat. Don't use the sandwich bag kind, as they have wires inside. Instead, save and reuse the plastic ones that come with your new cables. Another option: fabric stores sell Velcro strips by the foot, and two short pieces make a convenient adjustable loop. You could even glue Velcro patches to the back of a rack, then use Velcro loops to corral the cables. Don't wrap snakes in tape, which can leave a sticky residue.

- Collect a box full of handy hardware accessories that make life in the studio easier. This includes plug adapters that change one plug or jack type into another, female-to-female cable extenders, and cables and/or adapters that translate male into female in all formats. Also useful are Y-cables, 9V batteries and AC adapters for guitar effects, a test tone generator, and a low-power speaker you can plug into a headphone jack (like the type intended for use with portable tape/CD players).

Even when you understand the principles of proper cabling, figuring out which cables should go where can be a challenge. Try sketching out the different kinds of recording procedures that you'll want to use in the studio. Choose your most common applications and set up your studio in that configuration. Then when you're in a creative mood, things will be set up how you want them.

the AC line to provide a cleaner source of AC power. For example, MIDI Motor Hum Buster houses the equivalent of 10 isolation transformers, with matching AC outlets, in a rack box. Because each outlet is isolated, ground loops are not possible.

- Line Regulators. If your power is subject to brownouts, a line regulator can help prevent losing data in RAM if there's a momentary power dip. Regulators are cheaper than uninterruptible power supplies.

- Uninterruptible Power Supply. A UPS contains an internal battery that is constantly being charged. If the AC input voltage goes away, an inverter processes the battery's output to provide AC power for a limited amount of time (typically 10 minutes, more under light loads). This is usually enough time to shut down a computer system in an orderly way.

A basic industrial-grade UPS generally costs a little under $1 per watt of protection. More reserve time raises the price; consumer-oriented versions, such as those made by APS for individual computers, can run as low as 50 cents per watt.

Look for a unit with a pure sine wave output (cheaper models may generate distorted waveforms that are not suitable for sensitive gear), fast detection time (so it knows that the power has gone away), and fast transfer time (under 10 milliseconds) over to the auxiliary power. Manufacturers of these products include Sola, Stabiline, and TrippLite. Many products include insurance up to $50,000–$100,000 that covers the gear being powered, should damage occur due to electrical problems.

Where to Get AC Protection Products

Industrial-grade products are available from high-level computer stores and electronic supply houses. Consumer-oriented versions are available from mail-order and online computer stores such as PC Mall and MacWarehouse.

Studio Ergonomics

It's best to have all equipment needed for typical recording situations within arm's reach. Having to crawl behind or under something to access a front panel gets old pretty fast—give some thought to how you use your studio, how you flow among the various functions, and ways to minimize the amount of wasted motion that happens during the recording process.

Unfortunately, subtle ergonomic problems may go undetected, causing muscle strain, eyestrain, or minor irritation for months or years without rising above the threshold of awareness. So take a look around your studio with an eye to the following:

Lighting. Ideally, the main light source should be behind you to minimize glare; but position it so that your computer screen doesn't reflect the light. Lights should be bright enough that you can see what you're doing, but not so bright that the studio feels like the operating room at the veterinarian's office. (Unless, of course, you also operate on small animals as a sideline to your studio business.)

In the daytime, direct sunlight from a window can render an LED unreadable. Likewise, a window behind the computer screen will make the screen hard to see in full daylight—but too little light on the wall behind the screen can also be a source of eyestrain. Speaking of lighting, if you need to get behind your racks to repatch modules, you may find a high-intensity flashlight a useful studio accessory.

Dimmers are definitely not recommended, unless you buy the somewhat pricier types that include built-in filtering to minimize the amount of electrical "hash" the dimmer contributes to the AC line. Otherwise, you'll probably end up with nasty buzzes when you record guitar. Sometimes dimmer buzz can even work its way into mixers and recorders. If you're in a situation where there are dimmers, turning them up to maximum brightness will cut out most of the noise.

Traditional "tube" fluorescent lights can also be a problem, but the new, compact fluorescent bulbs are a different story. These are great for the studio as they generate very little heat, seldom require replacement, and the light they produce is quite soft. Although expensive, the savings in electricity and replacement bulbs more than offsets the difference. They're also more environmentally friendly than traditional incandescent bulbs.

Ventilation. If you decide on an extensive remodeling job, don't forget about ventilation. Air conditioners add background rumble that's hard to remove without acoustic baffling. One tip (thanks to Spencer Brewer at Laughing Coyote Studios) is to make the ducts larger than recommended. Smaller ducts increase the amount of air pressure, whereas with larger ducts, the air just sort of "falls" out, which creates less air motion. In any event, make any contractors fully aware of your needs before they start construction.

Some studio owners swear by negative ion generators as a way to create fresher air and reduce fatigue. Regardless of whether these claims are true, these devices also remove particulate matter from the air, which is indisputably beneficial. It's generally advised not to place them too close to computers, as the negative ions could gravitate to the high voltage connections present in monitors.

Also remember that humidity isn't good for your gear (in fact, some gear, including DATs and video transport-based audio recorders, will shut themselves off automatically if the humidity goes too high). A dehumidifier is a good idea, but even "passive" dehumidifiers (such as Damp Rid) that use moisture-absorbing crystals can be tremendously helpful.

Posture. Is your chair the right height for playing the keyboard? If you're shopping for a new chair or bench, take this question into account. Not all adjustable stands will adjust up or down as far as they should. Depending on your setup, you may want to pay extra for an adjustable-height chair. In a larger studio, a chair with casters on the legs may make it far easier to reach all of the modules. Does the chair provide proper back support? Chronic pain in your back or shoulders after a few hours in the studio is a good sign that you may have the wrong chair. Also, the computer's mouse pad should be positioned where you can get at it without reaching or twisting your torso.

Layout. If your master keyboard has enough empty space on its top panel, you may be able to place the computer's keyboard and mouse pad there. With a two-tier keyboard stand, the computer monitor could sit on the upper tier—but this will work only if the upper tier has enough depth that the monitor can be set back, away from your face. Having the screen within 18 inches of your eyes when you're playing virtually guarantees eyestrain.

Given that the three basic components of a typical digital home studio are the computer, the master MIDI keyboard, and the mixer, one will be in front of you, one to the left, and one to the right. This puts everything within arm's reach (note that with some hard disk systems, you may not need a mixer at all). Consider which element you will use most, and which needs to face the monitors in the "sweet spot," so that you can listen in stereo. If you have lots of keyboards, set up two keyboard stands off to the side as mirror images of each other, so they form a "V."

Doing control room vocals requires that you minimize ambient noise. Use external hard drives and put them below the computer table. Just putting them on the floor reduces noise; adding some carpet underneath the drives and on the underside of the table reduces the noise even more. Another noise abatement trick: use powered monitors without fans, instead of speakers and a power amp that includes a fan.

Keep guitars at right angles to the computer to reduce noise pickup. If there's a lot of interference, just turn off the computers and go directly to tape to minimize noise (or if you use a hard disk recording system, turn off the video monitor and do your recording with keyboard equivalents).

Creative Ease. Minimize the time it takes to get your studio up and running—for example, being able to power up the whole studio from one switch is great. If you normally use two or three main pieces of software, learn how to auto-boot them when the computer switches on (e.g., in Windows, place the program, or a shortcut to the program, into the Startup folder within the Windows directory).

Finally, keep a small, budget-priced portable cassette recorder with a built-in mic in the studio at all times—plugged in and ready to go—to "jot down" ideas quickly. Also, the small, dictation-type microcassette recorders are great for portable applications—stuff one in your shirt pocket, and you'll never lose a good idea again.

Studio Organization

A database program is a good idea for studio documentation, as it can store not only phone numbers and financial details, but what sounds are used in a given project, and where those sounds are stored. It also allows you to do keyword searches.

If you have many DATs, disks, and other storage media, a good cataloging system is essential. Label disks, and update your documentation as you go along. Later, you may not remember the details of a specific project. Many sequencer programs include a notepad utility, but if yours doesn't, there's always the one that comes with your computer (Stickies on the Mac, Notepad for Windows). And while taking notes on your projects, don't forget the SMPTE start time, if applicable, for each tune.

If you don't start each sequence track with a program change, note which program or programs are used for each track, and in which sections of the tune. If you tend to jump back and forth a lot from one tune to another, you might also find it helpful to keep an annotated, cross-referenced list of the patches currently in each synth's RAM. If you want to edit a particular patch for the tune you're working on, consult the list to find out whether that patch is being used in any other tune—and if so, the memory locations in which the new version can safely be stored. Better yet, maintain a separate Sys-Ex disk for all the instruments used in a song.

Once you've acquired a few synths or tone modules and some extra cards or banks of sounds, organizing the sounds can become quite a challenge. Factory banks usually contain a little of everything in each bank to show off the instrument better in a store, which can make it a real chore to find what you want. After going through your available sounds and deciding which ones you'll want to keep at your fingertips, organize your RAM banks to group similar sounds together—basses in locations 1 through 8, strings in 9 through 22, and so on (or follow the General MIDI protocol if you're a fan of standardization).

However, don't fill up the entire memory (if you're using a GM-based categorization, one possibility is to leave the effects sounds empty). Keep eight or ten locations empty as storage buffers for each individual project. For example, a given tune might demand an electric piano with wild chorusing. The right patch might be on a ROM card in a drawer somewhere, or you might have to create it by editing an existing patch. In either case, store it in internal memory at location 98 or 99. This way, you'll be able to access it with a simple program change command during the sequence—there will be no need to mess with bank select commands, or (heaven forbid) to swap ROM cards in the middle of a tune.

The music isn't the only element that you may want to document; consider storing the studio configuration itself in a word processor file, detailing your equipment and how it's hooked up. This is particularly useful with multiport MIDI interfaces, so you always know which gear hooks up to which MIDI channel. Another option is to put a small, removable label on each piece of gear's front panel showing the MIDI cable and channel number.

4

Recording

Basic Recording Tips

Many major recordings have been partially, and sometimes entirely, recorded in home studios. Granted, some of these home studios are quite elaborate, but hit records have been cut on nothing more than a beat-up Compaq computer and a few samplers. With a little knowledge, some decent gear, a smidgen of ingenuity, and a healthy heap o' talent, you too can create great-sounding recordings at home.

Getting Started. One of the greatest advantages of having a home studio is freedom. You never know when creative inspiration may strike. Always have everything hooked up in your studio and ready to go. It's not enough just to have a studio set up; it needs to be set up efficiently, as discussed in Chapter 3.

Unless your multitrack recorder generates SMPTE

time code (either by itself, or through an optional box), stripe one track with time code. Generally, hard disk-based systems can generate time code; low-end digital tape machines do not, although adapters exist that can extract time code from the recorder's timing circuitry so that it's not necessary to give up a track (as it is on the ADAT, for example). The time code allows synchronizing devices such as sequencers, automated mixdown modules, and even video to your audio.

Once the preliminaries are out of the way, it's time to start tracking your instruments.

Recording Electric Guitar. Many guitar styles thrive on earthy technology, and electric guitars in particular have a limited frequency range that survives low-end recording and processing better than many other instruments. Simply put, you don't need fancy equipment to capture great guitar sounds.

Recording Direct. A recording made by miking a cool amp with a good mic in a great-sounding room tends to sound deeper and more multidimensional than any direct recording—regardless of the effects used. But even with access to the above—and no volume constraints—there are times when a quirky direct sound may serve you better than a miked amp.

Guitar amps aren't neutral. A lot of what we traditionally love about electric guitar sound has to do with the idiosyncratic distortion and equalization curves they impose on your signal. Plugging your guitar directly into a mixing board or recorder input is like playing through your home stereo. You get higher highs and lower lows, but the tone may feel flat and unengaging.

If you overdrive your mixer or recorder's preamp and adjust the EQ, you start to reintroduce a guitar amp's distortion and coloration. You probably can't craft a convincing amp tone that way, but you may forge some compelling sounds. You can also create some useful direct sounds with just a few stompboxes or a multieffects; for example, a bit of compression, some midrange dips and spikes via a graphic or parametric equalizer, and some delay can deliver a handsome clean tone.

Although the better guitar-oriented preamps and effects may not seem to have the right "feel" as you record through them, you may be pleasantly surprised by the track's authenticity during playback. Effects are especially handy for crafting an appropriate tone when adding a guitar part to an already dense track. But a less specialized preamp—just something to add sparkle and clarity to your guitar tone before it hits the mixer—may be all you need.

Miking Amps. Place the mic a few inches from the speaker. Aiming directly into the cone yields the sharpest tone; to soften it, angle the mic slightly. Another common approach is to place one mic directly on the speaker and another a few feet back. Patch both mics into your mixer, listen on headphones to the close mic alone, then bring up the distant one. You'll hear the difference instantly—the more diffuse, echoey room mic adds depth and dimension to the closer mic's sound. You also may hear a sort of hollow, phasing-like sound as you adjust the relative levels, due to possible cancellations between the two mics. That isn't necessarily a bad thing—it can add texture to the track, helping it stand out in the mix. Expensive condenser mics are great for capturing the room sound, but you can get good results with a modest dynamic mic, or one of those flat PZM mics, which run about $50 at Radio Shack. A PZM situated on a hard floor a few feet in front of an amp can add character to a close mic, though a single close mic sometimes has the most impact.

Top-flight studios invest much time and money in tuning their rooms for optimum sound, but there's a lot to be said for exploring your workspace's random sonic idiosyncrasies. That too-full closet may be ideal for a punchy, dead sound; a small amp on a hardwood floor might offer the perfect brittleness. Try putting the amp in the shower (water off!), where the hard surfaces can lend an eerie harshness. You can get a dirty, claustrophobic tone by miking a tiny, overdriven amp inside a cardboard box, and a garage sounds, well, garagey.

It's tough to beat the tone of a modest combo amp. Obviously, you can get power-amp distortion at lower volume with a small amp. But don't overlook the possibility of running a distortion pedal into a quiet, clean amp.

Don't rule out using just plain _bad_ amps, which can lend a unique edge and character. Try playing through a cassette player, an intercom, or a walkie-talkie. And those toy Marshall half-stack amps are superb for creating hard, pinpoint tones that can slice through a dense mix (see Figure 1).

Recording Acoustic Guitar. To capture the true sound of a fine acoustic, nothing beats an expensive condenser mic. If you specialize in solo acoustic playing, your best bet is probably to find a great-sounding room—such as a church, or a woody-sounding front parlor—and record direct to disk or DAT through a pair of condenser mics and a couple of quality preamps (many guitarists favor tube preamps for their "warmth").

Figure 1

Recording from a small, overdriven amp can sound like a big amp.

Direct recording options are less appealing than for electric. The piezo-electric pickups built into many new acoustic-electrics are controversial. Some guitarists revel in their crisp sound; others find even the best systems irritating and quacky. Usually, proper equalization can bring up the lower midrange and bass, improving the sound dramatically. However, even unequalized piezo pickups can sound just fine when laid back in a mix, and that characteristic piezo "zing" can be just what's needed to stand out in a track.

Aiming a mic directly at the soundhole usually sounds too boomy. Try angling it toward the neck-body junction—even then you may have to roll off some low midrange frequencies. And because the acoustic's dynamic range is so much greater than an overdriven electric guitar, you may need some compression to capture soft passages at an adequate level without having loud parts exceed the available dynamic range.

Sticking a magnetic soundhole pickup on an acoustic and playing through an amp or amp simulator is a fascinating and under-explored approach. It doesn't sound anything like a miked acoustic guitar, but it can yield some spectacular sounds.

Using Effects with Guitar. Global warning: Effects tend to obscure the character of your instrument and the way you play it. Don't be afraid of them, but be aware of their tendency to make your guitar sound generic. Guitar tracks often need less distortion than you might think. Excessive distortion tends to wash out the guitar's entire frequency range. Context is everything—a moderately distorted tone can seem like the filthiest thing in the world after a comparatively clean passage.

Modulation effects like chorus, flange, and tremolo can animate a track or just dull your point with unnecessary detail. Chorusing thickens, but generally removes edge, though the animation of chorusing and flanging might draw attention to an instrument obscured in a mix. If you use a flanger you should probably record it to the multitrack rather than add it during the mix. This way you can record the sweep you like best. Another option is to sweep the effect manually while mixing, although this may be a problem if you're occupied with other aspects of the mixing process.

Think dynamically. For example, instead of using a bit of reverb throughout, try a relatively dry mix with just one intermittent part subjected to heavy reverb—that way you'll at least have some spatial and temporal contrasts. And don't be afraid to explore your own spaces—thousands own the same reverb chip, but only you have your tiled bathroom.

If you think you need reverb, first consider the delay alternative. Delays can add the spaciousness you seek without gumming up the entire track. Old-style analog delays have diminished high-end response, which makes them sound warmer, with the fuzzy echoes sitting neatly behind the direct guitar signal. You can fake that sound by splitting your guitar into two signal paths: One goes directly to the mixer, while the other goes to the mixer through the delay (set this for delayed sound only—no straight sound). Roll off some of the highs on the mixer channel carrying the delayed signal; you might also want to experiment with stereo placement (e.g., guitar panned left of center, echo panned right of center). Also try recording simultaneous miked and direct tracks, and separate them slightly in the mix.

If you have tracks to spare and want a "wider" sound, try doubling a part. Panning an exactly doubled part full left and right—a technique favored by everyone from acoustic strummers to death-metal riffers—is guaranteed to create an ultra-wide stereo image, but that extreme approach can get fatiguing, especially on a loud foreground part. Consider narrower panning, and don't rule out doubling in mono. But keep in mind that doubling doesn't necessarily make a part sound *bigger*, just wider.

Finally, don't forget to inflict your funky guitar effects on other instruments. Controlled distortion, for example, can sound amazing on drums, or transform a weenie keyboard preset into a terrifying roar. And you may be shocked by how wicked vocals sound through a dedicated guitar reverb—or a guitar amp.

The digital tape/hard disk popularity has spurred a renaissance in tube preamps and compressors designed to inject analog warmth, with a number of new devices aimed at the semi-pro market. These boxes can soften the sometimes clinical contours of digital recordings. You can record individual tracks through them—perhaps going straight to the recorder, bypassing the mixing board—or use them to warm up an entire mix. They impart a more tape-like sound to the individual tracks, as well as help them merge better.

Great mixes are dynamic. A nice sound isn't enough—it has to move. Give your mix a foreground and background; not everything can be loud. Explore contrasts of wet and dry, as opposed to cramming everything into one space, however attractive. Don't be afraid to use small sounds, which give big sounds room to exist (and make them sound huge in comparison). If the guitars are big, try small drums, and vice versa. Play left against right, near against distant, loud against soft, bright against warm, smooth against rough.

Don't be a perfectionist about mistakes. So many guitarists let their inspiration dribble away while chasing perfect takes. We tend to be more forgiving of others' flaws than our own—are you really bummed out by the small clams you hear on so many classic records?

Finally, don't be afraid of your naked tone. Let your fingers and frets come through; they are more compelling than any mass-produced gadget. Your personality is your greatest asset.

Recording Vocals. Vocals are a problem area for most home studios. Once again, it's hard for the humble home studio to compete with the expensive microphones, preamps, and outboard gear used by most professional studios. But with a modest investment in the proper equipment, and a little experimentation, it is possible to achieve good-sounding vocals at home. Get the best mic you can afford, and use (but not abuse) a compressor/limiter.

Try to use separate mics for each vocalist, so you have more control over the mix. If your recorder has a VSO (variable speed oscillator, sometimes called a pitch or speed control), you can use this to create chorus, harmonizing, or equalization effects that sound particularly effective on background vocals. For example, for a fuller sound, record the first vocal track at normal speed, the second track about 5% slower, and the third track 5% faster.

Experiment with different microphone positions before going for a killer take. Microphones can sound vastly different depending upon where they're placed in relation to the sound source, as well as reflective surfaces in the room. Once you've found the right spot, mark it with masking tape on the floor. It's also usually not best to record a vocalist by putting the mic right in his or her face. It should be at least eight or ten inches away, and a bit above the mouth in order to avoid pops and sibilance. A mesh pop screen, available at any music store, is a must.

Recording Drums. It is very difficult to record acoustic drums in a home studio. Even if you're lucky enough to have a large, good-sounding room to record in, you'll also need thousands of dollars' worth of microphones, preamps, and processors to achieve optimum sound quality—not to mention neighbors who can handle the noise.

Because of this, most people use drum machines in their home studios, but even these can be problematic. The biggest complaint is that drum machines often sound too much like machines. However, there are several strategies you can use to make your drum parts sound more realistic. See "Recording Electronic Drums" below for tips on improving the sound of your drums.

About Effects. The source should sound as good as possible before you record it. Use effects sparingly; when you sit in your studio for hours, after a while you'll get used to the reverb, so you'll want to add more. Eventually, you'll be swimming in reverb. Over-equalizing changes phase relationships to other sounds. You might want to use EQ to cut rather than boost; for example, if a sound isn't bassy enough, consider rolling off the treble rather than boosting the bass. This will give the EQ more headroom, and reduce the chance of distortion.

If you want a track with more presence and headroom, try using a compressor (but don't overcompress or the sound will be "smaller"). A noise gate, designed to eliminate system noise during moments when a given track is silent, can add space by removing unwanted noise or shortening decays.

Experiment with your signal processors. Although a pitch shifter is designed to create a clone of a track at an altered pitch, instead try using it to move the vocalist's reverb or delay a 5th above the pitch at which he or she is singing. Or, use a noise gate to eliminate a keyboard pad during the spaces between hi-hat hits (using the gate's key input).

Many engineers compress the full mix as a matter of course, particularly with beat-heavy music, to allow the kick and snare to dominate the sound without pushing the signal into overload. This is less effective with "bands" made up of sampled and synthesized sounds, because the sounds often start out tremendously compressed. And, of course, it may not be musically appropriate in other situations.

Try recording tracks with effects, and make sure the performer can hear the effects while playing. In these days of multi-processors and affordable multitracks, this isn't common practice; it's more likely that decisions about which effects to add will get postponed until mixdown time. But effects—delay, flanging, and reverbs of various sorts—can influence the performance, and you may well find that the two are better married if they're performed and recorded together. Also, a board that lacks lots of effects sends and returns for each channel will limit how many effects you can add during mixdown.

Performance vs. Perfection. All the emphasis on perfection nowadays has overshadowed one of the most important aspects of music: performance. While it doesn't hurt to spend a little extra time making sure everything sounds good and that you don't make any mistakes, always keep focused on the emotion and energy you're trying to convey.

Final Tips. When recording digitally, watch your levels. Once you go beyond true digital zero, it's all over (load). On the other hand, don't be too conservative or you'll lose valuable resolution. Every 6dB down from zero is the equivalent of giving up one bit of resolution. Therefore, if your peaks don't exceed –6 with a 16-bit recording medium, then your recording is actually a 15-bit recording, not 16-bit. However, if a piece of digital audio has just a few extremely short transients that hit maximum headroom, you can go a little over zero and (hopefully) not hear the difference.

Practice routine studio maintenance, as outlined in Chapter 3. With digital tape, clean the heads with a dry cleaning cassette every 100–200 hours. With hard disk recorders, defragment your disk after each session. Get the dust out of those pots and faders, too—a mixer cover is a great idea—and clean patch cords every four to six months.

Always remember that the arrangement is a critical element in the success of your production. A well-arranged piece of music can virtually mix itself if the tracks are recorded properly. On the other hand, a poorly arranged piece of music can be changed drastically by creative muting during the mixdown—that is, by "fixing it in the mix."

Don't worry about your gear's limitations. When it comes to recording, the most significant limitations are time, energy, and imagination. Where there's a vision and a will, there's nearly always a way.

Working alone in your studio provides great freedom, but the isolation can turn into a creative bottleneck. When you write, arrange, produce, and engineer everything yourself, you're not getting any new input. Working with other people, though it can be frustrating at times, often helps lift you out of creative ruts.

Recording Electronic Drums

Although electronic drums are instruments in their own right, for better or worse they are often compared to the real thing—and usually don't come out ahead. Let's look at some tips that will not only improve your recorded sound, but may improve the quality of the part as well.

Try triggering sounds and samples "live" rather than entering them in step time. If you're recording drum tracks in a sequencer, try to avoid using quantization. Play the part over and over, if you have to, until you get a feel that you like. Some drum modules let you use MIDI continuous controllers to make subtle changes in individual drum sounds. Used judiciously, controller modulation can definitely help. The track may not sound exactly like a real drummer, but it will sound less robotic.

Another approach is to buy a sample CD of drum loops, and create your part by looping the same rhythm over and over. Modern software, like Sonic Foundry ACID and Propellerhead ReCycle, allow you to time-stretch loops to fit most any tempo, and you can always overdub some percussion manually—tambourine, maracas, shaker, etc.—to add interest. Some of these CDs provide samples of individual drums from the same kit that plays the loop. You can use these to fly in additional snare drum hits, tom fills, and so on that are different in every bar.

If you're not a drummer, you may be able to find one who is willing to play a part on MIDI pads. The natural accents, and the part itself, will probably be more realistic than anything you'd come up with using a keyboard as an input device. If you record the part into a sequencer, you can clean up occasional fluffed notes without disturbing the live feel, but be careful not to over-edit. Get the drummer to play the track several times if necessary, and then cut and paste the best bits into one finished track. Or, borrow a good snare drum and sample it yourself. Take five or six samples with as close to the same tone quality as you can manage, assign them to adjacent keys on the sampler, then alternate between the keys to add variety to the snare sound.

Limited Polyphony. Most drum machines have limited polyphony: if you try to play too many sounds at once, voices may be "stolen" (i.e., newer sounds will cut off the sustains of existing sounds).

One solution with multitracks is to sync the drums to a sync track, and record a few drums per track (muting the other drum sounds) on each pass. Or, record some drums in your multitrack recorder, sync the drum machine to MIDI (or drive a drum tone module with a MIDI sequencer), and play the remaining sounds as "virtual" tracks during mixdown. But be careful: non-drummers frequently overplay parts, and have too many sounds going on at once. If you're running out of voices, that could be one of the warning signs of a bad drum arrangement.

One main voice-stealing problem is cymbals being cut off, as these have long decays. If possible, overdub real cymbals and forget about using the electronic versions, which generally sound inferior anyway. In fact, you can often fool people into thinking you're using real drums just by overdubbing real cymbals.

Separate Outputs. In addition to stereo outputs, most drum modules have individual outputs to which you can assign various drums. These outs are excellent for pulling the kick and snare out of the main mix and feeding them separately into the console. Typically, these two sounds are the foundation of a drum mix, and often benefit from custom EQ or other processing. It's also easier to change levels by moving a mixer fader than jumping into a drum module menu. Just remember to take any drums out of the main mix that you're feeding in separately.

Panning. Decide if the listener is behind the drums or in the audience, as this influences where you position the hi-hats and toms in the stereo field. Some prefer the audience viewpoint, where toms are on the left and the hi-hat is on the right. Figure 2 shows a typical drum setup and where you might pan individual drums in the left/right stereo field; keep your hypothetical setup in mind as you set the panning.

Instead of panning drums full right and left, try closing them in a little bit toward the center. This leaves some room for percussion instruments, which tend to go more to the extremes. Arrange the panning so that drums don't fight with respect to frequency response, but complement each other. For example, with hi-hats on the right, place tambourines and shakers—which also have a lot of high frequencies—toward the left. Since toms are on the left, pan bongos, dumbeks, timbales, and other pitched drums to the right.

The Problem with Processing. Be careful when processing electronic drums. Most manufacturers already add EQ, treble enhancement, compression, etc., to make their drums as wonderful-sounding as possible. It's often better to seek out the dry drum sounds and work with those so you can add your own processing.

A different reverb on each drum seems to diminish the power of the part. Instead, a combination of reverberation with short delays often works well.

Sequencing with Electronic Drums. If you want to avoid a mechanical feel, you need to think like a drummer. Here are more tips that should help.

Changing Tempo. Real drummers speed up and slow down to add expressiveness to a song. These changes are often subtle, but they have a huge effect on the emotional impact of the music. Your sequencer will have some option for varying the tempo—use it! Pull the tempo down one beat per minute (bpm) just before going into the solo, push it one bpm higher during the solo, and so on.

Alternating Pitches. No two drum hits by a player are exactly alike, but they are in the world of electronic drums. To get around that problem, try assigning the same drum sound to two different notes, and detune one very slightly compared to the other. Then use a "logical edit" function to move every other snare hit to the alternate drum sound. This is particularly helpful with drum rolls.

Track Shifting. Drummers often push or lag individual notes to create a particular feel. For example, pushing the ride cymbal a bit ahead of the beat is a common jazz technique, whereas rock drummers often

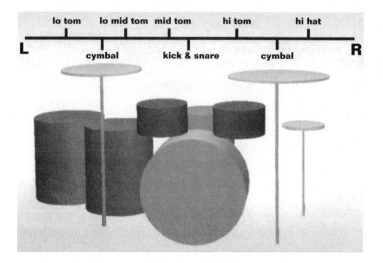

Figure 2

Proper panning greatly influences the impact and realism of a drum kit during the mixing process.

lag a little on the snare to create a "bigger" sound (subjectively, we naturally associate delay with distance). Sequencers generally include a track shift function that can move entire tracks forward or backward a certain number of MIDI clocks, which is ideal for this application. Others provide "groove templates," which can quantize drums to patterns other than traditional quantization templates. For example, these patterns might have been played by a real drummer or follow a particular type of rhythm (e.g., salsa or Brazilian), thus imparting some of the feel that only a human drummer can truly provide.

Timing. Drum machines usually respond faster to MIDI data than do synths (particularly workstation types running in a polytimbral mode). To bring all sounds "into the pocket," consider shifting the drum track a few clocks later to compensate.

Velocity vs. Controller 7. To change drum levels when sequencing, you have two choices: alter velocity or (with some drum machines) feed MIDI Controller 7 messages into the drum module. Controller 7 usually sets the overall volume, whereas velocity affects individual drums. With multisampled drums, velocity changes may also affect the timbre. To change individual drum levels without altering timbre, do so at the machine itself, using the available drum level mix option.

Finally, remember to keep it simple. You'll seldom hear anyone say a drum part had too *few* notes!

Synchronization

Synchronization allows two devices to work in tandem by providing a precise master timing source, which the devices use as a reference. When two devices are synced, one is the *master* (the source of timing information, which it generates internally) and the other is the *slave* (which receives this timing data and reacts accordingly). Under these conditions, the slave is in "external clock" or "external sync" mode, because it receives timing clock information from the master. In other situations, a dedicated master timing source may generate sync signals that all of the synchronized (slaved) devices receive.

For example, if you want to link two 8-track tape decks together for a total of 16 tracks, the tape transport mechanisms have to sync (lock) together. If they aren't synced—even if they start precisely at the same moment—sooner or later they will drift apart because of mechanical differences. This will create an echo effect of ever-increasing length as the devices slip further and further out of sync.

A common synchronization method for desktop musicians is syncing a sequencer to a digital multitrack tape recorder. Even if you're using a single computer to multitask a software sequencer with a hard disk recording program, the two must still be synchronized. Computer-based devices usually have far more precise timing than motorized tape decks, but the problems due to any lack of synchronization only get more subtle; they don't go away.

Synchronization Applications. Following is a list of common applications for synchronization in the studio.

• Synchronize multitrack recorders together (whether analog or digital tape, hard disk, MIDI sequencing, or some combination) to create more tracks. Press the transport controls on one machine, and the others follow along. You can also synchronize a MIDI sequencer to tape or hard disk and record MIDI data in the sequencer, along with audio data in the hard disk or tape recorder.

• Synchronize an automated mixdown system and/or signal processing system to a multitrack recorder.

• Interdevice MIDI communication. For example, sync a drum machine via MIDI to a sequencer that is itself synchronized to tape or hard disk.

• Synchronize two or more devices to create a multimedia setup (e.g., sync an audio recorder to a video recorder to create a soundtrack).

• Digital audio synchronization. Digital audio signals need to be synchronized to a master clock to prevent certain types of "jitter" that can degrade sound quality.

Synchronization Signals. Different applications require different types of synchronization signals. The two main references for sync signals are _absolute_ time (hours/minutes/seconds) and relative (musical) time (bars/beats). The two formats used for these are SMPTE and MIDI, respectively. First we'll cover the different kinds of MIDI sync signals, then SMPTE synchronization.

MIDI Sync

The MIDI Spec includes synchronization instructions in the form of digital timing messages, which are exchanged between pieces of equipment over the MIDI cable.

Start, Stop, and Continue. The most basic MIDI sync instructions are _start_, _stop_, and _continue_ commands. These synchronization messages are examples of System Common data (i.e., all instruments on all channels, not just individual instruments on individual channels, receive this data).

- *Start* tells the slave when the master has started so that the two units can start together. Start always causes a device to start at the beginning.
- *Stop* tells the slave when the master has stopped so that the two units can stop together.
- *Continue* tells the slave to resume playing from where it was last stopped so that the two units can continue together from that point.

MIDI Clocks. Once you press Play, you now need signals that will keep the units in sync. The simplest option is the *MIDI clock* signal. A master device transmits clock bytes over a MIDI cable at a rate of 24 ppq (pulses per quarter note), so the master MIDI clock emits 24 MIDI clock messages every quarter note. When a slave receives one of these messages, it advances its internal clock by $\frac{1}{24}$th of a quarter note.

In MIDI, clock messages have priority over all other messages to ensure accurate time keeping. Many devices, such as sequencers, further subdivide this clock rate internally so that events may be recorded with greater resolution (e.g., $\frac{1}{480}$th of a quarter note).

MIDI clocks are tempo dependent. If the master sequencer speeds up, it will transmit more MIDI clocks per second, and the slave will speed up too.

Song Position Pointer Messages. MIDI Song Position Pointer messages (SPP messages) identify precise locations in a song. They do this by keeping track of how many 16th notes have elapsed since the beginning of a tune (up to 16,384 total). An SPP message is usually issued just prior to a continue command, which provides autolocation. For example, suppose a drum machine is slaved to a sequencer. If you start the sequencer in the middle of a song (e.g., 724 16th notes into the song), as soon as you start the sequencer, the following events happen:

1. The sequencer issues an SPP message that tells the drum machine, "Hey, we're 724 16th notes into the song!"

2. The drum machine then autolocates to 724 16th notes from the beginning.

3. The sequencer pauses long enough for the drum machine to autolocate, then sends a continue message.

4. Both units play from that point on.

With SPP, you can record a sync track whose tempo varies; however, once the SPP data is recorded on tape, the tempo is fixed and cannot be altered.

Tempo Maps. What happens if you want the MIDI clock sync signal to change tempo at various points in the song? After all, a static tempo can be pretty uninteresting. The solution is a tempo map—a programmed series of tempo changes. Typically, you can change time signature at any measure and tempo at any time.

Tempo maps require that the MIDI aspect of the song be structured in advance, so it's best to start composing with the MIDI sequencer. If the MIDI sequencer syncs to MTC (described next), it will follow the sync signal but add any tempo changes that you created. With SPP/FSK sync, the FSK tone recorded as audio reflects the tempo changes, and on playback, the sequencer follows these changes.

MIDI Time Code (MTC). This part of the MIDI specification allows SMPTE times (see "SMPTE Time Code," below) to be communicated directly over MIDI, thus allowing MIDI devices to respond to absolute times if necessary. An example will help clarify why this is desirable.

Suppose you're scoring a commercial, and also providing some sampled sound effects to be played back from a sampler. You sync your sequencer to the video, and start creating the background music. Then as you see where specific effects are to take place—a car crash, crowd applause, etc.—you play the corresponding keys on the sampler that trigger those sound effects, and record those keypresses into the sequencer. Perfect—on playback, the tune is in sync with the video, and all the effects are triggered in just the right places.

Then the producer decides to speed up the song tempo by five percent. So you speed up the sequence tempo, but now the rate at which the sound effects occur speeds up too, and they no longer match the film. The problem is simple: the sound effects relate to absolute time—in other words, the door should slam at perhaps 12 seconds and 11 frames into the film, regardless of what the music is doing. The music itself relates to relative (musical) time.

With a MIDI time code-equipped sampler, you could create an *event list* of SMPTE time code cues, then trigger the samples via MIDI time code at specific times. Problem solved—you can change the sequencer tempo, yet the MIDI time code values remain constant, since they relate directly back to SMPTE. Therefore, the samples will be triggered at the specified times regardless of what happens with the sequencer.

When a sequencer is synced to MTC, it references its own internal tempo—in the bars, beats, and measures of musical time—against the absolute time. For example, if the tempo is 120 beats per minute, the sequencer knows that the 60th beat has to line up with 30 seconds of elapsed time. A sequencer that responds to MTC can change tempo or time signature at any time; the sequencer simply re-calculates where notes should fall with respect to absolute time.

MIDI Synchronization in Action. Syncing MIDI gear to tape (or hard disk) is the equivalent of two multitrack recorders operating in tandem. You need not record drum machine or sequenced synthesizer parts, because the multitrack's master clock (or "sync track") can trigger the drum machine and/or sequencer in real time. Thus, the slave's audio outputs are virtually equivalent to the tape track outputs: they play along just as if they were recorded on a multitrack, and feed into your mixing console just like any other track. In fact, the outputs from the electronic instruments are often called "virtual tracks" because they are "virtually" the same as tracks recorded in any other type of multitrack recorder (see Figure 3).

Sequencers are also useful for controlling automated mixing and signal processing. The sequencer could be a "stand-alone" type, or part of an automated mixdown system that runs concurrently with other MIDI sequencers.

Figure 3

Typical virtual tracks setup. The multitrack digital tape recorder provides a sync signal to which the sequencer synchronizes. The sequencer in turn drives two MIDI keyboards. As you start and stop the tape, the sync converter produces commands that start and stop the sequencer.

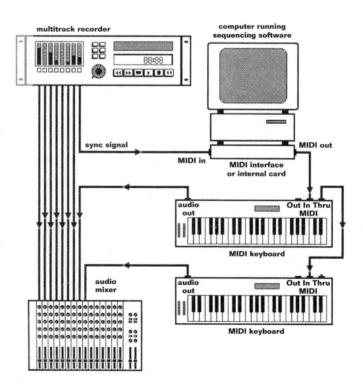

Not having to record sequenced synthesizer parts economizes on tape tracks or hard disk tracks. Many project studios use a digital or analog multitrack to handle acoustic instruments, and virtual MIDI tracks to expand the total number of tracks.

Hard disk systems, because they are computer-based, can often add some useful twists. For example, a MIDI sequencer might be built into the program, so it's unnecessary to sync an external device. The hard disk system might also generate MTC or SMPTE time code (as discussed below) to provide synchronization signals.

SMPTE Time Code

The most common of the sync signals referenced to absolute time is called SMPTE, after the Society of Motion Picture and Television Engineers, which took a time logging protocol developed by NASA and adapted it to film and video applications. SMPTE divides time into hours, minutes, seconds, frames, subframes, and user bits. A number of frame rates are used to accommodate film and video, which run a different number of frames per second. When syncing to SMPTE time code, you'll have to choose matching frame rates—for example, 24, 25, or 30 fps (frames per second)—for the master and slave devices.

SMPTE time code is an audio signal, and can be easily recorded and played back. It can't be sent down a MIDI cable directly, as MIDI is a digital signal. However, MIDI Time Code (MTC), as mentioned above, allows SMPTE data to be encoded in MIDI form and transmitted over a MIDI cable. Note that SMPTE and MTC don't provide start or stop commands, nor do they change tempo. They provide an absolute timing reference in minutes and seconds, rather than a music-related reference in bars and beats. If a sequencer is synced to MTC and you change its internal tempo *after* recording some tape tracks, it will still drift out of sync with those tracks, even if it's receiving MTC correctly from a SMPTE track that has been recorded ("striped") onto the tape. This is because the tempo is independent of the absolute time expressed by MTC or SMPTE.

SMPTE time code is a reliable and increasingly universal method of synchronization. With tape, if some slight damage occurs such that SMPTE data is lost, most SMPTE boxes will "guess" where the markers would have been until the real markers appear again. In contrast to Song Pointer-based tape sync, SMPTE is a standard. SPP boxes have their own proprietary way of translating SPP messages into audio tones, so you usually have to use the same device for recording and playback.

How SMPTE Works. A *SMPTE time code generator* generates "timing markers" that serve as a super-accurate index counter. Hard disk recording systems often generate SMPTE timing messages without requiring external hardware or a dedicated sync track. Sync control units for digital tape machines, such as the Alesis BRC, can also provide SMPTE messages.

A frame's duration varies for different applications. For film work, the standard rate is 24 frames per second (i.e., each frame equals $\frac{1}{24}$th of a second). For black and white video, the rate is 30 frames per second in the U.S. and 25 frames per second in Europe. For U.S.A.-standard NTSC color, the rate is 29.97 frames per second.

A *SMPTE time code reader* reads the SMPTE markers, and sends this timing data to other devices.

SMPTE-to-MIDI Conversion. A SMPTE-to-MIDI converter can convert absolute time (as represented by SMPTE) into "musical time" by reading SMPTE, then translating SMPTE times into MIDI SPP data. Although common at one point, these boxes are far less used today because most MIDI sequencers can follow MTC or SMPTE directly.

Advanced SMPTE-to-MIDI boxes accommodate tempo changes by letting you define a tempo map, where every time you enter or tap a beat, it is related to SMPTE time code (e.g., at 0 hours, 2 minutes, and 12 frames, increase the tempo by 2 beats per minute). On playback, the SMPTE time code provides a consistent reference point for the beat map. Many jingle and film scorers use the beat map feature to "fudge" the tempo a bit in spots so that particular visual cues, like cereal pouring out of a box, Godzilla eating Manhattan, etc., land exactly on the beat. In other words, if the cue lags a bit behind the beat, the tempo will subtly speed up for a couple of measures prior to the cue.

Many computer interfaces have SMPTE-to-MIDI conversion built in, which simplifies matters. Feed the SMPTE sync track audio signal into the interface's SMPTE audio input, and SPP messages magically flow out the interface's MIDI out jack. In today's studio, SMPTE generally provides the system master clock, while MIDI acts as an intelligent interface between various pieces of equipment.

Word Clock

Neither MIDI nor SMPTE provides enough accuracy for synchronization in digital audio recording. Governing the entire digital audio recording and playback scenario is a clock. This is referred to as a word clock. Every piece of digital gear has one—the word clock determines the sample rate and makes sure the samples are taken on a regular basis. Given how high (fast) sample rates are, the quality of the clock in a digital device is extremely important to the sound quality. If the clock rate isn't stable (a condition called jitter), the digital audio will be degraded.

When you're using only one piece of digital gear, the whole clock thing is pretty transparent. The digital gear references its built-in (internal) clock, and all is rosy. But when you start trying to hook two or more pieces of gear together digitally, things can get a bit hairier.

If you take it step by step, it's pretty easy to figure out how to clock your digital audio gear—and if you get it wrong, your rig will let you know by either not working, by flashing various indicator lights at you, or by emitting noxious digital flatulence.

The most basic scenario is when you want to hook together two pieces of digital-capable gear. Say you have a song all sequenced up in a keyboard workstation and you want to feed it digitally into the sound card on your computer. You hook the digital output of the keyboard into the digital input on the sound card, put your music software in record mode, play on the keyboard . . . and the software flashes an error message and won't record at all. Or maybe you get something that resembles music, but either it's buried in a wash of digital distortion and hash or you hear clicks and pops when you listen to it play back.

Here's the problem: In order for digital audio signals to be sent from one device to another, the sample words have to be transferred from one box to another at the correct speed and with the correct timing. In other words, the word clocks in the two boxes have to be synchronized. If you're hearing clicks, pops, digital hash, or—worst case—nothing, the word clock sync isn't happening.

Fortunately, the fix is easy. Our keyboard workstation, which is the device that's sending out the audio, operates as usual off of its internal clock. The sound card, the device that's receiving the digital audio, should be set so it's slaving to external clock. Look in the sound card's manual to see how to do this, or look in the Audio Preferences dialog box in your music software.

In this case, that's all there is to it—in all the digital interconnect formats we're likely to encounter (AES/EBU, S/PDIF, Lightpipe, TDIF, etc.), the word clock signal is embedded in the digital data stream and is sent along with the digital audio signal. This makes our lives much easier, since it eliminates having to run separate clock cables. However, clocking a larger system with multiple pieces of gear can be more of a challenge, and requires a dedicated clock signal to be run among the devices on its own cable.

As far as clocking and sync are concerned, word length (also called bit-depth, as in 16-bit or 24-bit) isn't an issue; the clock is concerned only with how fast the sample rate is (e.g., 44.1kHz vs. 48kHz) and locking the sample rates of multiple pieces of gear together. Normally, digital signal will still flow if the word lengths don't match between devices, although the audio quality may or may not be compromised, depending on how the mismatch occurs.

Converting Session Sample Rates. Once digital audio has been recorded at a given sample rate, changing the word clock or sample rate settings on the system won't help things. If you change the sample rate from the original setting, the pitch and timbre of the audio playback will also change.

Fortunately, we're not completely out of luck. Let's take a look at how we can get the incoming audio's sample rate to match up with that of the computer. It comes down to this: If you want to remain completely in the digital domain for the transfer, then you only have one choice: sample rate conversion. Sample rate conversion takes audio that was recorded at one sample rate and changes it so that it plays back at another rate without changing the audio's length or pitch. When the sample rate being converted is an even multiple of the rate it will end up at, such as when converting 96kHz to 48kHz, sample rate conversion is fairly straightforward and easy, and doesn't impact audio quality much. But when the two sample rates aren't multiples, such as when trying to change 48kHz to 44.1kHz or 96kHz to 44.1kHz, sample rate conversion can have decidedly negative audible effects on the resulting sound. (The story goes that this is the original reason for DAT recorders sampling at 48k and CDs playing at 44.1k; to prevent easy digital copies of CDs from being made.) That's the bad news. The good news is that sample rate conversion algorithms have gotten much better in recent years. In some cases, they're extremely good, depending on the source material that's being processed. There are several ways in which digital audio can be sample-rate converted:

• You may be able to beg, buy, or rent a stand-alone sample rate converter or other hardware box that has sample rate conversion capabilities.
• Some computer-based digital audio interfaces can sample-rate convert "on-the-fly" as signals pass through them.

• A computer application or plug-in can be used to sample-rate convert the audio after it's on the computer's hard drive. Most digital audio sequencers can sample-rate convert audio files, as can most digital audio editors. There are also real-time and non-real-time plug-ins that can perform this function.

It may take some time, but the best thing to do is to try all of the sample rate converters you have access to, whether hardware or software, and see which one sounds best. Sample rate conversion results can vary depending on the source material you're working on; try as many as you can and let your ears decide. Warning: Some sample rate conversion processes are "destructive"—they forever alter the original digital audio file—so make a copy of your audio file first and process the copy just in case things don't work as well as you'd like.

Ultimately, though, the best solution to this problem may be the "brute force" approach: Get the best digital-to-analog and analog-to-digital converters you can lay your hands on and do the transfer in the analog domain. Many times the sonic difference between the additional D/A and A/D conversion is much less audible than that of performing conversion from one sample rate to another. Once again, only your ears can decide.

Of course, the *real* best solution is never to put yourself in this position at all. Check and double-check all sample rate and clock settings when recording, doing transfers, and playing back. The little bit of extra time being careful takes is well worth it!

Quantization

Quantization, which shifts the start times of MIDI notes to a specific rhythmic "grid" (eighth notes, 16th notes, etc), got a bad rap back in the days of 24 ppq sequencers. If you didn't quantize, the clock resolution was so coarse that what came out of the computer was a little jerky compared to what you had played. So you quantized everything, and then the music marched along in lockstep. Lockstep is a wonderful thing for certain styles—but what if you want your tune to have that supple human feel?

One school of thought is, don't quantize anything. Play the part ten times if you have to, until you get it right. Again, for certain styles—classical orchestra simulations, say—that's unquestionably the right approach. But for pop music, consider using a mixed strategy.

Start by quantizing the kick and snare so that they're nailed to the beat.

That provides a fixed reference point for the listener, and for the other tracks to be recorded. What happens next depends on the music. Consider using percentage quantization to move the bass line 50% of the way to the quantization grid. In some settings it may be better to quantize the bass all the way when it's playing a purely supportive role, then use a 50% setting, or no quantization at all, when the bass steps forward to play a more melodic line. Ditto for chord comps and hi-hat patterns.

Stay away from the "human feel" utility, by the way. This generally randomizes the note start times—but humans don't play randomly. Inspect your own live-recorded tracks (or those of a world-class player, the next time one drops by) and you'll find expressive, non-random fluctuations. A real player will get excited, for instance, and jump on a fill a little ahead of the beat. Some players consistently play ahead of or behind the beat, or play certain licks such as grace-notes with a specific type of rhythmic displacement.

For the same reason, it doesn't make sense to quantize note durations. If you move the start time of the note by quantizing it, you may want to use the pencil tool to shorten or lengthen it slightly so that it ends exactly where it did before. Phrasing has a lot to do with the ends of the notes.

Hand Work. Another approach, which takes more effort but gives very musical results, is to leave a track unquantized and correct individual notes by hand. Open up the "piano-roll" notation window (see Figure 4), zoom in far enough to see clearly which notes are before or after the beat, and start playback. If either your ears or your eyes tell you that a note is too far away from the beat, stop playback, grab the note with the mouse, then rewind a couple of bars and start playback again.

When using this technique on fast triplets and such, it's often helpful to shorten some notes and lengthen others slightly while you're at it. This will give a smoother legato or the right sort of detached articulation, depending on what you want. If you're going to go to all this trouble, you may as well leave the velocity window open and fix any notes that are too loud or soft.

The big fill leading into a dramatic downbeat is often the place for a little extra hand work, even on a previously quantized part. Pushing the kick or tom note back so that it's a little late will add drama—and you might want to shift the crash cymbal so that it's a little early, even if you played it smack on the bar line.

Swing and Percentage Quantization. Two of the more common forms of quantization are *swing* and *percentage* quantization. When

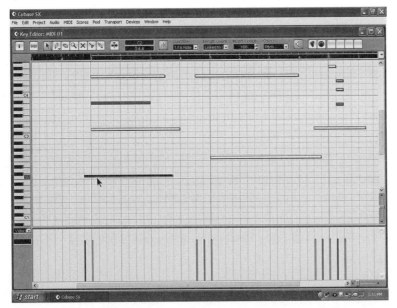

Figure 4

In the piano-roll, or graphical, edit window in Steinberg Cubase SX, the note that starts just before bar 4, beat 1, is about to be dragged to the right to bring it a bit closer to the beat. This is called quantizing, and can be done manually or automatically, on input or after the fact.

swing is applied, notes that fall in the second half of each beat are delayed by the swing amount, producing the dotted or triplet rhythm characteristic of jazz. In percentage quantization, notes are moved only part way to the chosen rhythmic grid: How far they are moved is determined by the quantization percentage or strength setting. For example, if a note is originally recorded 10 clock ticks before the beat, and the quantization strength is 50%, after quantization it will play back five ticks before the beat.

You can also quantize one track to match another. The reason for using this feature would be if you've crafted a rhythm—on a hi-hat, let's say—in which certain beats are pushed or laid back more than others. Even then, it's probably best to let that part occupy its own place in the mix by not cluttering up its attacks with exactly matching hits on other drums.

Looping—Steinberg ReCycle

"The recording's great, but can you change the tempo a bit?" This question has been posed since the days of steam-powered multitrack recorders, and there's seldom a pretty answer. Here's the problem: if you recorded a killer solo into a digital audio recording program at, for example, 120 bpm, changing the tempo will cause the part to be out of sync. Two measures at 120 bpm will last more than two measures at faster tempos, and less than two measures at slower tempos. And if you're into using loops, it's also a problem if the perfect loop for your 133 bpm song chugs along at 125 bpm.

One way to deal with this is to re-record the part. But hey, we have technology! Digital signal processing algorithms can lengthen digital audio by adding data, or shorten by deleting data. But it's difficult to do this without compromising the sound quality, especially with substantial timing shifts.

MIDI-based recording allows you to, say, record a kick drum trigger on each beat of a measure at 120 bpm. If you change the sequencer tempo to 130 bpm, the trigger still hits on each beat—the kick parts simply occur closer together. If you slow down the tempo, the kicks hit further apart. Great—but not everything lends itself to being recorded as (or converted into) MIDI data.

Enter ReCycle. Several years ago, Propellerhead Software devised an extremely clever time-stretching solution that applies MIDI thinking to digital audio, and is perfect for musicians who use sampled rhythm loops of any kind—drum loops, percussion accents, bass lines, etc. It doesn't actually do anything you couldn't do manually in a sample editor (or, for the really bold, from the front panel of your sampler), but it does it a whole lot faster.

ReCycle takes a piece of digital audio, cuts it into small segments ("slices"), notes where in the measure(s) these segments occur, then creates a MIDI file that triggers the segments at the appropriate times within the

Figure 5

ReCycle has taken the audio file in the bottom track and "sliced" it (top track), indicated by the vertical gird lines. The individual slices can now be triggered via MIDI note commands.

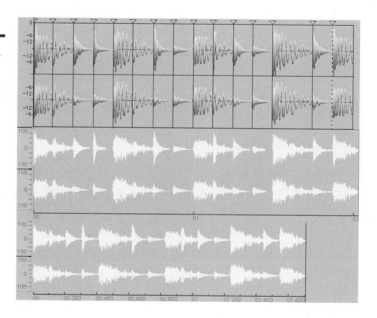

measure(s). ReCycle sets extremely accurate loop start and end points, and it makes it easy to integrate your sample loop into a MIDI sequence.

For example, Figure 5 shows how ReCycle separates the drum part (at the bottom) into individual slices (top), and how each slice can now be triggered by a MIDI note recorded in a sequence. When the sequencer plays back the MIDI notes at the original tempo, the various slices all play back in succession, at the original timings. With a slower tempo, the triggers that play back the segments are further apart; at a faster tempo, the triggers occur closer together. What this does is allow you to change a loop's tempo without changing pitch, yet doesn't use time compression/expansion routines, which often produce undesirable digital artifacts. The audio quality remains untouched—nothing is added or deleted, just triggered at a different time. Thus, it's theoretically (and often practically) possible to have ReCycle files whose fidelity is indistinguishable from the original, even when time-stretched. The program is easy to learn, so you can get results almost instantly.

Here's how simple the process is: Import any stereo or monophonic 16-bit, 44.1kHz sample file and then click a button to play the file back. As it plays, move an onscreen "sensitivity" fader—ReCycle then uses an intelligent algorithm that searches for transients in order to locate each of the individual sonic components within the file. If the sample file is a drum track, each of these slices will be an individual drum hit; if it is a bass track, each component will be an individual note. To preview the sound contained within each slice, simply click on it (the Mac version of ReCycle supports all Sound Manager 3.1-compatible hardware, such as the Digidesign cards, so you can preview in full 16-bit mode). Left-right markers appear at the file's start and end, and can be snapped to any slice start point, making it incredibly easy to set extremely accurate loop start and end points.

If ReCycle finds some false slice points (for example, in a drum flam it may find both hits), individual slice points can be hidden. Conversely, if it misses some slice points (as it may do at lower sensitivities), you can insert them manually. Zoom in/out tools make the process easy, and you can even use the audio scrubbing tool as well to help home in on questionable points.

Next, tell ReCycle how many bars and beats the loop contains and it automatically calculates the loop's tempo. At this point, you can either download the individual slices between the left and right markers to your sampler (assigned one to a key; currently supported samplers include

Digidesign's SampleCell and various Akai models, Kurzweil, E-mu, Ensoniq, and Roland samplers) or you can export them in a number of standard file formats (SDI, SDII, or AIFF in the Mac version; .WAV or AIFF in the Windows version). These samples can optionally be gain normalized to insure that each sample uses the maximum available headroom, but this also alters the dynamic balance between samples. At the same time, you can instruct ReCycle to generate a MIDI file that will play back the sample slices, one after the other, at the original tempo.

ReCycle also lets you specify a new tempo for loop playback, and the MIDI file the program generated will follow that new tempo. The magic of all this is that, by breaking a loop up into its individual components and triggering each component from a discrete MIDI note, you can alter the loop's tempo without changing its pitch.

One potential problem is that if you slow down the loop's tempo, there will be silences after each slice plays back. These silences may be apparent, especially if there is ambient sound in the sample. ReCycle cleverly addresses this problem through the use of a "stretch" function that adds short backward-forward loops to the end of each slice, thus extending each sample by a certain user-defined percentage. Since the end of a slice most likely contains only ambient sound (or, at worst, the tail-off of the sound), this works remarkably well.

It's not even so much what ReCycle does, but what it allows you to do after the fact that makes the program so impressive—the fun really starts after you've created and downloaded (or exported) all the individual slices and the MIDI file. For example, if your sampler provides multiple hardware outputs, you can route each component to a different output for additional mixing control, even applying different effects processing to each sample. Get bizarre by reversing playback of individual components (nothing like adding a few backwards snare or cymbal hits to an otherwise dull drum loop!) or experiment by substituting different sounds—simply assign a different sample to individual key numbers. In your MIDI sequencer, you can, of course, change tempo to your heart's content, and, if you're using Steinberg's Cubase Audio (or another sequencer that supports "groove" templates), you can even quantize MIDI tracks to the feel of the sampled loop.

The REX Factor. ReCycle saves the digital audio slices and MIDI information in a single file called a REX file. There are several types of REX files, but the most important, and recent, is the REX2 format (these types of files have a .RX2 suffix). Unlike earlier mono-only

FINDING REX FILES

Several sample CD companies produce REX file collections for use in programs that support the format. You can also use ReCycle to create your own REX files out of audio files.

Note that you don't necessarily need ReCycle; you can follow the same concept by cutting audio into slices, and triggering them from MIDI. However, ReCycle makes the process painless, and includes several features that optimize and enhance the process of converting a file into REX format.

Although some speculated that the REX file would drift into obscurity as programs like ACID (which offer on-the-fly time-stretching) appeared, that has not been the case. If anything, the REX file format is growing in popularity as more people recognize the advantages it can offer over "audio only"–based time-stretching techniques.

Who Supports It? Several products can read and interpret REX files. The most developed example is Propellerhead's own Reason, which includes a sophisticated REX file player module (for example, you can change the pitch of each slice). Cubase VST has an elegant REX file implementation; drag the file into the Arranger screen, and Cubase automatically knows what do with the MIDI and audio. Speed up or slow down the tempo, and the REX file data goes along for the ride—no tweaks required. Current versions of Logic and Performer also support REX files.

However, not all implementations are the same. For example, the Steinberg Halion sampler can accept REX files and map the slices across the sampler's keyboard—but you then need to load an accompanying Standard MIDI File into the sequencer driving Halion, so that it knows when to play back the slices.

There are also workarounds for gear that doesn't speak REX. SONAR doesn't read REX files directly, but is ReWire-compatible (ReWire is a protocol that allows soft synths, such as the ones in Reason, to integrate with sequencers and have their outputs show up in the sequencer's mixer module). So, you can load a REX file into Reason's Dr. Rex module, and have it play along with SONAR.

What's the Catch? REX files can be the perfect solution for many time-stretching problems. But like all other time-stretch options, REX files have their limitations. Here are the main ones.

- Slices have a finite, unchangeable length. Therefore, slowing down the tempo creates a gap between slices. If the sound decays before the slice ends, there's no problem. If the sound is relatively high at the splice point, ReCycle has a function that extends a sound's decay; however, it's not effective with all types of signals.

- Similarly, speeding up cuts off the end of segments. Fortunately, this isn't much of a problem because psycho-acoustically, you're more interested in hearing the new sound that's cutting off the old sound rather than the old sound itself.

- REX files don't work well with sustained sounds, or very complex sounds (e.g., a part with lots of repeating delays). Ideally, slices would have a quick attack time, and consist of a single "block" sound (like a guitar chord, synth bass note, or drum hit). This makes for an unambiguous slice—you know where it starts and where it ends. It's much harder, and sometimes impossible, to find good slices with a sustained sound.

- REX files aren't the only way to do time-stretching, but for certain applications, they are the ideal choice. Add them to your bag of tricks, and the next time someone wants to change the tempo, you'll be able to cope a little better.

ReCycle formats, REX2 files are true stereo. Interestingly, REX files usually take up much less space than their WAV equivalents.

All in all, ReCycle is a program that successfully combines stunning simplicity with incredible utility. If you work with sampled rhythm loops, do yourself a favor and check it out—it will not only save you valuable time but can also lead you to new creative outposts.

Compression

Compressors are some of the most used, and most misunderstood, signal processors. While people use them to make a recording "punchier," they often end up dulling the sound instead because the controls aren't set optimally.

What It Does. Compression was originally invented to shoehorn the dynamics of live music (which can exceed 100dB) into the restricted dynamic range of radio and TV broadcasts (around 40–50dB), vinyl (50–60dB), and tape (40–105dB, depending on type, speed, and noise reduction used). As shown in Figure 6, this process lowers only the peaks of signals while leaving lower levels unchanged. A second process—which could be a gain-normalization utility with software compressors, or an output volume knob on a hardware unit—then boosts the overall level to bring the signal peaks back up to maximum. (Bringing up the level brings up any noise as well, but you can't have everything.)

Even though media such as the CD have a decent dynamic range, people are accustomed to compressed sound. Compression is also useful to help soft signals overcome the ambient noise in typical home listening environments.

Compression can create greater apparent loudness. (Commercials on TV sound so much louder than the programs because they are compressed without mercy.) And of course, compression can smooth out a

Figure 6

The first section shows the original audio. The middle section shows the same audio after compression. The third section shows the same audio after compression and turning up the output control. Note how softer parts of the first section have much higher levels in the third section, yet the peak values are the same.

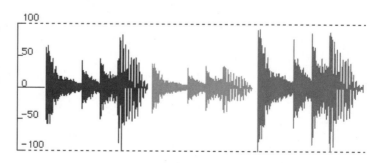

sound's dynamics—from increasing piano sustain to compensating for a singer's poor mic technique.

How It Works. Compression is often misapplied because of the way we hear. Our ear/brain combination can differentiate between very fine pitch changes, but not make minute distinctions in amplitude. So, there is a tendency to overcompress until you can "hear the effect," giving an unnatural sound. Until you've trained your ears to recognize subtle amounts of compression, keep an eye on the meters. You may be surprised to find that even with 6dB of compression, you don't hear much apparent difference—but bypass the unit, and the difference will be obvious.

Compressors, whether software- or hardware-based, have these general controls:

Threshold sets the level at which compression begins. Above this level, the output increases at a lesser rate than the corresponding input change. Bottom line: With lower thresholds, more of the signal gets compressed.

Ratio defines how much the output signal level changes for a given change in the input level when the input signal rises above the threshold. For example, with 2:1 compression, a 2dB increase at the input (assuming that the input is higher than the threshold) yields a 1dB increase at the output. With 4:1 compression, a 16dB increase at the input gives a 4dB increase at the output. With "infinite" compression, the output remains constant no matter how much you pump up the input. Bottom line: Higher ratios increase the effect of the compression. Figure 7 shows how input, output, ratio, and threshold relate.

Attack determines how long it takes for the compression to start once it senses an input level change. Bottom line: Longer attack times let more of a signal's natural dynamics through, but those signals are not being compressed. In the days of analog recording, the tape would absorb any overload caused by sudden transients. With digital recording, those transients clip as soon as they exceed 0 VU. With short attack transients, this may not produce any significant audible degradation. If there is distortion, lower the overall level with the...

Output control. Since we're squashing peaks, we're actually reducing the overall peak level. Increasing the output compensates for the volume drop. Turn this control up until the compressed signal's peak levels match the peak levels of the bypassed signal.

Decay sets the time required for the compressor to give up its hold on the signal once the input falls below the threshold. Short settings are great for special effects, like those psychedelic '60s drum sounds where hitting the cymbal would create a giant sucking sound on the whole kit. Longer settings work well with program material, since the level changes are more gradual and produce a less noticeable effect.

The *hard knee/soft knee* option controls how rapidly the compression kicks in. With soft knee, when the input exceeds the threshold, the compression ratio is less at first, then increases up to the specified ratio as the input increases. With hard knee (as illustrated in Figure 7), as soon as the input signal crosses the threshold, it's subject to the full amount of compression. Bottom line: Use hard when you want to clamp levels down tight (for instance, to prevent clipping in a power amp), and soft when you want a gentler compression effect.

Side chain jacks let you insert filters in the compressor's feedback loop to restrict compression to a specific frequency range. For example, inserting a high-pass filter compresses only the high frequencies—perfect for de-essing vocals.

The link switch in stereo compressors switches the mode of operation from dual mono to stereo. Linking the two channels together allows changes in one channel to affect the other channel, which is necessary to preserve the stereo image.

Figure 8 shows the fx:compressor module from Ultrafunk, a software plug-in for DirectX and VST plug-in formats. There was close to −12dB of noise reduction at the moment this screen shot was taken, as shown

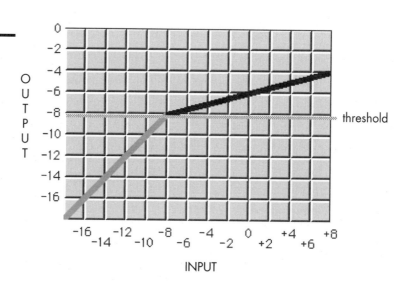

Figure 7

The threshold is set at -8dB, and the compression ratio is 4:1. If the input increases by 8dB (e.g., from -8 to 0), the output only increases by 2dB (from -8 to -6).

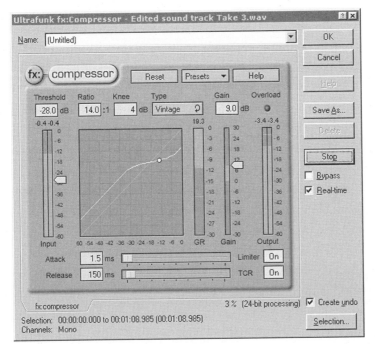

Figure 8

The fx:compressor from Ultrafunk

by the Gain Reduction (GR) meter. There are the expected threshold, ratio, attack, knee, release and gain controls; this module also includes a type section, and in this example a vintage-style compressor algorithm is selected.

Compressor Types: Thumbnail Descriptions

Compressors now come in both hardware varieties (usually a rackmount design) and as software plug-ins for existing digital audio-based programs. Following is a description of various compressor types.

- *Old faithful.* Whether rackmount or software-based, typical features include two channels with gain reduction meters that show how much your signal is being compressed. Hot tip: When compressing a stereo mix, blend in some dry, non-compressed signals for a livelier, more dynamic sound.

- *Multiband compressors.* These divide the audio spectrum into multiple bands, with each one compressed individually. This allows for a less "effected" sound (for example, low frequencies don't end up compressing high frequencies), and some models let you compress only the frequency ranges that need to be compressed.

- *Octal compressors.* These house eight compressors in a single rack space, which helps reduce the possibility of overload for signals going into your recorder, and brings back some of the tape compression effects associated with analog tape (minus the distortion). These units are overkill if you're overdubbing tracks one or two at a time (just get a good stereo compressor), but for live recording, they can literally save a session.

- *Vintage and specialty compressors.* Some swear that only the compressor in an SSL console will do the job. Others find the ultimate squeeze to be a big-bucks tube compressor, like the Demeter or Groove Tubes models. And some guitarists can't live without their Dan Armstrong Orange Squeezer, held by many to be the finest budget sustain box ever made. Fact is, all compressors have a distinctive sound, and what might work for one sound source might not work for another.

Whatever kind of audio work you do, though, there's a compressor somewhere in your future. Just don't overcompress—in fact, avoid using compression as a cop-out for bad mic technique or dead strings on a guitar. It is an effect that needs to be used subtly to do its best.

Backing up Your Data

Your floppy disk containing those killer sequences, the DAT master tape for your next CD, that S-VHS or Hi-8 tape that's backing up your precious multitracks where Trent Reznor came in and played a few guest licks—they're all going to be history, sooner or later.

The question is: How soon is soon? The answer: Sooner than you think, which is why backing up is crucial. This is particularly important with digital tape; unless your machine has an error indicator that chronicles the tape's gradual breakdown, you'll have no clue that it's about to become unusable. What's worse, unlike analog tape (where minor dropouts can often be tolerated), a minor dropout with digital can produce a rude, ripping sound.

Which backup method is the most reliable? Before getting to that, let's solve some problems in advance.

An Ounce of Prevention. Several steps can help increase the shelf life of digital tape, whether it's DAT or multitrack.

- Clean and maintain your machine. Use a dry head cleaner (e.g., Maxell's version for DAT) for periodic cleaning; every 20–30 hours seems about right. This should take at least the major pieces of gunk out of the tape path.
- Under normal use, have your DAT or multitrack professionally main-

tained once a year (for heavy use, every six months). Slight misalign-ments of the head blocks and other components are a major reason why tapes get "eaten."

- Use high-quality tape. Not all tape batches are created equal. With DAT, don't trust your precious music to recycled computer tapes. The latter are often thinner than audio tapes, which makes for a bad match with the transport. All things being equal, thicker tapes are more reli-able than thinner tapes.
- Pre-condition your tapes. Fast-forward and rewind several times before use (for ADAT, get a separate VHS tape rewinder so that any gunk that gets shed goes into the rewinder, not your tape machine). This unpacks the tape properly.
- Eject the tape during a silent section, as the greatest amount of tape handling inside the machine happens during insertion and ejection.
- Avoid cue and review modes when rewinding, as the tape is under more tension with respect to the head. Use the normal rewind and fast-forward functions.
- Store your tapes (and floppy disks) properly. Avoid excessive humidi-ty, heat, and cold. Safe deposit boxes and climate-controlled office buildings are good options. Also, it's generally good practice to play a tape through to the end before storing (a holdover from analog days, but it applies to digital tape as well). This precaution makes sense because the tape will be packed more evenly on the hub after normal-speed play than after a fast-forward or rewind, which could produce areas where the tape is packed more tightly than normal.
- Never put tapes or floppies on top of speakers, near transformers, etc. Any magnetic media can be erased if stored near a strong magnetic field. When shipping a tape, pack it in the middle of a relatively large box just in case it gets placed somewhere inappropriate during transport.

Backup Options. So what's the longest-lived form of backup? Sadly, if there's a fire or other physical damage, nothing works. This is why remote backups, such as a safe deposit box, are always prudent. Here are the options:

DAT was never intended as a robust, professional medium; the tape is thin and the tracks themselves are $\frac{1}{10}$ the thickness of a human hair (are you nervous yet?). You can count on a shelf life of at least ten years if the tape was good stock to begin with, and if you've been careful about han-dling and tape storage. Otherwise, you could start getting errors much sooner than that.

S-VHS tapes, as used in ADAT, tend to be somewhat less delicate than DAT. Still, there remains the issue of magnetic and plastic decay. Look at videotapes from 10 years ago: Those occasional streaks and "snow" might be a minor annoyance when watching *The Empire Strikes Back*, but if that was digital audio and the machine's error correction couldn't compensate, the cut would be toast.

Removable hard drives (SyQuest, Iomega, etc.), although theoretically more reliable than DAT, are still magnetic media. There are plenty of horror stories about cartridge reliability, but to be fair, these often come from people who don't keep the cartridges in their sealed cases, and throw them in the back seat of a car ("removable" doesn't mean "transport with impunity"). Cartridges are also fairly pricey, but there's another issue: If you pull a disk out of the archives in 10 years, will there be a working mechanism on which you can play it back? The multiplicity of removable cartridge formats is in itself a problem.

Magneto-optical cartridges boast very high reliability, immunity to magnetic fields, and large amounts of storage (1GB drives are commonly available). MO cartridges are the preferred backup medium if you need near-hard disk speed, transportability, and dependability.

CD-Rs are an excellent option. CD-ROM recorders need to be used with computers; whatever you back up has to be stored as a digital audio file, then transferred (usually through SCSI, FireWire, or USB) to the drive. Budget CD-Rs that simply record audio are another option. However, a CD-ROM writer lets you back up computer data, as well as make one-off CDs.

Initially, when a CD recorder wrote data to disk, that section of the disc could not be reused. CD-RW technology uses eraseable media, which, although more costly, are more environmentally friendly as they can be reused. There is one caution: most CD recorders are optimized to work with a particular type of recordable CD formulation. Find out which type your manufacturer recommends, and stick with that type.

Back Up Your Backups. Even CDs aren't perfect; no one really knows how long recordable CDs will last. Although some studies have said 70 years, exposing CDs to light or heat can shorten that dramatically, and CD-RWs are estimated to last no more than 50 years. Since no backup system is perfect, it's a good idea to do the following:

• Save to multiple media. For example, back up DATs to two tracks of an ADAT tape, and to a CD recorder. It's a good idea to back up really important data to multiple media of the same type. That way, if there's a problem with a tape, you can transfer the existing data into a hard disk recording system, and use an alternate tape to fill in the missing section(s).

- Re-back up periodically. As soon as you buy a backup medium, date it. After three to five years (depending on your level of paranoia), back up to a fresh tape. It's digital, after all, so you won't get any deterioration when you make copies (unless the number of dropouts is so severe that the error correction has to "fill in the blanks"). Even if you don't have digital ins and outs, at least back up through your DAT's analog I/O. There will be a slight sonic deterioration, but that's better than losing a piece of music altogether.

If you have only one DAT deck, you can re-backup by borrowing a DAT from a friend, or by digitally transferring over to a computer running a digital recording program, then sending the file back to a fresh tape. Use a consistent sample rate when backing up.

The bottom line is that an optical medium beats tape, but if tape is all you can afford, make multiple backups—and whichever medium you use, keep your fingers crossed.

Digital-to-Digital Transfers

One of the great aspects of the digital revolution is that we can now "clone" digital audio, transferring it from one medium to another without the deterioration associated with analog copying. You can blast signals onto CD, send them over to a hard disk system for editing, then transfer the best bits over to a sampler for triggered playback from a keyboard— all without degrading the sound. Try doing that with analog gear!

Although digital transfers are generally straightforward, there are still a few complications along the way—so here are some hints, tips, and cautions.

Transfer Protocols. Currently there are several common hardware/ software digital transfer protocols that you may encounter:

- AES/EBU. This protocol—the acronym stands for "Audio Engineering Society/European Broadcast Union," the two groups that collaborated on defining it—is a two-channel digital audio signal designed for professional applications. Signals are carried over wire cables that terminate in XLR (3-pin) connectors, or via fiber-optic cables. AES/EBU inputs ignore SCMS copy protection data. (SCMS, the Serial Copy Management System, is a misguided attempt to prevent copyright infringement. It prevents making a digital copy of a digital copy.)

- S/PDIF. This consumer-oriented version of the AES/EBU protocol was first adopted by Sony and Philips, hence the acronym, which stands for "Sony/Philips Digital Interface." S/PDIF (pronounced "SPIH-diff") uses RCA phono jacks or optical (TOSLINK) connectors; SCMS encoding is generally recognized, although some DAT decks and other devices with S/PDIF connectors allow you to defeat SCMS.
- MADI. Found in a few pro-level multichannel digital decks, a MADI fiber-optic cable can transfer up to 56 tracks of digital audio. The acronym stands for "Multichannel Audio Digital Interface."
- SDS. The world's slowest way to get digital audio from one place to another, SDS (the MIDI Sample Dump Standard) passes digital audio down a MIDI cable. It is used only with samplers.
- SMDI. This successor to SDS sends digital audio over the SCSI bus and associated control data over a MIDI cable, achieving a 50x increase in speed compared to SDS. The acronym stands for "SCSI Musical Data Interchange." Neither SDS nor SMDI is used much with standard digital recording.
- Proprietary. Not all recording devices follow a particular standard (as the old saying goes, "People must like standards...there are so many of them"). Instead, many of them implement their own proprietary transfer method. For example, the Alesis ADAT can transfer eight channels of digital audio over a fiber-optic cable; this has become such a common standard that other companies make ADAT-compatible gear (including mixers, synthesizers, and hard disk recorders) that can communicate using the same protocol. In fact, the ADAT Optical Interface has become a de facto multichannel digital audio interface.

Digital hookups are not that different from analog ones—outputs go to inputs—with one exception: These signals run at a much higher frequency than standard audio. Fiber-optic cables can handle this, but conventional wire cables should be low capacitance. In many cases, standard audio cables are not satisfactory because they distort the waveform, which may cause jitter (see below).

Level Setting. Digital-to-digital transfers require no level-setting. Sixteen bits of "full code" (maximum level) is 16 bits of maximum level, period; the same goes for 20- and 24-bit data. Don't worry too much if your DAT flashes the "over" indicator when it receives audio that is obviously not clipped. This simply means that the indicator triggers just *before* the signal goes into clipping.

The Clone Controversy. Some "golden ear" types insist that different digital clones can sound different. But digital just doesn't work that way; a stream of digits is a stream of digits.

If a few digits are lost somewhere along the line, error correction methods will kick in to replace them. But only in extreme cases (such as large tape dropouts) will this become audible. Some digital data formats, such as CDs, include redundant data or allow missing data to be re-read from the source medium, so that an error can be corrected with 100% mathematical exactness. As long as the transfer process is free of errors, you can clone digital data all day: Compare the bitstreams of the original and the copy, and they'll be identical.

Digital Processing During Transfers. There are times, such as when a mastering house loads up your DAT master prior to pressing your new CD, that digital EQ or other processing may be patched in during the transfer. In this case, we're no longer dealing with a clone.

Many processors claim "24-bit internal processing" even though the A/D and D/A converters at the analog input and output are 16-bit. The reason for the extra bits is because gain changes within the unit (filtering, compression, etc.) cause numbers to be multiplied and divided, which can create values that require a longer word length than the usual 16 bits. (To take a simple example, if you multiply 3 x 6 and then divide by 2, you only need one digit for the inputs [3 and 6] and for the result [9], but you'll get an incorrect answer unless you can internally store the result of the multiplication [18] as a two-digit number.) 24-bit devices can handle the extra math overhead without too much rounding off, but the more signal processing you add and the more that signals are truncated back to 16 bits for transfer to another device, the more errors accumulate. These affect mostly the very low end of the dynamic range, but anyone who has cringed at the sound of a non-dithered reverb tail breaking up during the final stages of decay knows that low-level artifacts can be a problem.

Sample Rate Conversion. Sample rate conversions face several technical problems, so it's best to choose a consistent sample rate throughout the recording chain. Fans of the "ADAT classic," take note: Although you can set the sample rate to 44.1kHz, this works by slowing down the overall system clock. If you're synching a sequencer with the BRC, the tempo will come out slower by a factor of 44.1/48. Either increase the sequencer tempo by 48/44.1 (1.08843), or just keep your system at 48kHz. Then, to achieve a final sample rate of 44.1kHz on the DAT master, mix down the ADAT signal through an analog mixer and set the DAT to record at 44.1kHz. Think of it as "analog sample rate conversion."

5

Digital Mixing

Basics of Digital Audio Mixing

You know that part in every good suspense thriller where the persevering hero unlocks the mystery, and all the characters, clues, twists, and turns fall perfectly into place? For the recording musician, mixdown—the last stage of the recording process—serves the same purpose. In a good mixdown, digital or analog, the jumble of musical parts comes together; sonic textures are sculpted, all the elements are blended, and what's left is a unique musical tale, played out on a unique soundstage.

Fortunately, giving your mixdowns a full, balanced, and professional-quality soundstage needn't be a big mystery, and digital technology only improves your resources over the audio domain.

What's a Mixdown? The song is written, the performances are captured on disk, sequencer, or tape, and the work is ready to come together. Mixdown is the process of bringing together separate tracks into a unified whole. The tracks can be audio tracks (from hard disk or tape), MIDI tracks (from a sound card, tone generator, or digital keyboard), or a combination of both. Usually, three or more such *source* tracks are mixed down to the left and right audio tracks of a stereo *mastering deck*, such as a stand-alone CD recorder, stand-alone workstation, or computer-based DAW hard disk (see Figure 1).

Before mixdown, your tracks are like pieces of a jigsaw puzzle spread out on the table: You can examine them one by one, and you even throw a few of them together loosely to get an idea of the big picture. But it's only during mixdown that you decide which piece goes where, so that your final mix—your master disk—has all the pieces locked in place.

The usual purpose of a mixdown is to create a "portable" master recording, which, for instance, can be played in a car or sent to a friend,

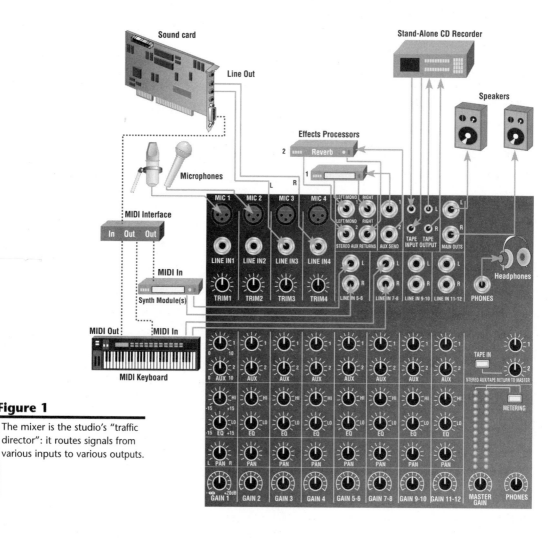

Figure 1

The mixer is the studio's "traffic director": it routes signals from various inputs to various outputs.

record label, or professional duplication house. But a stereo master tape or disc isn't the only fruit a mixdown can bear. Say you're creating a soundtrack for a QuickTime movie or Macromedia Director presentation; in this case, you may be mixing directly to your computer's hard disk, and you may prefer to do so in mono—especially if you consider that CD-quality audio uses approximately 5MB per minute of hard disk space in mono, as opposed to 10MB per minute in stereo.

What Happens During Mixdown? Mixdown can be the most creative—and decision-intensive—step of the recording process. It's where you determine the sonic qualities of each track, such as:

• Relative level, from loud to quiet, or sometimes silent (muted)
• Overall tone, using tools such as equalizers (EQs) and synthesizer filters or brightness controls (e.g., for MIDI virtual tracks)
• Location within the stereo panorama, from left to right
• Location in terms of "depth" and "room size" (from near to far), using reverb, delay, and other effects processing.

In essence, a mixdown is your opportunity to create a virtual soundstage. When you adjust levels, you're the conductor. As you adjust tone, you get to be an instrument designer. When you localize tracks in terms of depth and room size, you become an acoustical architect. And when you position the instruments from left to right, you place the musicians on your virtual soundstage.

Mixdown is also the last opportunity to correct problems that cropped up in the original recording, hence the phrase "We'll fix it in the mix." For example, it's common practice in professional recording studios to create composite vocal tracks by stringing together the best phrases—even syllables—from multiple vocal performances. Whether this sacrifices the flow of the performance in a quest for perfection is something only you can decide.

Incidentally, although mixing in a professional studio can involve scads of gear, with 48 or more audio tracks routed through gigantic mixing consoles (and towering racks of outboard signal processors) on their way to the mixdown deck, the principles of mixdown remain the same whether you're using a half-million-dollar console or simply a MIDI sequencer. Using just a computer and sequencing program, and a synth (or a high-quality, synth-equipped sound card), it's possible to craft surprisingly good-sounding mixes. The keys are your imagination, listening talents, and experience.

By the way, when we refer to mixdown as "decision intensive," don't let that sound intimidating or even final. Most hits you hear on the radio were mixed after days, if not weeks, of experimentation. If you don't like the results, you can always go back and mix it again. If anything, mixdown can be the most fun part of recording. After all, the musical performances are already captured, so the pressure to "perform" is off; a wealth of cool signal processing tricks is at your disposal, and what was previously rough and unappealing can be polished to a fine sheen (assuming, musically speaking, that's what you're after).

Analyze Your CDs. Before you touch a fader or grab a mouse, listen closely to some favorite CDs, both on speakers and headphones. As you mix your own music, switch back and forth between it and CDs of a similar musical style. How loud are the drums in relation to each other and to the rest of the instruments? How about the vocal or solo instruments? Strings? Brass? Sound effects? Note the balance of frequencies—a common mixing mistake is cranking up the high and/or low end, but too little of either is just as bad as too much, leading to dull or wimpy mixes. Close your eyes and try to pick out each instrument. Where is it in the room? Does it echo or reverberate? Does it seem to spread out beyond the speakers? Do instruments in the rhythm section (particularly bass and drums, but also piano and rhythm guitar) appear to be in the same space? How about other sections? Focus in on the snare drum sound, long a signature of recording engineers. Where does it fit in frequency and location? As we delve into specific mixing topics below, try to keep some of these big issues in mind.

Managing Levels. The most obvious function of a mixdown is adjusting the relative levels of your different tracks or MIDI parts. With few exceptions, the challenge is to strike a natural (or at least effective) balance between the parts, so that no one instrument sounds overly pronounced, and no instrument is completely buried by the others.

In practice, however, there may be times when, for subtlety's sake, one or more parts are thrown "deep" into the mix. These parts may not be obvious on first listening, but they nonetheless contribute to the overall texture of the tune. And there are times—during a solo, for example—when you'll want to bring an instrument way out in front temporarily. We'll tackle these issues below, when we look at designing a soundstage.

The Virtues of Virtual Mixing. If you work strictly with a sound card's MIDI sounds—or with an external MIDI module or keyboard—your sequencer may be able to handle all of your level-adjustment needs. Almost all modern synthesizers change their volume in response to

MIDI Controller 7 messages, which you can enter into a sequencer's event list window or often draw in with the mouse. (Multitimbral synthesizers, which can play several different sounds at once, should offer separate MIDI volume control of each of the different parts.) As the sequence plays back, these messages will change the track levels in real time. Individual MIDI tracks can be faded in, raised up during a song's chorus, lowered during its bridge, and faded out at the end. You can re-record these levels over and over, and change them whenever you like; no matter what, all of your automated levels are retained in the program's memory, allowing you to build the mix track by track.

Many programs feature on-screen mixers that let you automate the playback levels (as well as other parameters) of digital audio tracks you've recorded to your hard disk. The *pièce de résistance* is that you can also automate muting. With this feature, portions of tracks can be silenced, instantly and completely, for as long as you wish. (Muting is a perfect tool for cleaning up bits of unwanted audio, like lip-smacking on a vocal track or the hiss of a guitar amp heard before a song starts.)

Generally, sequencing programs let you use a mouse to adjust individual track levels, usually by dragging an on-screen fader knob, which is more intuitive than typing in Controller 7 values. You can select multiple faders to control with a single mouse movement, or you can use the program's *grouping* feature, which assigns several faders to a group master fader that controls the overall level for the group.

If you're one of those people who prefers to grab something physical, check out the JL Cooper FaderMaster or Peavey PC 1600. These external MIDI fader systems send out MIDI continuous controller data from each fader. Set each fader to transmit Controller 7 on a different MIDI channel, and you'll be able to adjust multiple tracks at once. High-end sequencers allow this incoming MIDI data to control their on-screen faders, providing a visual representation of levels. These fader boxes also sport buttons that can be programmed to control other functions, such as "record," "undo," or "mute."

Most high-end digital audio MIDI sequencers feature full automation mix capabilities. Check out "Digital Multitrack Automation" later in the chapter.

Know When Less Is More. One of the toughest mixing challenges is to avoid pushing every track's level up to the max—that is, to know when less is more. This is especially hard if you're also the musician. After all, it's only natural that you'll want to promote each deft lick by pushing up the level. Unfortunately, the result can be a jumble of licks and hooks, all fighting each other.

Instead, practice the art of subtlety. Not every catchy riff needs to be pushed to the front; maybe your song would be better if the riff is kept quiet (or even eliminated) except during the bridge between choruses. In fact, seasoned producers know that a great hook should be used judiciously, so that the listener is waiting for it, instead of having it repeated *ad nauseum*. Conversely, many musicians tend (perhaps out of self-consciousness) to mix their own vocals too low.

Add Dynamics to Your Mix. Don't let the faders stand still during a mixdown. Pump the entrance of keyboards just a bit. Push the fader up at the end of each vocal phrase. Bring the delay in and out during the guitar solo. Make the background vocals swell when they hold a note. This kind of activity can give your mix a kind of life that most "perfect" recordings, with their compressed levels and precision performances, lack.

Equalization

An equalizer is a frequency-sculpting tool. Even a simple two-band EQ, such as the bass and treble section of a home stereo, can alter frequency response dramatically. For instance, boost the treble a little, and you can make music sound "crisper" and brighter; cut it a lot, and you can completely muffle the music. Cut the bass and music sounds thin, boost it a bit to add some "kick," or boost it to the max if you want sonic mud (and maybe a blown speaker). Between those extremes, boosting or cutting specific frequencies within a sound allows you to tame obnoxious resonances or bring out subtle character. For example, boosting a vocal in the 3 to 8kHz region can emphasize consonants, aiding intelligibility.

Project studios typically have a variety of different EQ resources. Computer-based audio mixing programs offer *global* EQ that affects the entire mix, but this is not as useful as track-by-track EQ, since it's usually individual instrument or vocal parts that require EQ. More and more MIDI synths and sound cards offer built-in EQ, as do many external multieffects processors. With the latter, in particular, it's common to find relatively sophisticated types of EQ, such as three-band parametric. (Parametric EQ adjusts *which* frequencies are cut or boosted for each of the bands. On a home stereo, in contrast, the EQ frequencies are fixed—often affecting a wide band around 100Hz for the bass and around 10kHz for the treble. A graphic EQ has more and narrower frequency bands, but each band's frequency is still fixed.)

Equalization is a big topic—chapters have been written about it, and recording engineers regularly get into long debates about how EQ should be applied. But keep in mind these points:

• Start by making a "frequency inventory" of all the tracks you'll be mixing, to help you plan appropriate EQ settings. Strive for a balance of frequencies, which may require cutting as well as boosting different bands. Beware of *frequency masking*. An instrument that has been EQ'd to sound great on its own may not sound so great when it's in the mix. For instance, a muted guitar might sound nice and warm by itself but become lost when played back with keyboards, vocals, and other tracks in the same frequency range. This is because our ears tend to blend simultaneous sounds into a single, composite sound. When several instruments emphasize similar frequencies, those frequencies accumulate—and can either become overbearing, or can cause one instrument to hide or "mask" another (see Figure 2).

Figure 2

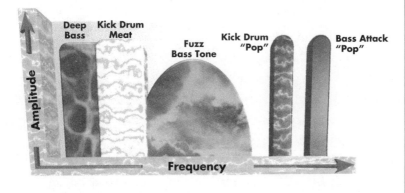

Figure 2 shows a rough graph of frequency vs. amplitude of the various voices used in a mix. This gives you a view of the frequency spectrum and the potential for one element to mask another, helping you sort out what sounds you might add, subtract, or substitute.

In the graph, there's no sign of a snare drum. That's because the snare drum, which contains a wide range of frequencies, would take up half the picture. If its frequency characteristics overlap those of the other sounds, why doesn't it drown them out? Because of its characteristics in the time domain: It decays to silence very quickly.

The meat of the snare drum falls right in the middle of the fuzz bass spectrum, but we hear the same fuzz bass both before the snare drum hits and after the snare drum decays. Because of its persistence, you hear the fuzz bass even though it's briefly obscured. Also, the drum's regular rhythm prompts the brain to expect to hear it at given intervals. The listener subconsciously gives less attention to the snare's spectral character than to its time-domain effect; namely, the groovy beat.

- Excessive use of EQ is rarely a good thing. Too much low-frequency emphasis, for instance, can turn a mix to mush; too much high-frequency cranking can sizzle your listeners' eardrums. Most pros will tell you that less EQ is more, and that if you need to add a lot of it to get the sound you want, maybe you need to change the sound at its source. For instance, a "boomy"-sounding acoustic guitar, which might prompt you to cut a lot of bass, might be better fixed by adjusting the microphone placement to a less boomy position during the initial recording. If you're mixing MIDI tracks, try substituting different patches instead of using EQ.
- As we'll learn below, high-frequency response can also play a role, in terms of depth, for placing an instrument or voice on a soundstage.

Panning

Listen to almost any current pop or rock music mix and chances are you'll hear the lead vocal, bass guitar, and kick drum all panned dead center, so that they all project equally from your stereo's left and right speakers. ("Pan" is short for panorama, and refers to a sound's left-right placement in the stereo field.) If you have any difficulty telling what's coming from where, use headphones. You'll also hear, perhaps, an electric guitar panned somewhat to the left, a synth panned slightly to the right, and the rest of the drums (and maybe a piano) spread out across both the left and right panorama.

Panning MIDI instruments is quite straightforward. If you're using a synth-equipped sound card, an on-screen utility may let you adjust each instrument's relative pan position. Alternately, or if you're using one or more outboard synth modules or keyboards, you can turn to your MIDI sequencer. Just as MIDI Controller 7 controls volume, Controller 10 sets panning. Generally, entering a Controller 10 event with a value of 0 will move a sound to the left speaker and entering a value of 127 will move the sound all the way to the right. However, some older synths aren't set up to respond to MIDI pan information. In this case you may need to program the pan position for each part within the instrument (read the manual for more info).

When working with audio tracks, you'll either need to adjust pan on-screen (if you're using a multitrack hard disk recording system) or with an external mixing console. There's one big advantage to adjusting pan on-screen: You may be able to automate the panning, as described earlier for volume. This means that you can have individual tracks move left to right over time. (For an interesting effect, try bouncing percussion sounds between the speakers. It can really add life to a mix.)

Stereo Imaging

If you're working with stereo sources, such as a stereo keyboard or drum machine, you may be able to adjust their stereo imaging, not just their localization. If you own an external mixer, it's easy to hear the difference between imaging and localization.

Take a stereo source, such as a stereo synth string patch. Route the synth's left and right outputs to two separate mixer channels, and pan the channels hard left and hard right. Then play the sound, preferably from a sequencer so that your hands are free for mixing. Adjust both channels' faders for equally loud levels. Now pan both channels to the center; the synth is now localized in the soundstage's center and has the narrowest possible stereo image: mono.

Next, again crank the pan controls hard left and right. Since our source patch is stereo, you'll hear its widest stereo image. The maximum width is determined by the width of the source and/or of any stereo processing, such as reverb, that you're using. Now here's the payoff: You can adjust the source's localization without adversely affecting its image. Let's move localization to the right by lowering the left fader's level. Notice that as long as the left channel remains relatively audible, the wide stereo image is retained, even though the source's position has shifted to the right.

So in general:

- A stereo source's overall stereo image is determined by the degree to which the left and right channels are panned oppositely; the greater the difference, the greater the stereo width.
- To maintain stereo imaging, localize a stereo source by changing the fader balance.
- A mono source's localization is controlled by its associated pan pot.

Au Naturel or Au Bizarre? With some music, the aim is to localize and image instruments as they sound in real life. Most acoustic jazz and classical music engineers aim for recordings that reproduce live concerts as closely as possible. In fact, these engineers often record their ensembles live with just a pair of microphones, or a single stereo mic, which results in a stereo soundstage that closely matches the real thing. If natural is what you want, you'll probably want to use pan controls with discretion.

In contemporary production, however, panning is more a matter of feel than rule—who says you need a "real" perspective?

Designing Depth: Localizing Parts from Hither to Yon

If you own a DSP-equipped card, instrument, outboard processor or plug-in, chances are you've heard how reverb can make it sound as if you are playing at the bottom of the Grand Canyon, or in Westminster Cathedral. If they're offered, you've probably also tried different delay (echo) settings, along with chorusing, flanging, and other "swirling" delay effects. Maybe you've noticed how these types of DSP can add a professional sheen to tracks, especially vocals or other instruments that may have occasional intonation problems. Unfortunately, many home recordists end up using far too much of a good thing. In fact, more than any other faux pas, excessive reverb and delay are the number-one give-away of a home-brewed demo tape.

The challenge, therefore, is to learn how reverb and other processing can place instruments on your virtual soundstage. The depth positioning chart opposite lists a variety of ways in which you can localize an instrument near or far, using adjustable reverb and delay parameters (these are programmable settings that many multieffects processors, synths, and sound cards allow you to edit), as well as a few mixing, EQ, and microphone techniques.

Reverb Settings. Let's take a brief tour of what these parameters are, and how to apply them. Keep in mind that not every processor or instrument is going to offer every parameter, and that the names may vary (e.g., "damping" on one reverb processor might be called "rolloff" on another). If you're in doubt, compare our descriptions with the ones in your product's manual.

Dry/Wet Level Balance. This sets the amount of the "dry," or unprocessed, signal relative to the amount of reverb. A big "wash" of reverb will position a track toward the back of the soundstage—though it may make the track sound muddy. For an extremely far effect, go 100% wet. For up-front, in-your-face tracks, especially vocals, go 100% dry. For most applications, the setting will be somewhere in between (for example, 25% wet).

Reverb Decay Time. This parameter adjusts how long the reverberation lasts; a good way to hear reverb decay time is to trigger a single dry percussive sound, like a clave, and listen to the reverb. Decay time is often

DEPTH POSITIONING CHART

Parameter	To Move a Sound Back	To Bring a Sound Closer
Reverb Setting		
Dry/wet level balance	Increase wet level	Increase dry level
Reverb decay time	Increase	Decrease
Reverb algorithm/room size	Larger	Smaller
Reverb pre-delay	Decrease	Increase
Early reflection delay	Decrease	Increase
ER density & level	Increase	Decrease
Diffusion & density	Usually higher	Usually lower
Color/reverb EQ	Darker	Brighter
Delay Setting		
Delay	10 to >1,000ms, no modulation	None
Chorus/flange/phase shift	0.5 to 30ms delay + modulation	None
Mixing Functions		
Overall track level	Decrease	Increase
Hard left or right pan	Avoid	Okay
EQ Settings		
Presence (800Hz to 6kHz)	Cut	Boost
Microphone Technique		
Mic placement	Far-mic (add room mic)	Close-mic

listed in seconds or milliseconds (thousandths of a second, abbreviated ms). If two sources have similar dry and wet levels, the source with the longer decay will sound farther back; if one source has considerably lower levels, then less decay will keep it positioned farther back. Keep in mind, as you crank the reverb past the five-second mark 'cuz it sounds so deep, man, that many clubs have a natural reverberation of about a half-second; many of the best concert halls have a natural reverb of around 2 ½ seconds.

Reverb Algorithm/Room Size. Digital reverbs use different algorithms (mathematical models) to simulate arenas, halls, clubs, and other "rooms." Some reverbs also offer control over room dimensions (either cubic volume or length). Choose smaller algorithms or sizes to bring a particular track forward on your soundstage; choose larger ones to push them farther back.

Reverb Pre-Delay. In most live concert settings, the first sounds you hear follow a path directly from the instrument (or singer, or PA speaker, or whatever) to your ears. This is the initial dry signal, and is free of natural reverberation. Right on its heels, however, usually 5 to 75 milliseconds later, come a number of reflections, which are sounds that have taken a more circuitous route to your ears—bouncing off the stage, a balcony, or a wall before they arrive at your ears. The total of these reflections make up the overall reverberation.

To simulate the natural lag between the initial dry signal and the first reflections, many effects processors offer a pre-delay parameter. Closer objects have relatively long pre-delays between the time their direct sound reaches your ears and the time you hear any reflected signals. Consequently, increased pre-delay times can help position some tracks closer. (If large amounts of reverb or early reflections follow their respective delay times, however, a track may still sound far away, particularly if the overall mix is so complex that the pre-delay might not be noticed.)

Early Reflection Delay. Early reflections are the first reflections to reach your ears, and sometimes sound distinct, like little echoes. Like pre-delay, closer instruments will generally have a longer delay between the initial dry signal and the first early reflections.

Early Reflection Density & Level. Sometimes we never hear direct, dry signals from far-away sources. If someone's singing in another room or playing a tuba at the bottom of a canyon (doesn't everyone hike with a tuba?), everything we hear will be reflected. So, if a source must sound really far away, apply mega-amounts of early reflections and reverb, with no dry signal. Such distant sounds usually have very tight early reflection patterns, so increase ER density to move sounds backward; decrease the density to bring them forward.

Diffusion & Density. These parameters control the number of later reflections, the spacing between them, and how distinct they sound. For sweet, smooth reverb, engineers prefer high densities and high diffusion. Reducing them, however, can help position a track closer (though the reverb might sound more "chattery" than smooth). Typically, percussion uses more diffuse and dense settings than vocals.

Color/Reverb EQ. In real life, high frequencies tend to lose energy more quickly than low frequencies—that's why fog horns can be heard for miles. Reverberation from distant objects usually has fewer high frequencies, and sounds "darker" than reverb from closer objects. If your reverb offers a color or EQ control, try experimenting. (If it doesn't, and you're using an external processor, you could adjust the reverb's EQ at the mixing console.)

Delay Settings. Multieffects processors usually offer a delay (or echo) function. Delay times greater than 50ms will be heard as distinct echoes, which, when mixed with reverb, simulate super-distant placements.

Chorus, flange, and phase shift are all *modulated* digital delay effects, which means the delay time varies in a (usually) slow, periodic manner (in some devices, the delay time varies randomly, or in accordance with input level changes). The swirling sounds they create can sometimes make the sound appear wider than, or emanating from in front of, the speakers.

Mixing Functions. Mixing a track dramatically quieter or louder than other tracks can position it without having to use reverb or delay. As long as there's enough musical "space" around the track—that is, there aren't so many similar sounds playing that the track gets lost—it can be placed way back on the soundstage and still sound defined.

Panning can also influence depth. In real life, you'll hear a source in just one ear only if it's right up against your ear. To position a mono track far back in the soundstage, don't hard-pan, regardless of how much reverb you add to it. (For a stereo source, like a synth or drum machine, it's okay to pan both outputs left and right respectively since the sounds have already been panned to intermediate locations within the machine.)

EQ Settings. Intelligibility is a hallmark of up-close instruments or vocals. Consequently, boosting a track's "presence" helps bring the track forward. Presence correlates to the range of frequencies from roughly 800 to 6,000Hz; this is usually adjustable with either a midrange or high-frequency EQ control. Cutting the same frequency range adds authenticity to tracks already positioned by reverb or room ambience.

Microphone Placement. To add natural ambience to audio tracks that have been recorded with a microphone, place the mic at a distance of three feet or greater from the source. You can also mix in the sound of a "room" mic—a microphone six feet or farther from the source—to position a source farther back. Keep in mind, however, that it's impossible to remove room sound once it's been recorded with a track, which is why it's often better to add the reverb artificially during mixdown.

Surround Sound in the Project Studio

The audio industry has been re-energized with the coming of surround sound, and with that renewed enthusiasm comes a slew of new technologies and buzzwords. But let's examine what it really means. The essence of surround sound is the recording and playback of six discrete channels of audio. Five of those channels are sent to full-range speakers that appear in the soundfield at the left front, center (front), right front, left rear, and right rear positions. The sixth channel carries only low-end frequencies (thus the ".1" in the 5.1 spec) and goes to a sub-woofer, which, because of its inherent non-directionality, can be placed in a variety of positions in the soundfield.

Most people who have experience with multitrack recording have little trouble understanding the concept of recording and playing back six channels through six separate speakers. Heck, you can do that with an ADAT and six powered monitors—and still have two channels left over. But in practical terms, the art of surround mixing (which is where most of the "art" lies) is much more. And unless you really think through recording, monitoring, playing back, mixing and bass-managing that subwoofer, the logistics can be a little confusing.

Following is a primer in the basics of surround sound and some practical advice on how you can get your project studio surround-ready.

Since its launch in late 1997, DVD-Video has proven to be the fastest-growing consumer format ever (even faster than VHS or CD). But it's the imminent arrival of DVD-Audio (with its much higher quality multi-channel audio) that's caused studios around the world to begin investing in surround sound gear. Major producers and engineers including Elliot Scheiner, George Massenburg, Dave Tickle, and Bob Margouleff are spending a good deal of their time doing surround sound remixes of classic albums and TV music specials, and new productions are beginning to make their appearance in 5.1 format (DTS-encoded CD and/or DVD-Video) as well as in traditional stereo format. But surround sound production need not be the province of the high-end studio alone. Here we'll take a look at what you need to add to your project studio to make it 5.1 compatible—you may be surprised at how little it actually costs.

Let's begin with the basic requirements. To get started doing surround sound mixing, you need the following:

A mixing board or audio interface with six buses in addition to the stereo bus. This could be just about any of the new digital boards, or a multi-output computer DAW. In a pinch, you could use *any* mixer that has at least six aux sends, but that's an awkward and somewhat inelegant solution.

A place to store eight tracks of audio. This could be a dedicated 8-track MDM (such as a TASCAM DA series or Alesis ADAT), but it could also be any six-track-or-more hard disk recorder, or any analog multitrack, for that matter. Bear in mind that these six "master" tracks have to be *in addition* to the multiple tracks you'll be mixing, though they don't have to necessarily reside in a separate machine. For example, if you have two ADATs (which provide a total of 16 tracks), you can use ten of those tracks for recording the song and the other six for storing the surround mix. On the other hand, it's good to have a dedicated eight-track recorder at your disposal for this purpose, since you can put a synchronized stereo mix on the other two tracks, allowing you to quickly switch between the two mixes for comparison purposes.

Five full-range monitors and at least one subwoofer, plus appropriate power amplifiers to drive them. If possible, the five full-range speakers should be the same make and model. But if you have two great stereo speakers that you want to integrate into the system, by all means do so, and then buy another three speakers that are as much like them (in terms of frequency range and response) as possible. While one subwoofer is sufficient, you'll get your money's worth with two: one for the front three speakers, one for the rear two. Self-powered monitors simplify setup by eliminating the need to run speaker cables; just send a line-level signal directly to each monitor.

A healthy dose of creativity. Surround sound mixing is a whole lot more than just deciding which guitar track to put in front of you and which to put behind you. There are numerous pitfalls to avoid but there's also a whole new universe of sonic possibilities waiting to be explored.

The best aspect of mixing to surround is that there are no established rules for using the six speakers. You can elect to have just the room sound come from the rear speakers, which places the listener facing a band on a proscenium stage. Or you can have different families of instruments assigned to each speaker (brass in the left rear, woodwinds in the right rear, high strings in the left front, low strings in the right front, etc.), which places the listener in the middle of the orchestra. To get acquainted with some different approaches, go buy some surround-mixed CDs, like Steely Dan's *Gaucho*, the Eagles' *Hell Freezes Over*, Lyle Lovett's *Joshua Judges Judy*, or any number of albums from Paul McCartney, Sting, Marvin Gaye, Chick Corea, Eric Clapton, Vince Gill, Debussy, Mozart, Tchaikovsky, and others (check out www.dtsonline.com for more titles in the DTS format).

One thing you *don't* have to necessarily buy is an encoding device, though it can be helpful to monitor through an encoder just to see how the conversion will affect your audio. Ultimately, encoding will probably be the province of the mastering studio; all you have to do for now in your project studio is get your six-channel mix together (in addition to—not instead of—your stereo mix).

Now let's cover the topics of equipment interconnection, bass management, speaker placement and calibration, downmixing, and encode monitoring.

Bus Assignments. The interconnections for a surround sound rig aren't particularly complicated if you keep in mind the main goal: to route signal freely to any or all of the six channels and to route each of the six channels to its own dedicated track and loudspeaker. There is no set busing scheme, but the Dolby Digital standard (also the SMPTE standard) is:

Bus 1 = left front
Bus 2 = right front
Bus 3 = center
Bus 4 = subwoofer (also called the "LFE" channel, for "Low Frequency Effects")
Bus 5 = left surround (rear)
Bus 6 = right surround (rear)
Just to make things complicated, the DTS busing scheme (also used by the Yamaha 02R) is different, as follows:
Bus 1 = left front
Bus 2 = right front
Bus 3 = left rear
Bus 4 = right rear
Bus 5 = center
Bus 6 = subwoofer
It really doesn't matter which of these two bus assignments you use—in fact, you can even make up one of your own—as long as you stick to

it. Just be consistent and carefully label the resultant mixes so that the mastering engineer knows which track is meant to be routed to which channel.

Once you've decided on your layout, the idea is to send line-level signal from each of the six buses to both the associated track on your mixdown recorder and the power amplifier driving the equivalent speaker (or powered speaker). For example, the Bus 1 Out of your mixer needs to be connected to both the Track 1 In of your ADAT or hard-disk recorder (whatever you're using to hold the final surround mix) and to the left front speaker.

There are several ways to accomplish this dual routing. One way is to use Y-cables, signal splitters, or patchbay mults to send the signal from each bus to both the recorder and power amplifier. Alternatively, you can connect the bus solely to the recorder and then route the recorder's outputs to the appropriate speakers (i.e., Bus 1 Out to Track 1 In, and Track 1 Out to the input of the first power amplifier). With the latter approach, you'll have to set the recorder to monitor the input signal arriving at each of the six tracks while you're mixing.

An even better solution is provided by digital consoles that have a provision for expansion cards. These cards allow a single bus out signal to be routed to multiple destinations. Here's one example of routing a digital multitrack for surround: make a two-way Lightpipe connection between the ADAT cards in an 02R and three ADATs. This allows signal from the 24 tracks to be input to the 02R, and at the same time allows the surround mix to be sent back to the first six tracks of each machine.

Bass Management. The line-level analog routing is slightly more complicated, because of an important principle called _bass management_ (sometimes called "bass redirection"). You could simply connect the bus 1–6 outs from the D/A card in the 02R to the five main nearfield monitors and a subwoofer, but that would mean that the subwoofer was receiving signal only from the LFE channel, and that's not a great solution for two reasons: one, since nearfield monitors typically only have limited bass response, you won't be able to hear any subsonic anomalies that may exist in those five tracks; and, two, that's not the way most end users will listen to surround sound (most consumer receivers take all low-end signal and send it to the subwoofer).

Your job as engineer is to make sure that what you're delivering is technically correct, and that means that you need to be able to hear the full frequency range of _all_ channels. The solution is to route low-frequency signal from all five channels as well as the LFE channel signal to your subwoofer, and that's what the term "bass management" means.

A bass management system uses filters to ensure that frequencies below a crossover point (typically 120Hz or 80Hz—the Dolby Digital and DTS standards, respectively) are combined with the LFE channel input and routed to the subwoofer output, while frequencies above the crossover point are routed to the full-range speakers. There are stand-alone "bass manager" boxes that do this, but it can also sometimes be accomplished within the mixer itself by circuitry inside the subwoofer, or by an outboard signal processor or software plug-in (e.g., Kind Of Loud Woofie). Genelec 1092 subwoofers, for example, have this capability. You could connect the front left, front right, center, and LFE bus output channels to a 1092 subwoofer, and then connect the 1092's front left, front right, and center channel outputs to the corresponding full-range speakers, like the Genelec 1029As. The bus outputs from the two rear channels can connect to an additional 1091 sub and its left and right outputs can then connect to the two rear 1029As. With a connection scheme such as this, signal from the five main channels goes to a subwoofer (along with the LFE channel) while signal routed to bus 1 is sent to both track 1 of the ADATs (in the digital domain) as well as to the left front speaker (in the analog domain); signal routed to bus 2 simultaneously goes to track 2 and to the right front speaker, and so on. It's much harder to describe it than it is to do it!

The Surround Monitoring Bugaboo. This makes, however, for an interesting dilemma: how to set the recording levels and monitoring levels independently. Most mixers—even those touted as supporting surround mixing—don't have surround *monitoring* capability. Monitoring for surround requires a dedicated six-way potentiometer, so that the level of all six channels can be adjusted simultaneously and *separately* from the bus send levels. There are a number of third-party surround monitoring controllers available from manufacturers such as MartinSound, Audient, Otari, and Baldwin Products, but these are aimed primarily at the high-end market and carry a hefty price tag.

There are workaround solutions to this problem, although they may not be perfect. On an analog 8-bus console, for example, you could use the eight subgroups to feed the monitors—but you'll have to be very careful to balance each output's level accurately. If you're using a computer-based DAW with an audio interface that features multiple outputs that you can access independently, you could use its outputs to feed the speakers directly; though you'll have to control volume from within your software as opposed to with a physical knob.

On a digital console such as an 02R, you could use your external aux sends. To set independent monitoring levels, assign the D/A card outputs 1–6 to aux sends 1–6 (instead of the default assignment of buses 1–6). Next, assign the tape returns from the target recorder (in our example above, an ADAT) to the aux sends *instead* of the stereo or bus outs—track 1 to aux 1, track 2 to aux 2, etc. Finally, group all six faders together for master volume control, and you're in business.

Other systems may provide different routing possibilities; take a creative look at your rig. If all else fails, you can simply use the volume controls on your power amps or self-powered speakers to set monitoring levels.

Speaker Placement and Calibration. Needless to say, speaker placement for surround monitoring is important, though perhaps not quite as critical as some audiophiles would have you believe. Let's deal with the five "main" (i.e., full-range, or non-subwoofer) speakers first. The front three speakers should be placed in an arc, with the left and right speakers at a 30–35° angle from the listener (finally, a use for that $1.49 plastic protractor you were forced to buy in high school!) and toed in slightly. If possible, the rear speakers should be angled in as well. The accepted practice is to set them at about 110° relative to the front center speaker, but some surround mixers prefer them at a steeper angle for improved phantom imaging (135–145°). (See Figure 3.) Ideally, you want all five speakers to be at the same height (ear level is best), though, again, this is largely a matter of taste.

Each of the five speakers should be at an equal distance from your

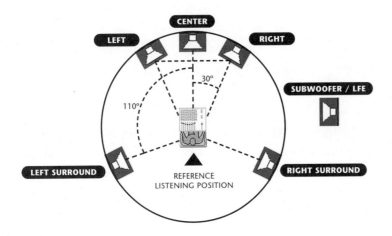

Figure 3

This aerial view shows the recommended placement of the six speakers in a 5.1 surround system. The subwoofer can go anywhere in the room that produces the ideal balance, and the rear speakers can be moved back even further behind the listener to improve the sense of surround and *phantom imaging* (where a sound seems to emanate from between two speakers).

normal mixing position. If this isn't possible, you can compensate by making distant speakers slightly louder (by turning up their power amp) and/or by slightly delaying the signal arriving at closer speakers. The basic rule of thumb for this delay is about one millisecond—that's one thousandth of a second—per foot. This means that if your rear speakers are six feet away and your front speakers are four feet away, you should delay the signal to the three front speakers by about two milliseconds. This is easily accomplished in most digital mixers or ADATs, where individual channels or tracks can be delayed precisely.

In practice, you'll find that slight distance variations like this are virtually imperceptible. In general, as long as all five main speakers are close to equidistant from the mix position, you're not going to have any problems. The vagaries of your project studio might dictate that, say, your rear speakers are about three feet further away than your front speakers and slightly off-center as well. By simply making them a little bit louder than the front speakers, you can achieve a good listening balance without having to delay the front speaker signals at all.

You can set the relative levels of the five main speakers with a reasonable degree of accuracy with the use of an inexpensive Radio Shack SPL meter. Simply position it at the mix position, set it to C-weighting (slow response), and feed a noise source into one speaker at a time, setting its power amp so that the SPL meter reads the same level (85dB SPL is the film standard listening level) for each.

Fun and Games with Subwoofers. Subwoofer placement and level calibration is a bit trickier. A subwoofer should fill the room, like some gaseous ooze, and each room is unique, so you'll have to experiment with subwoofer placement to find the spot in the room where the cabinet appears the loudest. Often a corner is good, because you can use the walls as a 90° wave guide. If you're using two subwoofers, be careful that you don't face them toward each other, as phase canceling can occur. Often you can place them next to each other, but if that's impractical try them on different walls at the edge of the room.

One of the most important factors in calibrating the subwoofer level is its acoustic phase alignment at the crossover point; incorrect alignment can cause a drop in the frequency response of the whole system at the crossover point. Some subwoofers offer a built-in phase matching control that allows adjustment in precise steps. If yours does, feed in a sine wave at the crossover frequency and adjust it to the point where the sound is loudest at the mix position. If your subwoofer does not have such a control, try repositioning the speaker until the signal is loudest at the mix position. While there is no industry standard as yet, experts such as Tomlinson Holman recommend that the subwoofer provide 10dB more headroom than the main speakers. This can be accomplished by setting its level so that it delivers approximately 4dB SPL above the chosen reference level when playing back band-limited pink noise (low-pass filtered at 120Hz). If you calibrate your full-range speakers to deliver 85dB SPL at the mix position, the subwoofer should be set to deliver 89dB SPL.

A number of surround sound speaker calibration tools are starting to find their way to market, including TMH Corporation DTRS-format multichannel test tapes and Kind Of Loud Tweetie Pro Tools plug-in.

Downmixing and Encode Monitoring. _Downmixing_ is one of the most dreaded words to the discriminating surround sound engineer. It describes a process by which the 5.1 mix is automatically reduced ("folded down") to stereo or even mono under the control of unseeing, unfeeling circuitry that has no sense of aesthetics or taste. Truth be told, no professional really trusts downmixing. Despite the fact that the DVD-Audio spec provides for something called SMART (System Managed Audio Resource Technique) Content, which allows the producer to set and embed various "downmix coefficients" (such as level, panning, etc.) within each track, it's best not to rely on it. Instead, you should plan on doing a separate stereo mix in addition to your surround mix. Fortunately, since most of the space on a DVD-Audio disc is reserved for audio data, there's plenty of room to store both mixes, and data compression can always be used if the program material is too long to fit. Most of the surround sound monitor controllers mentioned above allow you to hear the (usually disappointing) results of downmixing to stereo or mono at the touch of a button; Kind Of Loud Tweetie plug-in also provides one-click downmix previewing from within Pro Tools.

If your music will be released on DVD-Video, the surround mix must first be encoded into Dolby Digital, MPEG, and/or DTS formats (an encoded data stream is optional for DVD-Audio releases). All of these algorithms are "lossy" perceptual encoding schemes (as opposed to MLP, which is a "loss-less" data compression scheme), meaning that some of the audio data is actually discarded. In theory, the data that's thrown away is audio you wouldn't hear anyway (for example, low-level signals buried beneath louder ones, or portions of sounds masked by others in the same frequency range), but no matter how great a job the algorithm does, the audio is going to be compromised to some degree.

Fortunately, there are steps you can take in the mixing process to minimize the degree of degradation—for example, frequency-specific limiting in some bands can sometimes help reduce "spittiness"—so it's helpful to be able to preview your mix through an encoder in order to make these compensations. Standalone hardware encoders are available from Dolby and DTS, and there are a number of computer-based MPEG encoder cards (most of which run only under Windows NT) that allow real-time monitoring, but these all tend to be relatively pricey. A less expensive alternative is provided by the non-realtime software encoders available from a number of manufacturers, including Sonic Foundry and Minnetonka, as well as Kind Of Loud SmartCode Pro plug-ins.

Once you get your hardware set up and a feel for mixing in a six-channel soundfield, you can focus on the aesthetics. With a surround sound mixing program (like Cubase SX and Nuendo, Digidesign Pro Tools, MOTU Digital Performer, and Emagic Logic Audio) and automation, you can try out different approaches. But perhaps the best education you can provide yourself with is to simply buy a DVD player with both Dolby Digital and DTS playback capabilities. They're less than $400 as of this writing, and they'll only get cheaper and better. So spend the money you save on surround-mixed discs (an excellent source is www.dtsonline.com) and listen to the sound that is all around.

Preplanning Your Mix

With so many ways to localize tracks on your imaginary soundstage, it's easy to wind up with a cluttered mix. It's also easy to position tracks formulaically, without thinking. Fortunately, some preplanning can open new creative doors onto your soundstages. Preplanning your soundstage is cheap, and makes good engineering sense. After all, you wouldn't build a real stage without blueprints, would you?

Sketch Placements. Many engineers start off a mix by panning tracks in a familiar manner—for instance, kick, snare, bass, and lead vocal center; keys to the right; acoustic guitar to the left; etc. Feeling inspired, they may vary one or two of these placements, but not much. Similarly, they'll use reverb with a familiar approach: wet-sounding snare, a moderate amount of reverb on the vocals, no reverb on the bass, and so forth.

If this sounds familiar, you, too, may be in need of a creative kick. So next time you mix, reach for a pencil before you reach for a pan control.

Make a diagram of the soundstage you are about to create (see Figure 4) and sketch out the following details for each track:

• Left-to-right placement (pan)
• Depth positioning (reverb amount and other positioning techniques)
• Stereo width (for stereo sources, or tracks with stereo reverb)
• Acoustic space (reverb room algorithm or size)

By using your mind before you use your ears, you'll approach the mix from a different point of view. As an added benefit, the visual reference map can help you avoid a cluttered mix.

Plan Acoustic Spaces. Remember, the primary way to control depth positioning is to adjust the amount of reverb. If your aim is a natural-sounding mix, say for acoustic jazz or classical music, usually it's best to use just a "global" reverb setting—with a single room algorithm (hall, cathedral, etc.) and a single decay time that's applied to all instruments. Then, the simplest way to position tracks near or far is to adjust each track's reverb send level: more reverb to position a track to the rear, less to bring it forward. After adjusting the reverb sends of the individual instruments, pull back on the master reverb output level until you can hear all of the instruments clearly.

However, if you're mixing modern pop/rock music, and your sound card or synth allows for effects processing on a track-by-track basis (or you're using a mixer in conjunction with multiple processors), it's common to combine a variety of room algorithms and decay times. "Big" drums, for instance, typically call for an arena algorithm with a long decay time; an up-front vocal might call for a plate algorithm with a

Figure 4

Sketch out your instrumental placements before you start to mix. Not only will this help you identify potential problems, but you might also find that using a visual approach gives added inspiration.

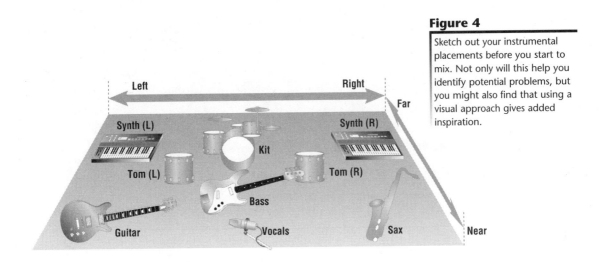

rapid decay. You can also achieve "big" sounds using a smaller room with a long decay, and setting the wet/dry balance to relatively wet. (However, if you're unlucky enough to have a cheap, gritty-sounding reverb, like the ones built into many sound cards, it's advisable to keep things on the dry side.)

When using multiple room algorithms, it's helpful to draw size diagrams for each track in your soundstage, as shown in Figure 5. Doing so may inspire novel-sounding mixes as well as help you avoid clutter. And it will make it easier to identify tracks that can share reverb channels—an important consideration for anyone with fewer reverb units than tracks.

Non-Automated Mixing. Automated mixing is wonderful, but some of us are still doing it the old-fashioned way, by moving the mixer's faders up and down during playback (see "Digital Multitrack Automation" for automating with digital recorders). Try keeping track of levels with colored pencils. If there's a smooth surface, you can mark directly on your mixer's panel with a grease pencil. (Make a test mark first in an inconspicuous corner and try rubbing it off. If you use isopropyl alcohol to clean the marks off, also test it first. Some chemical

Figure 5

Visual representation of some of the mix elements from Peter Gabriel's "That Voice Again."

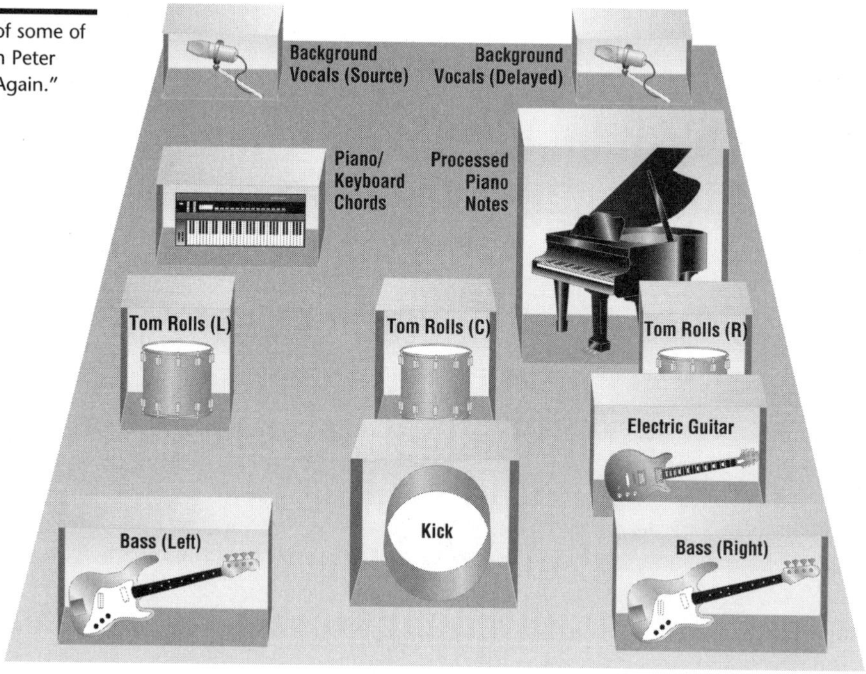

cleaners will degrade some types of plastic panel.) Or put white artist's tape alongside the faders, and mark on the tape.

Plan your mixing moves. Try recording the tracks with natural dynamics, so you don't have to change levels constantly. If you're recording a quiet sound for the background, record it at a lower level, consistent with staying above the noise floor. Try to record tracks with gaps between the events so you can make your moves without panicking.

Quality Counts. Ultimately, it's the quality of your music that really counts, and not so much the mix. Listen long enough to any radio station and you'll hear mediocre songs packaged oh-so-nicely in gloriously slick mixes. While a great mix might make a hit, a great mix does not make a great song.

But the flip side also applies. It's not just enough to have a great song, especially if you're hoping to have it noticed. Record label execs frequently pass up absolutely terrific material because of a poor mix, even though they're expected to listen to the music and not the production. So if you believe in your music, think as a playwright might, and choose to have your story told on the most appropriate and flattering stage you can create.

Digital Multitrack Automation

One of the benefits of using a digital audio recording system is that you're often given very detailed automation control over various track parameters. Even plug-ins (on computer-based systems) can be automated, which means effects can benefit from automation as well as the more normal channel-strip controls like volume, EQ, effects-send level, panning, and mute.

There are four basic types, or methods, of automation in a digital recording device. Depending on what type of system you have, they are:

• **Graphic envelope control**. Also known as the "rubber band" method, this is used primarily in computer programs, and involves drawing an envelope (contour) on the screen for each track.

• **MIDI-based automation**. This method is suitable for mixes that use "virtual tracks" of MIDI synths and samplers, whose output levels can be controlled using MIDI volume controller messages. It's also used in mixers that offer external MIDI control of fader levels. MIDI-based automation requires a MIDI sequencer playing back in sync with whatever audio tracks are being mixed.

• **Snapshot-based automation**. Often found in stand-alone

recorder/mixers, this method involves storing a series of "snapshots" or "scenes," each of which records the positions of all of the mixer controls at a given point in the music. After recording the snapshots (or while recording them), you assign them to specific points in the song (such as the beginning of the chorus). They're called up automatically while the song plays back.

- **Moving fader automation**. In some hardware recorders, such as the Yamaha AW4416, the faders are motorized so they'll move physically when an automated mix is being played back. But even if the faders don't physically move without human aid, the idea behind moving fader automation is the same: Fader moves are recorded while the music plays. After being recorded, they're reproduced each time the music plays, as if ghostly hands were pushing the faders up and down. Fader moves can be recorded in a number of passes, edited, punched in, and so on. Moving fader automation is preferable to snapshot-based automation, because it allows you to do smooth fades between higher and lower volume levels. The fadeout at the end of a song, for instance, can't be automated using snapshots. However, some snapshot-based automation systems offer a hybrid approach in which you can program a transition, or "fade time," between one snapshot and the next. This does allow for smooth fades.

Level, or volume, remains one of the most useful and powerful parameters to automate. Most musicians use level automation to set the volume at the beginning of each track, and leave it at that. But because you're putting tasks under machine control, which is faster and more accurate than human fingers, there's much more you can do with level automation. Here are three level-based applications for digital automation that would be difficult to impossible to execute manually, or without a dedicated processor.

Dynamics. The dynamics in many pop performances can leave something to be desired. This is especially true with performances on electronic instruments, where you look for the same type of dynamic shaping you'd get from, say, an accomplished vocalist or string or horn player. The best way to achieve a more expressive performance is with careful performance or sequencing, but you can use automation to enhance the dynamics of the performance even more. An example might be to swell the volume of various tracks as a build from the verse of a song into its chorus.

Automation can be used to bring up a passage that's too quiet, or to bring down a passage that's too loud. There are also situations where, in an otherwise acceptable track, there's a note or two that jumps out or fades back into the final mix because of the dynamics of the backing tracks. Rather than use a compressor to even out the levels, experiment with either momentarily turning the backing tracks up or down slightly (done carefully, you won't even hear the results) or turning the offending notes in the lead track up or down (see Figure 6). You may find that controlling a few errant notes in this way is superior to compressing the whole track.

Compression. You can use level automation as a substitute or replacement for hardware or software compression. The problem with compressors is that you're forced to come up with a setting that's the least common denominator for the track, and then apply it to the whole track. The compressor usually isn't smart enough to take into account the fact that the track is always changing, and that the setting should be changing (whether subtly or dramatically) to compensate. You end up with parts of the track being compressed too heavily, and some parts not being compressed at all.

There are ways you can use level automation to correct for this. The first is to go into the track, turn down peaks that need to be controlled, and raise low-level signals. The beauty of using computer-based automa-

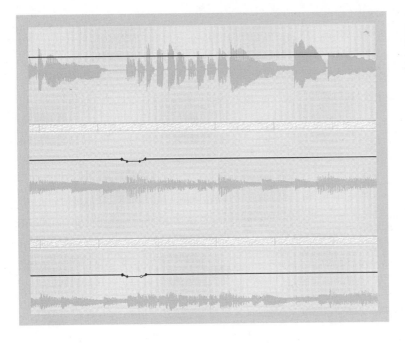

Figure 6

Automation compensates for notes that drop into or jump out of the mix. You can either turn the offending notes up or down, or, as in this case using tracks recorded in Mark of the Unicorn AudioDesk software, momentarily adjust the level of the backing tracks. If you're careful in drawing the automation curve, you won't hear the level dip in the backing tracks; the lead track will naturally fill in the volume drop.

tion for this is that you can be extremely accurate in controlling just the worst peaks or valleys (see Figure 7). Once you've done this, you can turn the whole track up without fear of overloading or distorting, accomplishing the same thing as running the signal through a compressor or limiter. If you're tweaky about drawing in your automation curves, you won't be able to hear the effects of the "compression" at all—a real bonus in many situations.

You can be as detailed and thorough about doing this type of automation as you like, but don't spend hours and hours drawing detailed automation curves that don't really make any discernible difference in the final mix. Use your ears.

The other way that this kind of automation can be used is in conjunction with a hardware or software compressor. Once you've used automation to bring down the worst peaks and raise the volume of the lowest levels, a compressor can often be applied subtly with much better results. The signal being fed into the compressor is more consistent, so compression is applied more evenly.

Guitarists often use stompbox compressors to enhance the sustain of their instruments; the box turns down the peaks and turns up the sustain portion of the notes, increasing the instrument's apparent sustain time. You can accomplish the same thing with automation. While you may not need to go through a track and apply a volume boost to the sustain portion of each note, you can get in there and turn up the decay on notes that particularly need to ring out.

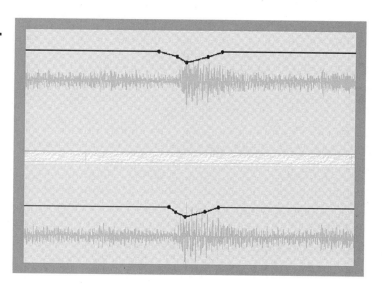

Figure 7

By carefully automating levels to compensate for transients and peaks, you can accomplish much the same thing as a compressor or limiter, but with far greater control and often with less audible results. In this case, only the worst part of the peak has been automated down; the general shape of the transient hasn't been affected, resulting in a very natural, uncompressed sound. You can be extremely detailed and accurate with your automation curves. In this example, raising the position of any of the automation points by even one notch results in a digital clip.

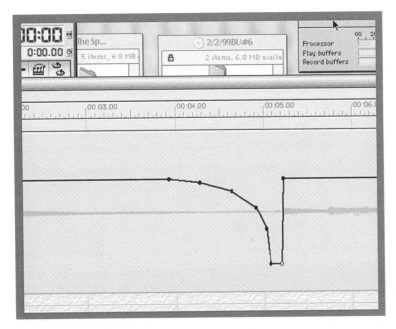

Figure 8

Using automation to gate noisy tracks. Here, the automation curve has been set so that the desired signal is not affected, but the subsequent noise is turned down to an acceptable level. Note that the noise hasn't been turned down completely. Allowing a bit of noise to bleed through can make the track sound more natural than it would if sudden silences and gaps appeared. In a dense mix, you could probably drop the noise out completely, but in an exposed track a sudden silence would be very noticeable.

Gating. As with compressors, the problem with using noise gates is that you're forced to apply the same gate setting to the whole track being processed. This often results in extraneous noise getting through in certain places, and in the desired audio getting chopped off in others. Before automatically invoking the gate plug-in or strapping on an outboard unit, go in and *automate* the noise out with level control. Cleaning up the track this way achieves the same results as a gate, but with some benefits: Your automated-level "gate" never chatters or flutters as the signal passes the threshold. You have complete control over the envelope, so desired sound is never affected adversely. You can also specify with great control whether the region drops to complete silence, or whether a little bit of the background ambience is allowed to get through.

Gating or automating down to complete silence often sounds unnatural. (This is one reason you shouldn't just cut out the noisy region entirely.) By carefully establishing and possibly even shaping the background noise level that's allowed to bleed into the gaps (see Figure 8), you can keep the track sounding natural, while reducing the noise to an acceptable volume.

Do-It-Yourself Snapshot Automation. One side benefit of digital recorders (tape or hard disk) is that they have brought back the art of premixing, or bouncing tracks. Part of this is from necessity; because track counts are typically limited, you'll probably need to premix if you want a complex, layered sound. But also, digital audio makes quality premixing possible. Unlike premixing with analog machines, no longer does the process build up noise and distortion.

Our snapshot method uses two unused tracks on your digital tape or hard disk multitrack to hold the final mix. The downside is that with an 8-track, you now have only six tracks available for basic recording, so this method works better if you have 16 or more tracks available. However, the advantages of this type of mixing are quite compelling (especially with 16 or more tracks), as it gives you snapshot mixing "for free" and can be employed on machines that don't have any automation features (ADAT, DA-88, etc.). Here's how to do it:

1. Connect the system as shown in Figure 9, where the recorded tracks go through the mixer to two unused tracks. (If you use a stand-alone workstation, you can do the routing internally, but the diagram still visually represents what's happening.)

2. Go to the beginning of the song, put the unused tracks into record, and start mixing.

3. As long as the mix is okay, keep recording.

4. As soon as you want to change the mix, stop the multitrack and rewind prior to where you wanted the mix to change.

5. Play back the multitrack and adjust the mix levels, EQ, etc.

6. Rewind the multitrack to about 10 seconds before the point where you want these changes to kick in.

Figure 9

A mix can be recorded in sections onto two unused tracks of a multitrack digital recorder.

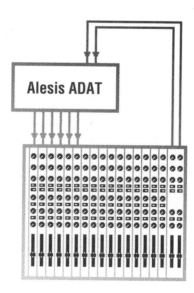

Alesis ADAT

7. Punch in on the mixdown tracks at the precise moment where the new mix should take over. *Unlike analog tape, digital tape doesn't leave a punch-out gap to fret about.* (You can optionally use a rehearse mode, if available, to set and audition the punch points.)

8. Repeat steps 4 through 7 until the entire song is mixed.

9. Your final mix is now located on what had been two unused tracks. Bounce them over to your mastering machine using the analog or digital outputs, and you're done.

This is really a great way to mix, as it gives the advantage of intuitive, real-time mixing up to the point where you need to make a change, at which time you reset a few controls and carry on.

Sure, fully automated mixing that re-creates all fader and control moves is convenient and effective. But when you have to do more with less, the above approach can give you a perfect mix without too much effort—and with very little cost.

Mixing with Effects

Synthesizers, audio recorders, and effects processors are turning increasingly digital, but when it comes to hooking all this outboard gear together, it's frequently still an analog mixer that does the job. The flexibility, number of patch points, and hands-on control remain appealing, as does the cost. However, in many ways these venerable boxes remain underutilized, particularly regarding effects. Here are several tips designed to increase the synergy between mixing and signal processing.

Full-Feature Effects Returns. If you have enough mixer channels, bring your reverb returns back into two mixer channels rather than the dedicated effects returns. Using mixer channels gives you control over the returned signal (EQ, panning, sends to other effects, etc.) that the returns usually don't have. When using this patch, be careful not to turn the return channels' corresponding send(s) up, as this would create a feedback loop.

Keeping Your Straight Sound Straight. Although mixer input channel effects loops are convenient for patching in effects, some processors alter the straight (dry) sound as the signal passes through them. Fortunately, you can preserve the integrity of the straight signal yet still add the desired effect; the patching option you'll use depends on your mixer setup.

In any case, the first thing you need to do is derive a send from the input channel signal. There are three ways to do this:

- If your mixer has separate loop send and receive jacks for each channel, patch into the send. This should not break the normaled channel connection that allows the straight signal to pass through to the stereo mixdown bus.
- Most mixers use a TRS (tip-ring-sleeve) stereo jack to handle the insert and effects send/return. Plugging a cord halfway into the jack (so that the plug tip contacts the jack tip) should provide a send without breaking the normaled connection. A quick glance at the manual will tell you if your mixer has this capability.
- If you don't have loop jacks, then use an aux bus to provide a send from the channel.

Patch the send into the processor, which should be set for effected sound only (no dry signal). Then bring the effects output back to a separate channel, or to two channels if it's a stereo effect, and mix in the desired effects blend at the mixer (dry sound on the original channel, processed signal on the additional channel or channels). As a bonus, using this approach lets you modify the effects signal with panning, reverb, aux sends to other effects, and all the other input channel options.

Better Reverb Pre-Delay. For more control over your reverb sound, patch a delay line between the effects send and reverb input. This provides more control than the pre-delay found in most reverbs. For example, adding a bit of feedback to the delay line can create a more complex reverb effect. Again, set both the delay and the reverb to an effect-only (100% wet) setting.

Bigger Stereo Images for Piano and Guitar. Here's an effect that Alex de Grassi uses a lot on his guitars to create a wider stereo image with two mics, and it also works well with piano. Split the main right and left channels to two additional channels, using either a Y cord, a direct out, or an effects loop send. Pan the main left and right channels hard left and right, and center the other two channels (see Figure 10) but bring their levels down about 5–6dB (or to taste). This fills in the center hole that normally occurs when the two main signals are panned to the extreme left and right.

While you're at it, experiment with adding reverb in different ways— only the main channels, only the middle channels, weighted toward the left or the right, etc.

Save an Effects Send. Most stereo reverbs are not true stereo, but sum the two inputs together to mono and synthesize a stereo field from that.

Therefore, there's no real need to use two sends, as the original stereo imaging is lost anyway. However, do use stereo returns.

Undead Compression. If you're using compression as an effect (as opposed to preventing tape saturation or some other "utilitarian" application) but don't like that squashed sound, patch the signal to be compressed through the main channel and send its direct out or effects loop out to the compressor, then return the compressor to a separate channel. Use the compressed channel as your main signal, then bring up the unprocessed channel to restore some of the dynamics.

Aux Bus Fun and Games. Get creative with your aux send processing—no law says you can use only reverb. Some favorites:

• Add a mild distortion device (tube preamp, etc.) and send it to drum tracks, bass, whatever. The distortion can add a nice edge and warmth; bring it back at a fairly low level just to add a bit of "crunch." Or patch the send to a guitar amp, mic the amp and the room, and bring the mic signal back into the board as an "effects return."

• Feed one aux bus to a vocoder carrier input, and another aux bus to the vocoder's modulation input. Note that this requires a real vocoder with two inputs, not the digital simulations that have only one input (with perhaps an additional input for MIDI control). This allows any signal to modulate any other signal, which can provide a very cool effect if you choose something percussive for the modulation input

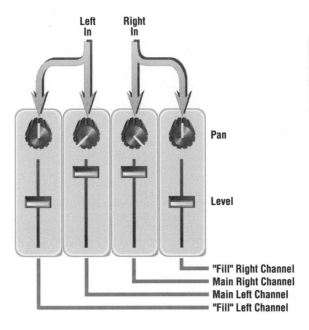

Figure 10

For a fuller stereo image, take two additional feeds from your left and right source signals, and pan them both to the center.

and use it to trigger a more sustained part, such as bass or long piano chords, which feed the vocoder carrier input.

- Miss that vintage tape delay sound? For that unmistakable tape echo, patch a pair of aux sends to an analog, two-track, three-head recorder set for record. (You can pick up these behemoths of yester-year at garage sales and online auction sites for a song.) Roll the tape, and patch the playback head outputs to the effects returns. You'll end up with a slapback echo that has that warm analog quality. If the deck has multiple speeds and variable pitch control, so much the better. For a truly grungy delay, use this technique with a three-head cassette deck.

- For some audio excitement, you can patch an "audio exciter" into an aux bus send/return rather than use it inline on the entire mix. Although these types of devices were originally intended to process an entire mix, these days it's not uncommon for samples to already be "excited" (particularly drum samples), and adding more exciter on top of that can give a really tinny sound. Adding an exciter selectively using the aux bus controls gives a much more controlled mix. Note: Some of these devices do not allow for cutting out the straight signal so that you have processed sound only—a necessity when using an exciter in an aux loop.

MONITORING TIPS

What's the biggest impediment to a well-balanced soundstage? Probably the loudspeakers you use as you record and mix, and the room in which you work. Almost all speakers accentuate certain frequencies and underrepresent others. Even with expensive "studio monitor" speakers, the acoustics of the listening room conspire against them—especially with the proverbial bedroom/spare room/living room/garage studio that lacks acoustical treatment. For these reasons, the monitor system is universally the least accurate component of any studio.

The problem gets even worse if you use a typical pair of home stereo speakers as monitors. Maybe you think they're fine, because all your commercial audio discs sound great when played back through them. Unfortunately, that's the problem: Most home stereo speakers are designed to sound good, not accurate, so they'll frequently boost the low end for a bit of thump, and boost the high end for a bit of sizzle. Mixes made on speakers like these can sound bass-shy and muffled when played back on somewhat more accurate speakers.

The good news is that there are a number of ways you can compensate for your speakers' shortcomings to help ensure a mix that sounds good in lots of different playback settings.

Use a variety of references. Listen to your mix through a car stereo (the favorite reference place for many producers). Car stereos have funky frequency weightings to compensate for the acoustics of the car interior. This is a good test to see just how flat your mix really is—if nothing totally unexpected (typically a low-midrange guitar) suddenly dominates a mix that sounded relatively subdued in the studio, you're in the clear. In addition, the auto environment is rife with background noise. Songs with a wide dynamic range can fall beneath the noise floor during the quiet parts. This isn't to say you should emulate the hyped-up, piped-in, compressed-to-kingdom-come sound of your local hard rock radio station. It just drops a clue that the quiet parts may need something else to help them pierce through a noisy environment, such as a boost to the high frequencies or less reverb.

Play your mix on a boom box, a friend's hi-fi, and through a DiscMan. Let your alternate references teach you how to mix. If the music sounds good in your studio but too bassy on your friends' stereos, you may be overcompensating for your monitors' lack of bottom end, and need to learn to mix with less low end. Also, home stereos—especially those with built-in effects or surround sound—have a way of exaggerating audio spatialization. That dreamy echoed guitar solo can turn into a splatter of disjointed frequencies on a loud home stereo, indicating that you should go back and pull back on the effects.

If your mixes sound excessively bright everywhere but in your studio, perhaps your monitors' tweeter controls are turned way down, or worse yet, the tweeters are fried. If your music sounds good through most or all of these references, you know you're on the right track.

Use professional near-field monitors. For $200 to $500, you can get a pair of monitor speakers that are more accurate than many expensive home stereo speakers. Be sure to buy near-field monitors, designed to be placed within a meter or two from where you sit (to minimize interference from the room's acoustics). If you're serious about your music, good monitors are money well spent.

When you're seated at your mixer, the space between the two speakers and your ears should form an equilateral triangle, about one meter on each side. Angle the speakers slightly toward your ears, and keep them at eye level. To widen the sweet spot, place the speakers on their sides with the tweeters to the outside.

Compensate for your studio's compromises. Since you probably don't have several thousand dollars to have your studio professionally "tuned," when using near-field monitors the best way to reduce the impact of your room's acoustics is to hang drapes or acoustical foam (like

Sonex) over hard walls and windows, throw carpets on hard floors, and generally do your best to "deaden" the studio.

Get intimate with your tracks. Hear beyond the obvious. To ensure that the reverb on your lead vocal is decaying smoothly, listen to just that track (all other tracks should be muted). Solo all of your MIDI tracks one by one, and mute, erase, or repair any musical clams. If you're recording audio to hard disk or tape, clean up the tracks before you mix by erasing unwanted sections, or if necessary by using a noise gate, which can silence hum, clicks, and other low-level junk. Many on-screen audio editing programs offer built-in gating; several compressor/limiters designed for use with a mixer also include gating functions.

What about headphones? Don't monitor exclusively through headphones, though they're indispensable late at night or when you're recording with a microphone. But committing yourself to a mix while monitoring through headphones is a mistake. On the other hand, you can hear details through headphones that you might miss through speakers, so they're a good way to "proof" individual tracks and complete mixes for stereo imaging, any glitches or pops, and other details. For best results, go back and forth among several different sets of speakers as well as headphones to get as complete a picture of your mix as possible.

Vary the perspective. Listen at moderate to quiet levels. (It's okay to listen at loud levels for short periods, but be aware of room interference and your ears' health.) To avoid "listener fatigue," take a 10-minute break every hour. Don't make final decisions at 3:00 A.M. after hours of mixing. Close your eyes. A common engineer's trick is to go behind the speakers and put your head in between them; this can reveal unheard details. Walk around the room. Turn your back to the speakers and listen carefully. Any of this might reveal something new.

Spare the loudness. While a professional power amp is best, a home stereo amp or receiver can be used for near-field monitoring—assuming it's a quality product with 30 to 50 watts per channel minimum. If you go this route, beware the temptations of the Loudness button. This is actually a variable EQ circuit, which boosts highs and lows at quiet to moderate listening levels, and it can make you think you're mixing with more bass and highs than you have. Make sure the loudness control is off before doing any critical mixing.

6

Burning and Mastering

Now that CD recordable drives and blank CD-R discs are affordable to even those on limited budgets, what computer-owning musician can resist? Demos recorded on CD have the same pristine quality as a DAT tape, but the person you send them to won't need anything other than a standard CD player. If you have a few fans who'd like to buy your album, but not enough to justify duplicating CDs in mass quantities, with a CD-R you can "burn" (record) just enough discs to satisfy demand. Recordings archived to CD-R won't degrade as quickly as analog or DAT tape (though exactly how long they will last is a matter of some contention).

Most CD-R drives (also called CD writers) can produce not just audio CDs but CD-ROMs that hold up to 650MB of data, so you can use them to archive completed digital audio projects, create sample and patch library discs, or even run off some discs for sale—there's probably somebody out there who'd pay big bucks for that 300MB of didgeridoo samples you've spent years collecting and indexing. You can even back up your hard drive to CD-R as well, now that CD-rewriteable discs (which can be used over and over, as opposed to being "write once") are available. A CD-R drive can also hold multimedia projects such as enhanced CDs, karaoke, and video CDs.

Equipment You'll Need. You don't need a lot of fancy equipment to record your own CD (see Figure 1). But you do have to make sure the gear you have is optimized for the process of creating CDs.

Burning CDs requires a relatively powerful computer—many a disc has been wasted because a system was too slow overall, or had a weak link in its speed chain. With a Mac or a PC, you'll need either a computer with a built-in CD-RW drive or, if your computer is at least 400MHz, a CD-R drive and card or interface (such as USB or FireWire) supported by the software you plan to use.

Figure 1

You don't need a state-of-the-art studio to make a CD at home. This modest desktop setup allows author/musician Jon Chappell to master CDs with abandon. He records directly into the laptop via the TASCAM US-428 audio interface/control surface, working in MOTU Digital Performer. When it's time to burn, he attaches an external FireWire CD-RW drive to the corresponding port on the back of his laptop.

CD-R Drive. If your computer doesn't already have a built-in CD-R/CD-RW, connecting an external burner is usually just a matter of plugging it in to the appropriate computer port. If you buy a writer designed for internal mounting, you'll have to open your computer, but a SCSI conflict is the most difficult problem you're likely to encounter. Usually, fixing this is as simple as changing an ID selection switch to a different ID number. In extreme cases you may have to open the unit and move jumpers.

Mount a CD-R unit on a stable surface, as close to level as possible. Nearly all manufacturers provide a list of do's and don'ts (usually printed on a separate slip of paper in the box or in a help file), as well as lists of compatible SCSI controllers, drivers, and media. Some CD-Rs use a disc caddie rather than a retractable tray. The caddie keeps discs a bit more stable, which is crucial for error-free writing.

SCSI Controller. All Macintoshes from the Mac Plus on have included SCSI, so the following pertains only to Windows systems.

Even if you already have a SCSI card, you may need an extra one if you've maxed out your current SCSI chain with a gaggle of hard drives, scanners, removable drives, and the like. If you have an old or cheap controller (like the one that came free with your scanner), you might want something better—an inexpensive card might work, but you're probably better off buying a good Fast or Ultra Fast SCSI-2 controller by Adaptec, Future Domain, or Atto. It will handle your CD-R and provide improved SCSI-2 hard disk performance. To all you IDE/ATA folks out there, sorry, but you'll have to move up to SCSI to burn your own CDs.

As for cables, SCSI cables are usually pretty short (two or three feet) but you can get them up to six meters (19.6 feet), which is the limit on the total cable length in the SCSI chain. For best results, put the CD-R next to or inside the computer. And don't forget about proper termination (see your computer manual for the arcane art of SCSI termination).

Hard Drive. You'll need a hard drive with less than 15ms average access time, sustained data transfer rates above 800KB/sec (for double- or quad-speed recording, you might want something a bit faster), and a high rotational speed (7200 RPM or higher is optimum, although somewhat noisier on average than drives with slower rotational speeds).

Depending on the software and type of writing you're doing, you may also need enough free hard disk space to hold a complete one-for-one copy of the data you intend to write, plus a little extra. So to fill a 650MB disc, you need roughly 1,300MB free on your hard disk drive.

Since it's important to leave some free space on your drive, 1.5GB is a good choice for a minimal system.

Software. CD-R software comes in flavors for just about every type of computer and level of experience. Packages are available for Mac, Windows 3.1/95/NT, OS/2, Novell, Unix, Sun-OS, and DOS. Most manufacturers sell separate versions for different platforms.

Just about all CD-Rs bundle software that lets you pick which files to put on disc does some special formatting, and controls the recorder's mechanical operations (with the exception of packet-writing software, you can't just copy files to a CD-R as you can with other media). Most mass duplicators require a disc-at-once master, where the entire CD is written at once, as opposed to a multisession disc, where different sections of the disc are written on at different times.

Burning Basics. Assuming your hardware meets the needed requirements, using CD-R software is pretty straightforward. In most cases, you simply tell the software what type of disc you want to make (Red Book audio, CD-ROM, multimedia, etc.), drag and drop filenames or complete directories into a special window using a file-manager-like utility (many PC packages actually use Windows' File Manager itself), specify a writing speed (1x, 2x, 4x, etc.; higher speeds place higher demands on the hardware), and then tell it to go. You can usually initiate a "test run" first, where the system determines whether the hardware is up to the task at the specified write speed. If your system passes the test, odds are that the CD-burning process will create something other than a coaster. Caution, though; these tests are not infallible, and any one of a number of hardware ills—from something as obvious as a power outage to as subtle as a misplaced interrupt—can interfere with the writing process.

At 1x speed, it takes a little more than "real time" to write a CD (e.g., if you're recording 30 minutes of music, the process will take a little over 30 minutes). The extra time is required for the CD writing process to close out the file after writing. A 2x writer takes about half the time, a 4x writer $\frac{1}{4}$ of the time, etc.

Of course, a lot more is happening under the hood, but the software should make this all pretty transparent. If you're curious about the CD-burning process, refer to the "For Further Reading" section at the back of this book.

Buffer Underruns. When writing, CD-R drives need a continuous stream of data. An interruption that lasts long enough for the cache to run out of data, called a "buffer underrun," ruins the disc. To reduce the likelihood of buffer underruns, observe the following:

- To handle momentary breaks in the data flow, CD-Rs have onboard RAM caches of 512K or more. Buffers of at least 1MB are preferred for CD recording.
- Reduce the number of devices on the SCSI chain to a minimum, and make sure the bus is properly terminated.
- Avoid running other applications while burning CDs, since every application that accesses the disk narrows the bandwidth available for transferring data to the CD-R drive. Even disk cache utilities that would speed up most applications can screw up a CD-R burn, because you want data to flow in a continuous stream, and not be cached on the way to the CD-R. Keeping Mac control panels and system extensions to a minimum will also help (use Extensions Manager to disable all extensions that aren't absolutely necessary). For Windows machines, disable add-ons like Norton Desktop or Microsoft Office Fast Find (which constantly "polls" your hard drive to maintain a current catalog of files), and also turn off CD-ROM Auto Insert Notification. To do this, open the System icon in the Control Panel and select Device Manager. For each item under CD-ROM, select the device, click on the Settings tab, and uncheck the Auto Insert Notification checkbox.
- If the CD-R burning software allows, increase the buffer size to reduce the chance of an underrun (this buffer is not the same as the computer's disk cache).
- Turn off any screen savers. These can cause havoc with some digital audio programs. If you're going to be away from the computer and don't want to turn off the monitor, just reduce the brightness.
- Don't do anything else with the computer while recording. With Windows machines, there may be some programs running in the background, such as routines that monitor software installations. Press CTRL-ALT-Delete to bring up a list of currently active programs. Click on any program you don't need and select End Task.
- Defragment your hard drive, especially for on-the-fly recording. (With "on-the-fly" recording, the CD-R picks up data from the hard drive as needed in the process of creating the CD. With "disk image-based" recording (see below), the program creates a file that duplicates the data exactly as it will go on the CD, thereby alleviating some processing that can be problematic with slower computers.) Even with a

fast AV drive, you should defragment periodically. Fragmented drives slow disk access speeds and eventually lead to buffer underruns. Occasionally reformat the drive you use for CD images to guarantee a clean slate.

• Record from an ISO "disk image" file rather than on-the-fly. Running a disk image will often let you know if an underrun would've occurred under real-time burning conditions, thereby avoiding the creation of a coaster. Exact disk images also are great for archiving projects that will be used to create multiple discs. The potential downside is that you could need as much as 650MB for a CD-ROM or 740MB for an audio disc when using a 74-minute blank.

• Always scan for viruses before burning CD-ROM discs. Commercial software has been released with viruses immortalized in polycarbonate. With a little extra care, you can avoid doing the same. Once you know a drive is virus-free, quit the virus scanning program so it doesn't unexpectedly "wake up" while recording a CD.

• Watch for virtual memory settings that cause swapping, unusual network activity, and background data downloads or faxes. Because Windows is a multitasking operating system, it makes extensive use of caching. Caching shuttles data into memory, where it hangs out until the cache (also called buffer) fills up, whereupon the data's "released" (e.g., to the hard disk or CD-R). Caching interferes with sending data to a hard disk or CD-R as a continuous, unbroken stream. As a result, most digital audio programs recommend limiting the cache memory.

Cleaning and Maintenance. If you want your CD-R drive and the data you write onto it to live long and prosper, then you must be stringent about equipment maintenance and cleanliness. CD-Rs have been rejected by CD duplicators because of a single speck of dust that was present on the blank CD-R before it was recorded. When the laser writes data to the disc, the dust speck causes a shadow that prevents the pits from being formed correctly. This results in an uncorrectable error on playback.

Important points to keep in mind when producing CD-Rs:

• Handle blank CD-Rs by the edges. Never touch the recording surface.

• Never set the blank CD-R down anywhere except in its original jewel case or the CD-R recorder's tray.

• Use Dust-Off or some other compressed air to remove dust from the CD-R and its carrier (if required) before each recording session.

- For the lowest possible error rate, use only the brand or type of blank CD-R media recommended by your drive's manufacturer.
- Choose a recorder that will produce the CDs appropriate for your requirements. Older CD-R units can have small buffers, record only in track-at-once mode, or leave a mandatory muted space between cuts.
- With most media, recording at 2x gives a lower error rate than either 4x or 1x.
- If your recorder takes longer than expected to recognize the inserted blank CD-R, then the laser lens is collecting dust. Clean it with compressed air, or take it to a repair center to have it cleaned. Do not use cleaning CDs; they can knock the laser out of alignment.
- Record the disc in disc-at-once mode, rather than multisession or track-at-once. This ensures that the greatest number of drives can read your disc.
- Doing crossfades in real time doubles the amount of data crossing the SCSI bus, so when you use them always do a test run first. If the test fails, circumvent the problem by writing a disc image and burning from that.
- Do not allow the CD to have prolonged exposure to sunlight. The error rates will increase.

Mastering

The art of mastering, where songs are adjusted for their optimum level, sequence, and tonal balance, is an art form in itself. It is usually done prior to creating a CD, but nowadays, it's just as likely that you'll create the CD first, live with it for a while, take notes on what needs to be changed, then master it before creating the finished product.

Highly paid and technically skilled mastering engineers often make a significant contribution to a song becoming a hit, almost as much as the songwriter, musician, or recording engineer. The mastering engineer makes sure that a tune can translate to a variety of playback systems, and can often correct for problems that creep into the recording process (such as mixing in a room with bad acoustics that leads to mixing with, perhaps, too much bass).

Several programs are designed to help with the mastering process: These are often plug-ins that work in conjunction with a host digital audio editing program. The host program can't be all things to all people, nor can it accommodate all needs. Plug-ins can fill the gap—they're like accessories for a car, such as a pickup hitch—crucial for some people, useless for others. Some mastering tools are available as rackmount boxes that insert between a mixer output and DAT, or include a digital interface that allows for doing a DAT-to-DAT digital transfer while adding particular types of processing (such as equalization or compression).

One important element of mastering is limiting a tune's dynamic range so that it is perceived as being louder (when a commercial comes on TV that seems far louder than a movie's dialog, you're hearing limiting at work). It may seem counterintuitive to squash your music's dynamic range, but just because the CD can reproduce a wide dynamic range doesn't mean that the listening environment can handle it. Many people listen to music in their cars, and a song's quiet parts can get lost in the road noise. Similarly, on the dance floor or on the radio, a song that is not as loud as others is psychoacoustically perceived as "weaker."

One common mastering tool, the Waves L1 Ultramaximizer plug-in, isn't used solely for music but for multimedia and game applications as well. This "look-ahead" limiter analyzes a signal and reduces the dynamic range so the whole track can be turned up louder (see Figure 2). The loud parts are still loud, but the quiet parts are louder than they were. The overall mix doesn't sound any different, just more energetic; in short, it kicks (although if you over-limit, it also annoys, and leads to listener fatigue).

Figure 2

In the original guitar recording (top window), the average level is fairly low, and there are wide level variations. After the file was processed with Waves L1 software, the spikes were tamed, allowing a significant overall level boost without adding distortion (bottom window). These screen shots were made in BIAS Peak for the Mac, though L1 runs on a variety of platforms.

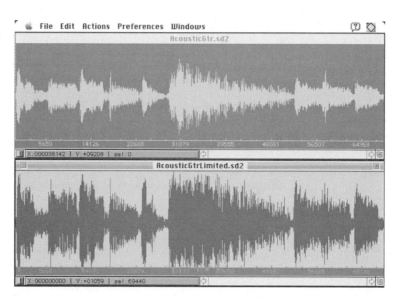

Some programs include a multiband dynamics processor that divides a signal into separate frequency bands and compresses each band independently. This kind of tweak requires a lot of practice and experience to use effectively. In general, it's best to use DSP tools sparingly, and let your ears be your guide—assuming, of course, that you have well-educated ears. Otherwise, it's probably best to entrust your music to a professional mastering engineer who can really bring out the best in your work.

Normalization in Mastering. Normalization is one of the most important mastering functions to perform on your music. It ensures that levels are matched among cuts in a final, sequenced CD master. This process ensures that different digital audio files (or portions of files) reach the same peak levels and take full advantage of the available headroom.

When you invoke normalization (which is usually a menu option on digital audio editing and multitrack recording software), the software scans the specified digital audio file or file region and notes the level difference between the highest signal peak and the theoretical maximum (called "full code"), which defines the upper limit of the available headroom. The program then raises the file's overall level so that the highest peak reaches full code.

For example, suppose that a file's highest peak is 7.2dB below full code. Normalization will apply +7.2dB of gain to the entire file so that the highest peak now reaches the maximum level. Note that this process does not improve the resolution of the audio. If it was recorded digitally at a low level and is later normalized, the excess background noise and quantization artifacts created by the digital recording process will be boosted in level right along with the music.

Variations on this particular theme include being able to normalize to somewhat less than the maximum (e.g., 95% of maximum, or something like "normalize to -1.5dB below the maximum"). Another variation is the "supernormalize" function found in Ensoniq PARIS, which adds a bit of extra boost, causing very short, very high-level transients to clip. These transients would otherwise set a limit as to how much the file's amplitude could be increased through normalization. Supernormalization will add bite to drum sounds, but this isn't usually perceived as clipping distortion, since the clipped peaks are so short.

Average or Peak? It seems logical that prior to mastering a CD, you'd want to normalize all the individual cuts so that they'd be at the same level. But this isn't recommended, because normalization is based on peak levels, whereas our ears respond to a signal's average level.

This is not a new concept. Analog VU meters show average levels, whereas LED VU meters generally show peaks. If you've ever recorded a percussive instrument such as tambourine into an analog recorder, you may have noticed that the tape would go into heavy distortion even with the meter registering at around -15VU. That's because a tambourine puts out huge, short, high-level transients that the analog meter is not fast enough to indicate, due to the pointer's mechanical inertia. (This is why many analog meters include a "peak" LED to show when the input exceeds some arbitrary amount, such as +5VU.)

Our ear, which is more interested in average levels than peak levels, reacts more like an analog meter than a digital one. Here's an easy experiment you can do:

1. Load a drum loop into a digital audio editor and normalize it. This is the "reference" file.

2. Copy the normalized reference file, and apply a level change of 150% to the copy to create a significant amount of clipping. If the program won't allow you to add this much gain, try using a clip or distortion function to clip the file at about 66% of full amplitude, then normalize the clipped file.

3. Compare the apparent level of the two files.

The clipped one will sound dramatically louder, because it has an extremely high average level, even though the peaks of the two files, being at 100% of full code, are the same.

Now, About Mastering. A well-recorded ballad, with lots of dynamics, can have high peaks but a low overall average level. A speed-metal song with everything slamming up against the top of the available headroom will have a very high average level. Normalizing both will result in two songs that are perceived as having radically different volumes.

So what's the best approach? In many cases, the best option is not to normalize, but instead to take your mixdown CD with all the tunes that need to be mastered to a mastering engineer, who will make sure that the levels are balanced properly. If you intend to master the tunes yourself, use your ears to make sure that all the tunes are at levels that sound right in the context of the whole CD. Another possibility is to normalize the song that sounds the quietest, then use that as a reference for setting the levels of other songs.

A Peak Experience. When files are being normalized, one common complication is the presence of a few "rogue transients" (e.g., the one place in the song where all the musicians hit on exactly the same beat) that are significantly louder than the rest of the tune. These prevent normalization from adding much of a boost.

You could limit or compress the file to bring down those peaks, but then you're stuck with a compressed sound, which is falling more and more out of favor these days—especially in styles of music where you're going for a natural sound. A better option is to track down the rogue peaks and lower just those peaks using your software's gain change or level change function. You can then normalize the entire file and obtain a much higher overall level—without compression, and without destroying the dynamic range.

To do this, you can take advantage of the fact that several audio editors have a "find highest peak" function. (You can also just locate peaks visually, but make sure you're zoomed in pretty tight. When you're zoomed out, sometimes the peaks are too narrow to show up in the waveform display.) Zoom in as tightly as necessary to see the peak clearly, then click and drag across the peak, which will often be only a single cycle or half-cycle of the wave, and use the program's "gain change" option to reduce the peak so that it's more in line with the other peaks. Typically, this requires a 3 to 6dB level reduction.

Find any other peaks that are excessively high, and similarly lower them. Usually the peaks will be so brief that the changes you make will not be audible. Now you can normalize the entire file (see Figure 3).

Why Be Normal? Although normalization can definitely be useful, be careful not to apply too many processes that alter the file (normalization, compression, filtering, etc.) or re-apply the same process several times. Every time you process a file, round-off errors may accumulate that color the sound. With 24- or 32-bit internal processing this is less of an issue than with 16-bit processing, but in general, the less processing you apply to a signal, the better.

Remember that your ears remain the best pieces of test equipment ever designed for analyzing audio. Use them, not meters, to match levels of different cuts, and you'll end up with more musical results.

Mass Production

Making custom CDs works well for small quantities, but it's time-consuming and relatively expensive. Also, since recordable CD media aren't entirely reliable, you really should test each disc before you try to sell it. Given the prices offered by CD manufacturing houses, it makes a lot more sense to mass-produce if you're making more than 100 CDs. Still,

Figure 3

The upper window shows a file
normalized in BIAS Peak. Note
how a single transient hits the
maximum headroom, while the
rest of the audio is significantly
lower. The lower window shows
the same file after the peak has
been pulled down a few dB and
the entire file normalized.
Although the file in the lower
window has a dramatically higher average level, because we've
only modified a single "rogue"
transient the original dynamics
are preserved.

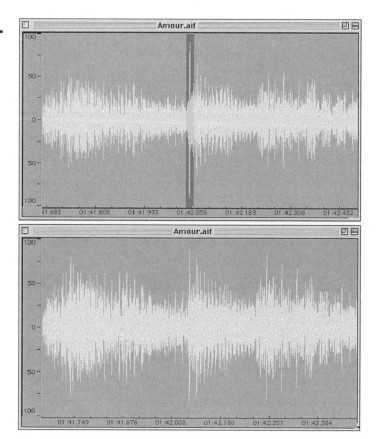

owning a CD recorder with the proper software can save you a few hundred dollars on the cost of limited-run duplication if you have more
time than money.

For a successful manufacturing run, it's a good idea to check out the
information on the Disc Makers web page at www.discmakers.com. The
site includes hints on master tape preparation, answers to frequently
asked questions, and templates for artwork to download. They even provide helpful tips for building contacts for distribution and sales. Also be
sure to visit www.cd-info.com, a wonderful source of CD-R information and links.

Disc Makers stresses listening to your master submission to make sure
you like everything about it. Most problems, they say, result when their
customers trust the engineer in the recording studio and don't bother to
master the music properly before sending the final product out for
duplication. The first time they hear it is when they receive a reference

copy from the CD manufacturer. You can expect the manufacturer to make sure the recording fills a CD's entire dynamic range, but unless instructed otherwise, they will simply duplicate what they are given, without any mastering. Also, if clicks or false starts haven't been trimmed out, don't expect the manufacturer's engineers to clean them up. Unless you provide explicit instructions about changes you want implemented, the engineers have to assume you want the material duplicated exactly as presented.

It's helpful to list the contents of your master as thoroughly and precisely as possible, including track start and stop times and anything that needs to be fixed. If there's a click between two songs and you want it removed, note its exact location. If all the songs are separated by silence but you want particular cuts to butt up against one another on the final disc, tell the disc manufacturer not only the song titles, but their exact lengths and even what the audio is doing at that point (e.g., "snare drum reverb fades to zero"). The better the documentation, the more likely you are to get what you expect. Duplicators often complain that timings from home and project studios are never right; do your best to prove them wrong.

Disc Makers formats their CDs using a Sonic Solutions system. They capture the master tape or home-burned CD digitally, convert the sample rate if necessary to 44.1kHz, make any explicitly requested edits, then enter subcode data. Then they burn a CD just like the one you pulled out of your CD recorder, which goes to the customer for reference. If the reference isn't right, they do it again (and charge extra). Once the customer approves the reference disc, they make molded plates from it, stamp out the discs, and ship them to your doorstep within a couple of weeks.

It may seem silly that you provide a finished, mastered CD and they recapture it and give it back to you as a reference disc. Assuming you have a cool piece of CD-burning software, you can probably bypass this step. The upside: You save a couple hundred bucks. The downside: You take a crucial step in the production process upon your own shoulders and eliminate one opportunity to catch errors before they cost you a lot more dough. Unless you like to gamble, always ask for a reference disc.

If you have any doubts about your ability to format a disc for commercial use, it may be cost-effective to use the manufacturer's mastering service. You'll pay a few hundred dollars, but you'll gain from the expertise of people who have mastered many musical projects. Then again, no one cares about your music more than you, so if you're ready to climb the relatively steep learning curve required to master music with technical accuracy and artistic finesse, go for it.

PRACTICAL FAQS FOR BURNING YOUR OWN CDS

Q: What do different CD-R recording speeds mean?
A: The "speed" rating of a CD-recorder determines how fast it can record or play back data. Ratings such as "1x," "2x," "4x," and "8x" define multiples of the original speed of first generation CD-ROM players. These data transfer speeds translate to about 150K per second (1x), 300K per second (2x), 600K per second (4x), and 1200K per second (8x), etc.

Q: What are "disc-at-once," "track-at-once" and "multisession" writing modes?
A: *Disc-at-once* is a writing mode that requires the data on a CD to be continuously written, without any interruptions. All of the information is transferred from hard disk to the CD in a single pass, with the lead-in, program, and lead-out areas being written in a single event. Some CD-R drives don't support disc-at-once recording.

Track-at-once is a writing mode that allows a session to be written as a number of discrete events called "tracks." With the help of special software, the disc can be read before the final session is "fixed" (a process whereby the disc's overall lead-in, program data, and lead-out areas are written), allowing all of the data contained on the disc to be read by any CD or CD-ROM drive.

A *multisession* disc differs from track-at-once in that several sessions can be recorded separately onto a single disc (with each session containing its own lead-in, program data, and lead-out areas). Thus, data can be recorded onto the free space of a previously recorded CD. (Note that some older CD readers can read only the first session of a multisession disc.) A CD-R that supports multisession can record a number of discrete sessions onto a single disc, and a CD-ROM drive that supports multisession can access the data that was written within any of these sessions.

Q: Can CD-R discs be used as masters for stamping?
A: Yes. If you're planning to do this, first speak with the mastering facility about its specific needs. This facility will help you ensure that no "uncorrectable" or E32 errors are present on your disc. This is important because the software used in the glass mastering process to drive the recorder's laser beam is often set up to terminate the mastering process upon encountering an E32 error. Traditionally, the mastering facilities will require that you record the disc in the disc-at once mode, because it eliminates the linking and run-in/run-out blocks associated with multisession modes. These often are interpreted as uncorrectable errors during mastering.

Q: What is "digital audio extraction"?
A: Certain hardware/software packages can transfer CD audio tracks directly to your hard disk as stereo 44.1kHz .WAV or AIFF files (depending upon your computer operating system).

Q: What are the options for CD-R printing?
A: CD-Rs can be labeled in several ways, depending on what level of professional look you want and what you can afford.

- Using a felt-tip pen is the easiest and fastest way to label a CD-R. However, you should never use a permanent marker pen that contains a solvent, since it can actually permeate the disc surface and cause damage to either the reflective layer or dye layer below the surface. Two recommended pens are the Sanford Sharpie Ultra Fine and the Dixon RediSharp Plus.

- The next least expensive alternative is stick-on labels. You can buy sheets of labels at any office supply store, and various templates are available for all types of printers (laser, inkjet) so you can design and print your own labels. However, if you misalign the label or don't smooth the label down and there are air bubbles under the surface, your CD-R runs the risk of spinning out of balance, which could cause reading and tracking problems. Several companies have created label-positioning devices that claim to solve the above problems (such as Stomp Inc. CD Stomper). Stick-on labels are one of the least expensive professional-looking labeling methods, but be aware that some adhesives can "outgas" over time, and, over the long haul, these solvents can adversely impact the disc. Sticky labels are OK for references, but are not recommended for masters or archival copies.
- Special inkjet labelers can print four colors onto a custom-faced disc directly from your PC. This is a great option for those who burn lots of discs that have to have a professional look and feel.
- Finally, companies exist that can custom silk-screen your discs. This method uses the same process as mass-replicated discs and only makes sense when dealing with quantities of 100 or more. Note that it takes time to have them printed, and this is the most expensive "personalized" option. But the results are crisp, clean, and professional.

Q: Are there Web sites where I can find out the latest info?

A: OSTA (www.osta.org) is an international trade association that's dedicated to promoting use of writeable optical technology for storing computer data and images. Also, the http://www.roxio.com/en/support/discs/ site includes detailed facts on many technical issues regarding CD burning.

The Afterburn

It's easy to forget that your final product is more than music. Without a package that features eye-grabbing artwork, your babies will probably just sit on a shelf. Many musicians have great ideas about packaging but lack experience turning a visual concept into a finished product. Most CD manufacturers are associated with graphic artists, either in-house or independent, who understand how colors translate from a computer screen into print, what screen resolutions work best with various printing processes, and other arcane matters. If you decide to use these services, again, document everything you want done as clearly as possible and exercise the patience necessary to answer questions thoroughly. The less guessing the graphic artist has to do, the better the odds that the package design will reflect your artistic sensibility.

And don't forget to trademark your band name and copyright your compositions. Trademark searches can be expensive, but there are ways to work around the big legal fees by doing your own search. In the U.S., contact the Federal Patent and Trademark Office at www.uspto.gov/ for information. For copyright forms and information, call the Copyright Office Hotline at 202-707-9100 or check out their web page at http://lcweb.loc.gov/copyright/. To apply for a UPC code that distributors and retailers can use with their barcode readers, call 937-435-3870 or see the UC Council site at www.uc-council.org/.

BY THE BOOK

In 1983, Sony and Philips presented the first specification for CD-Audio to the ISO (International Standards Organization). Being enclosed in a red binder, the spec became known as the Red Book standard. The more technical name for the Red Book spec is ISO 9660.

To differentiate it from audio, the first CD-ROM spec was bound in a yellow cover and became known as Yellow Book. Then came Green Book (CD-i), White Book (Video-CD), Pink Book (Photo-CD), and finally Orange Book (CD-R and MO-R). A few other variations have cropped up to deal with technologies like multisession recording (the ability to stop and restart a writing session), enhanced CD (in which CD-ROM data is added at the end of an audio disc rather than writing it in the first track), and packet writing (enabling data to be written in small increments rather than all at once).

Welcome to the Web

For many of us, the process of creating and recording our music is its own reward. While few of us would turn down Warner Bros. or Sony Records if they came calling, becoming a rock star isn't really our goal. Still, wouldn't it be nice to get your music out to a larger audience than your immediate family and friends? Wouldn't it be cool if the masses could enjoy your tunes? And what would be wrong with maybe making a buck or two off of your efforts?

Until recently, exposing your music to a large audience was a costly proposition best left to the professionals. But as with many aspects of modern life, the Internet has changed the picture. Using the Web you can make your music available to an incredibly large potential audience. No one can guarantee that just posting your songs to the Web will result in people hearing them or in your making any money, but hey, at least there's a reasonable self-promotion avenue available for you to exploit! Putting music on the Web may seem like an unapproachable task best left to cellar-dwelling Web hackers with questionable personal hygiene, but in fact it's a pretty easy task. Let's look at what it takes to prepare your music for the online experience.

To get things started, you're going to need your music in some finished form. It could be on cassette, DAT tape, or living as audio files on your computer hard drive. If your tunes are recorded and ready to go, then you're well underway. The next step is to figure out whether you want to create your own Web site or let someone do that work for you.

When in Doubt, Delegate. The easiest way to get your music online is to have someone else do it for you. Many Web sites offer online promotion and distribution for independent musicians (see the sidebar "Popular Promo Sites"). You simply fill out an agreement, tell them about yourself, provide a photo or two of your smiling face, and supply them with your finished music. They'll convert your recordings into the right types of digital audio files and create a page on their site containing the information about you and your music. They'll offer your songs for download to visitors either for free or for a fee, depending on the agreement. Some offer short demo clips to visitors to give them a taste of your music, and then sell copies of your CD (if you have one). MP3.com is a very popular site that has a range of deals to offer independent musicians (see Figure 4).

Figure 4

MP3 is the file format, MP3.com is the Web site. Both are household words to online music aficionados who encode music and seek cyber-glory and recognition through online distribution.

In exchange for these services, you'll have to fork over some cash. Some sites charge a set annual fee that can range from $99 to $300. Others won't charge you anything unless you actually sell some music; then they'll take a percentage of the sale—sometimes up to 50 percent. This type of arrangement can be worth it if you don't want to hassle with putting a Web site together yourself.

If you decide to go with one of these promo sites, you can exit here— no need to read any further. But if you're interested in doing some or all of the tasks involved in putting your music online yourself, read on.

In addition to the "commercial" promo sites discussed above, there are sites that let you promote your music for free. They give you a free Web page so that you can post information about your music as well as a link to your Web site (if you have one). And they'll give you free disk space so that you can offer your songs to visitors for download. But since the services are free, you'll usually have to take care of all the details yourself. This includes converting your recordings into digital audio files.

You can also choose to create your own Web site and post your songs to it. If you need information on how to create a Web site, check out *Creating Cool Web Pages with HTML* by Dave Taylor (http://intuitive.com/coolweb) and *Poor Richard's Web Site* by Peter Kent (www.poorrichard.com).

Let's take a closer look at what's required to get your music ready for the online experience. We'll also sift through the more popular Web audio formats, and take a quick glance at what's required to put the audio files on your site.

What Do I Need? You probably already have much of the gear and software you need to get your songs ready to go online (assuming that your songs are recorded and ready to be distributed). For starters, you'll need a computer, sound card, and digital audio editing software.

To put your music online, you also have to have access to the Internet. This usually means forking over $20 a month for an ISP (Internet Service Provider) account.

If you're going to create your own site, you'll need somewhere to store your Web pages and your digital audio files. The agreement you have with your ISP may entitle you to storage space on their Web server. If not, you can sign up with a dedicated Web hosting service, which can cost $20 or more each month. Before signing up with a Web hosting service, check to make sure that they're set up to allow your fans to download audio files in the format(s) you'd like to supply, and that the amount of space you'll need for the audio files on the site won't cost you extra. If your songs already exist as sound files on your computer, you can skip to "What Format?" below. Otherwise, you'll need to get your music into your computer. The process of converting the songs from DAT or CD to digital audio files is quite easy. Simply connect your tape or CD player to your computer's sound card and play each song one at a time, recording them using your digital audio recording software. Then save them as 16-bit/44.1kHz resolution WAV or AIFF files. These are the standard digital audio file formats on the PC and the Mac, respectively.

What Format?

After you've finished converting your songs into digital audio files in WAV (in Windows) or AIFF (on the Mac) format, you need to decide what file format(s) you're going to use to put them online. Technically, you could upload you files as is, but not only will you quickly run out of space on your Web site, no one will download the files because they'll be much too big. CD-quality (16-bit/44.1kHz) stereo audio takes up about 1MB of disk space per minute. This means that a five-minute song will be around 50MB in size. It could take hours for someone to download a song of that size, even if they have a fairly speedy modem. To get around this problem, audio files are usually data-compressed down to a more reasonable size using a variety of audio technologies and file formats. Each of these has its strengths and weaknesses, so you may want to offer your songs in more than one format.

MP3. If you'd like to make sure your files retain near-CD-quality sound while only taking up about 1MB (compared to 10MB) of disk space per minute, then consider using the MP3 format. MP3 uses what is known as "lossy" data compression. This means that it reduces file size by throwing away parts of the audio signal that listeners theoretically won't miss. In practice this works surprisingly well, although no one claims that MP3s are suitable for critical, golden-ear listening. What you end up with is a much smaller file that can be sent quickly over a modem connection. Your listeners will still have to spend some time downloading the files, but with MP3 it will take minutes instead of hours. The other advantage is that many computer users are familiar with MP3 files, and will likely have the necessary software for playing them back.

Streaming Audio. If you want to provide your listeners with the added convenience of not having to wait for your audio files to download, then consider using a streaming audio format. Streaming audio allows your listeners to immediately hear your music while it's being downloaded. This means no more waiting for downloads, but it can mean lower sound quality. Users downloading your music will also have to have the necessary player software in order to listen to your songs. In most cases, this isn't a big problem: The players are free and readily downloadable on the Web. A number of streaming audio technologies are in use, the most popular being RealAudio, Liquid Audio, QuickTime, and Windows Media Technologies. As with MP3 files, streaming technologies use lossy compression to reduce file sizes to a more modem-friendly level.

As of this writing, RealAudio is the most popular format being utilized, with over 80 million downloads of the RealPlayer software. Many feel, however, that the best-sounding format is Windows Media Technologies. Using WMT you can potentially achieve FM stereo radio-like quality on a 28.8K modem connection, though many factors can affect the final quality of the audio the end user receives. Be aware that there's a hidden aspect to streaming formats: The audio files must be stored on a server that has software capable of providing streaming capabilities. In most cases, you'll pay extra for streaming capabilities, although there are ways around this requirement (see sidebar "For Tech Heads Only: HTTP Streaming").

Pre-Processing. If you plan on using a data-compressed audio format, you may want to consider tweaking the sound of your files before you encode them (turn them into streaming files). Creating streaming files directly from your original WAV or AIFF files may work just fine. But since the streaming audio formats use such massive amounts of data compression, a little pre-processing usually helps.

File Editing. The first thing to do is to use your audio editing software to remove any dead air from the beginning and end of your song. Once your file is edited, make a copy of it. This copy will be useful later as a reference point.

DC Offset Removal. Before you make any changes to the sound, you should remove any DC offset that might have crept in during the recording. DC offset is low-frequency, inaudible noise that usually occurs because of an improperly grounded sound card or a bad connection between the sound card and another device. If you don't remove DC offset, your files may end up noisier when you encode them.

Compression. This isn't the same as data-compressing a file to make it smaller for downloading or streaming. Audio compression affects the volume of the sound, not the size of the file. This type of compression takes the loudest sections of a sound and reduces their level while at the same time raising the level of the quietest sections. Compression reduces the dynamic range of the music, giving it a more even volume level, which is better when it comes time for encoding. Your digital audio software should include some type of dynamics processing function that allows you to set a compression ratio (see Figure 5). Usually, a good ratio is between 2:1 and 4:1. The setting you use will vary with the content of the audio, but if you can get away with a 2:1 setting, that's usually best. Too much compression can make the music sound dull and lifeless. Use the reference copy of your audio file you created earlier to assess the effects of the compression. If the compressed version sounds worse than the reference copy, back up and try again.

EQ. Because the streaming audio encoding process removes a lot of the high-frequency (treble) portion of an audio signal, some EQ (equalization) is usually needed. Again, your digital audio software should include an EQ function. As when you added compression, break out

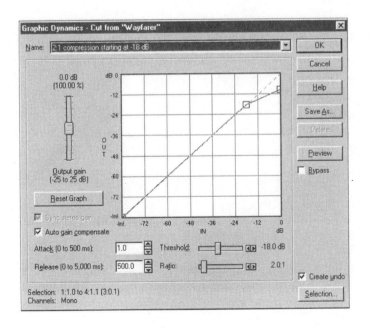

Figure 5

Audio compression affects the volume of the sound, not the size of the audio file.

Compression takes the loudest sections of a sound and reduces their level by a certain amount. This gives you room to turn up the entire signal, raising the overall average level. In this example, signals above the 18dB threshold will be compressed with a 2:1 ratio.

your reference audio file to assess the effects of EQ. Once you've encoded the file (see below), you'll want to listen to it to check the effects of your EQ. Experiment with different EQ settings until the encoded file sounds good to you. Often you'll find yourself giving the audio a midrange boost of about 6dB at around 2.5kHz (see Figure 6).

Normalize. The last step before encoding is to normalize the audio file. Normalization raises the volume of an audio signal as high as it can go without causing any distortion. If your software allows it, normalize your files to 95%, rather than 100%. This will leave a small amount of headroom in case the encoding process needs it.

Once you're finished processing, save the file (be sure to use a new name so you keep the original file intact) in WAV or AIFF format, and you're ready to encode.

Encoding

To encode your files, you'll need special software. Depending on the file format you've chosen, the software may or may not be free. The actual encoding process varies with each format, but you'll find that documentation that will step you through it comes with most of the software out there. Many times, the default encoder settings work just fine.

MP3. There's plenty of free software available for encoding MP3 files—your digital audio editing software may even be able to export files

Figure 6

To compensate for the loss of brightness that can occur when a sound file is converted into streaming audio, equalize the file prior to encoding it. In this case, a 6dB boost is being added at 2.5kHz.

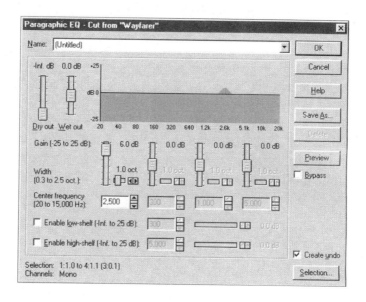

in MP3 format. One of the most popular free encoders for the Windows platform is MusicMatch Jukebox (www.musicmatch.com). Mac users are particularly fond of the MPegger (formerly MPecker) Encoder (www.proteron.com/mpegger/). You may also want to consider spending a little money on one of the commercial MP3 encoders. Why? Because encoders aren't all created equal. While there are some excellent freeware encoders available, their commercial competitors tend to produce better sounding files in a shorter amount of time. One is AudioCatalyst (www.xingtech.com), which is available for both PC and Mac.

RealAudio. To encode files in RealAudio format, you have to go directly to the company that created the technology, RealNetworks. They provide both free players and commercial encoding software. The player and commercial encoder (RealProducer Plus) are available for both Windows and Mac.

QuickTime. Although Apple's QuickTime is more often used for video content, the latest version of this technology sounds as good as it looks. QuickTime can produce high-quality streaming audio, but unfortunately there aren't any free encoders available. Still, at about $30, the QuickTime Pro encoding software (available for both Windows and Mac) isn't terribly expensive. You can purchase a copy online at www.apple.com.

Media Technologies. The only totally free streaming audio format on the market today is Media Technologies from Microsoft. A whole suite of free tools for creating Media Technologies files is available for download at www.microsoft.com. There's just one catch: The tools are only available for Windows.

Liquid Audio. The great thing about Liquid Audio (www.liquidaudio .com) is that it's a secure format, which means people won't be able to make copies of your music files and distribute them without your permission. The tracks are "watermarked" to allow ownership tracking, and encrypted so that only the authorized listener can play them. Only the player software is free. The encoding software for this format is Liquifier Pro (available for Mac and Windows), which will set you back $100.

Post-Process

After you've recorded, processed, and encoded your files, it's time to get them up on the Web. Posting your files to your site is pretty easy. All you need to do is upload your files to your Web server, and then create standard links to them on your Web page(s). The HTML code for the link might look something like this:

```
<a href="mysong.mp3">Click to hear my song!</a>
```

FOR TECH-HEADS ONLY: HTTP STREAMING

If you want to provide your listeners with the convenience of streaming audio files without paying for the privilege of using streaming server software, there's an alternative called HTTP streaming. RealAudio, QuickTime, and Media Technologies all support HTTP streaming. For QuickTime and Media Technologies files, you can simply upload the files and place standard links on your Web page(s). The QuickTime and Media Technologies player software will take care of streaming the files automatically. RealAudio files require a bit more effort to take advantage of HTTP streaming.

First of all, your Web host's server must be set up to support the RealAudio MIME type. Many already do. If yours doesn't, it's a simple matter for them to configure this for you. The other trick is to create what's called a "metafile." A metafile is actually just a plain text file referring to the RealAudio file that you want to stream. You simply create a standard link on your Web page to the metafile, and you're done. When your listeners click on the link, it will launch the metafile, which in turn will start the RealAudio file streaming. For complete information, visit the RealAudio Developer Resources (http://partners.real.com/developer.html).

POPULAR PROMO SITES

While there are literally hundreds of music-related sites on the Internet—not including the thousands of sites devoted to individual musicians and groups—below are listed some of the more popular ones. Some of these sites offer a full line of services; all you need to do is supply them with your music, and they'll take care of giving you a Web presence. Others will host your music for free, but you'll need to take care of creating your own audio files, etc. Even if you decide to create your own Web site, it might still be a good idea to place your music on some of the sites listed here. It will help steer traffic to your site and expose your music to a wider audience.

www.amp3.com

www.dmusic.com

www.iuma.com

www.mp3.com

www.resortrecords.com

www.ubi.com

As mentioned earlier, in order to use streaming audio formats, your Web host's server will need to have special streaming software installed; usually you'll be charged a premium to use this capability. Using the server software makes the files stream (or download) reliably, and allows a large number of listeners to access the files at once. (For an alternative streaming method, see sidebar "For Tech-Heads Only: HTTP Streaming.")

Thanks! I'll Try It. Putting your music online is a great way to make it available to a potentially huge listening audience. If your music is recorded and ready to be heard by the anxiously awaiting masses, why not join the thousands of musicians who have already put their music online? Who knows, you might even make a buck or two—would that be such a bad thing?

7

Troubleshooting

When you hook up a bunch of equipment to a computer, there's no guarantee that it will all work perfectly the first time you turn it on. When making music with technology, Murphy's Law ("If anything can go wrong, it will") prevails. The question is, when something doesn't work, what do you do about it?

• Don't panic. Trace your signal flow, both audio and MIDI, from point to point, and think carefully about what's supposed to happen. Make sure all of the relevant devices are turned on, their audio outputs are plugged into the mixer, and their volume knobs are turned up. Check that the MIDI cables are hooked up properly, with each Out or Thru connected to the next In in the chain. Is everything on the right MIDI channel?

• With software, investigate the status of the

relevant drivers (PC) and extensions (Macintosh). Examine every item in the Options and Preferences boxes. To give just one example of a possible snafu, MIDI may be arriving at the computer's hardware input but never reaching the sequencer software because you haven't selected the hardware input as a MIDI source. If all else fails, try de-installing other software (and hardware) that you're not using at the moment. Simplify the system until it works, and then re-install one piece at a time until it breaks. This key technique in troubleshooting will tell you which item (or conflict between items) is causing the problem.

- Read the manual, but even more importantly, check for any README files that may come with the distribution disk or CD. Manuals are printed before a product is shipped, and unexpected bugs and conflicts generally don't appear until after the product is out in the world. The README files often contain invaluable information gleaned from real-world experience; reading these can save you many hours of frustration (or time spent waiting on the line while calling tech support).

- Scan the classified ads in magazines like *Keyboard*. Third-party manuals, videos, and instructional books are available for some of the more popular synthesizers and computer programs.

- When all else fails, call the manufacturer. Unfortunately, tech support hotlines are often swamped, so be ready when you get through. Be sitting at your equipment, with everything turned on. Try everything you can think of before you call, so as not to waste the tech's time. Describe the problem in as much detail as you can—and make sure you understand the answer before you hang up. When they're in a hurry to answer more calls that are stacked up, techs will sometimes try to give you a quick answer that doesn't actually apply to your situation. Don't expect the tech to instruct you in, for example, MIDI basics; they will usually provide information only on their own products.

  And do try to be polite with them, no matter how frustrated you get. The tech didn't design the product, and isn't responsible for its failure to perform as you anticipated. If you're dissatisfied, though, either because the owner's manual doesn't explain things clearly or because the product won't do what you need it to, it's perfectly okay to respectfully tell the tech what you think. Part of their job is passing on complaints so that the next generation of products can be improved.

- Be patient. There isn't anybody in the business, no matter how expert, who hasn't been mystified on occasion because of strange malfunctions and odd phenomena. There's always more to learn.

Noise

Eliminating noise from home recordings is a many-faceted challenge. Microphones can pick up passing cars or planes. Older components and deteriorating cables can degrade system performance. And then there's the ever-present hum from AC lines.

Noise, which we'll define broadly as unwanted sound, may consist of non-periodic sound waves (e.g., hiss, rumble, clicks) or periodic waves (e.g., hum, interference from monitors, etc.). It can manifest as a distorted or grainy sound, or as artifacts such as clicks, pops, chirps, or warbles.

In whatever form, noise is perhaps the most pervasive, aggravating, and puzzling problem in any recording situation.

Noise can have many causes. For instance, digital devices might drop a few bits here and there, creating strange "ripping" sounds. Then there's acoustic noise (such as sound waves that come from the computer's fan, a creaking floorboard, or passing traffic) which travels through the air to your mic. In contrast, electromagnetically induced noise (electromagnetic interference, or EMI) starts not as sound but as electromagnetic waves, which silently assault audio signals as they're traveling down a wire—with unpleasantly audible results. The ugliest of all noise, however, is digital distortion. This can happen while recording, if an error occurs during file backup, or during signal processing—even when the goal of the processing is to remove other types of noise.

Digital Audio Dropout Culprits: Disk Caching and Thermal Recalibration

Digital sound files are big. When you're recording multiple tracks, or playing several tracks while recording another one, the sheer bulk of data can be too much for your computer's hardware or software. A momentarily overwhelmed computer may drop bits of audio that it should be recording. On playback, the resulting discontinuities usually sound like clicks or pops. This situation is most likely to arise if you're using disk caching, a system that saves data in RAM and then writes it to disk in large chunks. During the writing process, the computer may be too busy to store incoming audio data. This is why it's usually recommended that you shut off disk caching during a recording session.

Many older drives also take time out to do a "thermal recalibration," which adjusts the positioning of the drive's read/write head to compensate for the slight expansion of the drive's platter as it heats up. Though thermal recalibration takes only a matter of milliseconds, it can cause noticeable audio dropouts, or even lock up your recording software. Thermal recal dropouts are an annoyance during playback, but during recording, they can destroy a great take. Some manufacturers build drives that will not interrupt read or write operations by postponing thermal recalibration until idle periods. These are given the designation "A/V" drive, which indicates suitability for audio/video applications.

You may need a faster hard drive, one that postpones thermal recalibrations, or a computer with a faster CPU or bus. Before you get out your checkbook, though, learn all you can about optimizing the operating system and digital recording software. It's also important to make sure you're using up-to-date drivers (which are usually free for downloading from the Web) for your drives and SCSI card.

Acoustic Noise

Once you've been working with computers for a while, your mind begins to filter out familiar sounds like whirring fans and clicking hard drives. But your microphones don't, and your music can come out sounding like it was recorded live on a runway at the local airport. No wonder: Some computers have as many as four "propellers" going all the time, such as fans for the CPU, the power supply, any external drives, and maybe even some add-in cards.

Proper placement of directional microphones can help reduce pickup of unwanted sound. And, of course, computer noise won't be a problem if you have an acoustically isolated control booth. That's not the case with most home studios, though.

The simplest, although crudest, solution for home miking (aside from remembering to close the window while you sing or play) is a good noise gate (see Figure 1). Some multi-effect devices offer a gate algorithm. A gate won't eliminate noise that bleeds through while you're singing, but it may clean up the gaps between phrases. If most of the noise comes from one direction, such as a street, using a cardioid (directional) microphone rather than an omni-directional mic may squash the grunge by a few dB. Recording late at night or early in the morning is another way to avoid traffic noise.

When environmental noise does get onto the tape, you often don't hear it in the mix unless you solo the vocal track. The rest of the music will often "mask" the offending noise.

Before recording a track that you may want to keep, try recording just the mic output with no music going through it. Take a look at the residual noise waveform on the screen, or listen to it through headphones, to determine whether you have a background noise problem.

One common solution for eliminating fan noise is to isolate the computer (by putting it in an adjacent room, for instance), place the screen and keyboard in the control room, then use special extension cables to connect the peripherals to the computer. Even placing the computer under a table, and attaching sound-absorbing material under the table-top, will help a little. However, don't put the computer in a closet or any kind of enclosure without adequate ventilation, as components (particularly the power supply and processor) can overheat and fry.

PC users have another option: a very-low-noise computer like the Quiet PC from Decibel Instruments. The Quiet PC has just one ultra-quiet low-power fan; to compensate for the reduced ventilation, the power supply incorporates extra heat sinking. Also, the Quiet PC's hard drives are encased in a rubber-like material and have special heat sinks. Unfortunately, the Quiet PC costs considerably more than a comparable "noisy" PC.

Another way to eliminate computer fan noise is to turn off the computer, then record your acoustic tracks direct to DAT tape or to a digital multitrack tape deck. Tracks can then be transferred digitally to some computer-based recording systems with no loss of fidelity (see Chapter 4, "Digital-to-Digital Transfers").

Figure 1

A noise gate, such as this dbx 1066, mutes the signal fed through it when the signal's level falls below a preset threshold. This is a quick way to remove hiss between songs or noise entering a microphone between vocal phrases.

Once you've dealt with the noise-making parts of the computer, you can use insulation (such as fiberglass or acoustic isolating foam) in or on the walls to prevent other noises from leaking into your studio. Other devices that address acoustic noise include acoustic tiles, baffles, and traps, which alter the reflective/absorptive qualities of walls and ceilings. But before you nail up 200 empty cardboard egg cartons on the walls, consider the distinction between soundproofing and sound diffusion. The only way to stop sound from passing through a wall is with mass; cement blocks are ideal, and egg cartons will have little effect. What egg cartons do is create a non-reflective surface inside the room, which may help give the room a flatter frequency response and a lower overall level of reverberation. Hanging heavy blankets or rugs several inches away from the wall can help reduce sonic reflections as well. For further reading, check out *How to Build a Small Budget Recording Studio from Scratch*, by F. Alton Everest and Mike Shea, or *Building a Recording Studio*, by Jeff Cooper.

Electromagnetically Induced Noise

Electric guitarists know that a guitar will hum when held near a transformer. The coils in the guitar's pickup act as an antenna, picking up electromagnetic waves created by the AC current. The coils convert those waves into a voltage, which the guitar amp turns into hum.

Electromagnetic waves can induce currents in your audio cables, too. Radio frequency (RF) waves from power supplies and monitors can travel through the air for many yards to infect cables. House current produces lower frequency waves (60 cycles per second in the U.S.) that can usually travel only a few inches through the air. But a few inches is more than enough if the house current gets into an audio cable.

Here are some straightforward precautions you can take against electromagnetic noise:

- Don't run audio or digital signal cables next to power cords or transformers ("wall warts"). Audio cables can pick up hum. Even digital audio signals can be affected, though this is less likely. Some experts even avoid bunching audio cables together. If you must place an audio cable next to a power cord, make sure it crosses the power cord at an angle rather than running parallel.
- Look out for "unterminated" audio cables that don't connect to anything on one end. They have a particular tendency to act as antennas. If there's nothing connected to one end of a cable, unplug it from the other end as well.

- Keep your audio cables as short as possible. Short cables pick up less RF energy, and what they do pick up is mostly in the higher frequencies. A two-foot length of cable may pick up only noise frequencies that are too high, with levels that are too low, to cause any problems.
- Avoid standard fluorescent lighting in your studio (fluorescents produce considerable acoustic noise, too). Dimmer switches are also problematic. However, compact fluorescent lights are acceptable.
- Try not to connect heavy appliances, such as refrigerators and air conditioners, to the same circuit as audio equipment. The heavy current they draw makes them potent noise sources. Smaller appliances with motors (blenders, hair dryers) are also offenders.
- Try moving a sound card to a different slot in the computer. The inside of a computer is full of electromagnetic noise, and the sound card may just be in a bad spot.

Tracing Hums and Whines. Okay, what if you've taken these precautions and still hear a hum or whine? Usually, one cable, power cord, connector, or piece of equipment is responsible, but it can be hard to find out which one, since EMI tends to spread throughout the system. A computer monitor may produce RF interference, for instance, that is picked up by every cable in the system. Similarly, a single bad connector may cause 60-cycle hum in multiple cables and devices.

You may be able to eliminate RF interference just by reorienting the source—turning your computer monitor 90 degrees, for example—and/or moving it farther away from the "antennas." If reorienting doesn't help, you may need to adjust, repair, or replace the offending piece of equipment

Luckily, RF problems are relatively rare. AC hum, on the other hand, is as common as the proverbial cold.

Symptom of a Blocked Ground Path. Hum can come from poor grounding (see "Hums and Ground Loops," below). If you run short of outlets, you can plug a computer or sequencer into a different outlet than the synths and mixer without creating ground problems, as long as the only connections between the two components are MIDI cables. Theoretically, MIDI cables aren't supposed to make a ground connection—but never assume anything (the cable or MIDI connector may be defective). Check those connections if all else fails.

What can clog up a ground path? The list is long: A bad connector, improper house wiring, corrosion on the third pin of a power cord or in the wall socket, or a power cord that has no third pin are likely candidates.

In Figure 2, having equal, low-resistance paths to ground for both the mixing board and the computer should result in a quiet, safe system. On the other hand, if corrosion in the mixing board's plug or socket raises the resistance of the ground path, current flowing through this resistance will create a voltage; given that many components in an audio system connect to ground, this voltage could end up catching a free ride to your signal path. The worse the corrosion, the greater the resistance, and the greater the chance for hum. What's worse, this corrosion may take on the electrical properties of a diode, which can turn radio frequencies into audio frequencies (this is the principle behind the crystal radio) and cause even more interference.

Of course, this assumes all your equipment combined draws no more current than can be supplied by one circuit—a fair assumption for most home studios. If you're concerned about how much current your equipment draws, here's how to suss it out: Look on the back of each device to determine its wattage (this is usually printed on a plate or label next to where the AC cord enters the unit), then use the formula *Amps = Watts/Volts* to figure out its amperage. For instance, a 25-watt device running on a standard 120V circuit will draw 25/120, or about 0.21

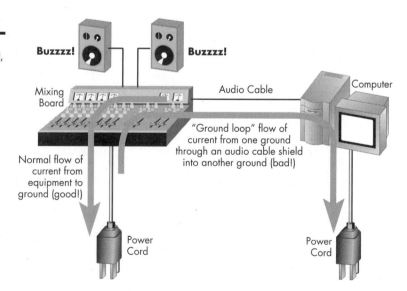

Figure 2

When an electrical signal has several possible paths to ground, there can be voltage differences between these paths. This can allow for the current to flow in the system's ground connections, resulting in the dreaded 60-cycle hum.

ampere. Add up the total amperage of your system, and compare this figure with the ampere rating of your breaker box's circuit breaker.

Reassemble your complete audio system one component at a time. If hum suddenly appears, look at the most recent piece of equipment you installed, its power cord, audio cables, and connectors. If one particular analog audio cable is causing problems, you may be able to improve its performance by using a product such as DeoxIT, from Caig Laboratories, to clean the connectors.

Gain-Staging

Optimizing mixer settings (or, more generally, the audio settings in your studio) for the maximum headroom and minimum noise is called gain-staging. For starters, set any audio source to produce the maximum possible volume, short of distortion. If it's a synthesizer, crank the volume knob all the way up. Then use your mixer's input trim controls to reduce the level of the signal in that mixer channel. Turning down the input trim reduces any noise added by the audio cables as well.

If the input trim is set too high, the incoming audio will distort. (Some mixers provide a clipping indicator on each channel so that you can see at a glance where the distortion occurs. If you don't have clipping indicators, check to see whether you can switch your mixer's output metering to monitor one input channel or bus at a time to help isolate the distortion's source.) Conversely, if the input trim is too low, you won't take advantage of the mixer's available headroom, which may add noise to the mix. To set the input trims properly, turn up each one and play the loudest audio that will be handled by that channel. When clipping occurs, turn the trim down just far enough to cause the clipping to disappear, then turn down just a bit more to add a little safety margin.

Noise Prevention and Removal

You cannot completely prevent audio systems from generating and picking up noise. A certain amount of noise, particularly hiss, is inherent in audio equipment.

Detective Work. To analyze the electronic noise in your system, turn up the power amp and master output volume sliders as far as possible. (and be extremely careful not to feed in any input signals!). This will magnify the hiss and hum in your system. Next, turn down one mixer channel at a time while listening closely to the noise, or turn them all down and bring up one channel at a time.

If you're able to isolate an especially noisy channel through this procedure, figure out why it's noisy. Is a trip to the shop in order, or is a bad cable perhaps at fault? Check the audio cable's path to make sure it doesn't lie alongside a power cord. Some distortion and chorusing algorithms produce audible noise even when no notes are being played; you may be able to remedy this problem by switching the noisy instrument to a different setting, or bypass mode, when it isn't playing.

Here are more tips to minimize or remove noise:

- Avoid cheap equipment. You can do Windows-based hard disk recording with a consumer-level sound card, but one designed for pro applications will be quieter. Generally, an indication of pro audio gear is balanced instead of unbalanced jacks: AES/EBU instead of S/PDIF for digital signals, and XLR instead of phone jacks for analog signals. (Note that phone jacks are sometimes set up in a balanced configuration, but XLR connectors are almost always balanced.)

- If you're adding MIDI tracks to your recording, don't rely on MIDI volume control messages to mute a channel. MIDI instruments often generate the same amount of hiss regardless of MIDI volume control messages—and even if they don't, the cable between the synthesizer and the mixer could add some noise to the system. Use your console's mute buttons, or automation in your hard disk recording software, to mute the audio channels of unused MIDI instruments.

- You can use noise removal software for the Mac or Windows. Some of these programs are available in stand-alone form, while others are plug-ins for host programs. To use these, you first take a sample of a track where there is no recorded material—just before the music begins, for instance. Any sound on the track at that point is pure noise. Once that sample has been analyzed, the software goes through the entire track and digitally removes that noise pattern. Use these types of programs judiciously, however, or they may introduce other artifacts such as warbles and chirps.

You can also use hardware or software equalization (EQ) to reduce the level of an offending frequency. For example, if you have a hum or whine at a particular frequency, use the EQ on your mixing board or hard disk recording software to attenuate that frequency. This will obviously affect whatever musical material is in the same frequency range, so the best EQ settings will be those that affect the narrowest possible band of frequencies. Ideally, you'll catch the whine or hum while setting up or doing a test recording, so the noise will never get on your final recording. You may be able to determine the frequency and the amount of attenuation required by a little experimentation.

Digital Clipping

With digital recording, you need to listen to your tracks carefully after recording to make sure that transient peaks didn't cause even momentary clipping.

Clipping occurs when the input signal exceeds the system's maximum headroom. This cuts off the peaks of the input signal, turning rolling hills into mesas (see Figure 3). Analog recorders can also clip, and it sounds bad. With a digital recorder, however, clipping sounds particularly obnoxious.

The most natural way to prevent digital clipping is simply to turn the input signal down until it no longer produces clipping. But in certain situations, such as a live band recording, this may not be practical. If your source material has a wide dynamic range, turning it down also has the effect of reducing the low-level signals to an undesirable level.

Compression. To prevent clipping while preserving a hotter overall signal level, you can run the signal through a compressor before it hits the recorder. A compressor reduces the signal's level when the level rises above a certain threshold level (see "Compression" in Chapter 4). Typically, you set the threshold level to reduce only the loudest sounds. You also set a compression ratio. For instance, you could reduce all sounds above -10dB by a ratio of 3:1.

However, you need to be aware of clipping on your compressor's inputs. If you're squashing the signal, use the output level control to

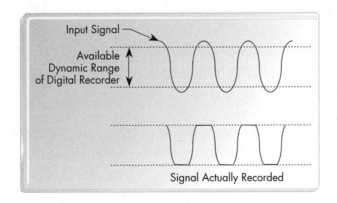

Input Signal

Available Dynamic Range of Digital Recorder

Signal Actually Recorded

Figure 3

Clipping occurs when the input signal (top) has a level that exceeds the maximum dynamic range of the system. The outer edges of the sound wave are "clipped" off (bottom), which drastically changes the harmonic content of the sound. Momentary clipping usually sounds like a pop or click; when a whole area of the wave clips, your music will be inundated by thick, grinding, static-like noise.

maintain the desired output level. If you feed too high a signal into the compressor to maintain a loud output, you could overload the compressor's input.

Compression does alter the sound of the material. For instance, rock bands often put heavy compression on drums to squash and "tighten up" the sound. If you're going for a natural sound, however, you'll want to keep the threshold relatively high (thus bringing compression into play as seldom as possible) and the compression ratio as low as possible (thus minimizing the effect of the compression when it does come into play).

Limiting. If the compression ratio is infinite, then nothing louder than the threshold will get through the compressor. In that case, the compressor becomes a limiter. Almost all compressors can also function as limiters. Many units add expander, noise gating, EQ, or de-essing functions as well. (De-essing reduces the amount of sibilance in vocal material. Sibilance is a hissing or whistling sound often associated with an "s," "ch" or "sh" sound. Often considered undesirable in vocal material, sibilance can be reduced by cutting down particular frequencies. Some software programs also include de-essing algorithms.)

Quantization Noise

The digital audio equivalent of "jaggies" (in computer graphics, this refers to the choppiness you see in curved lines) is called quantization noise. And just as visual jaggies show up most clearly on fine lines, quantization noise is most apparent with low-level signals. It's also present in louder digital audio, but any noise will be completely masked by the music.

Dithering. Digital audio engineers use a process called "dithering" to minimize quantization noise. Strange as it may seem, dithering involves adding a bit of controlled noise to the audio signal. This smoothes out the transitions from one level to another, thus giving a subjectively more pleasing sound. Dithering is often done when converting 20- or 24-bit signals to 16-bit. Just cutting off the last few bits doesn't sound as good as adding dither to them.

Noise is a beast that can never be entirely tamed, and it often comes snarling out of its cage when you least expect it. Defend yourself with knowledge, perseverance, and careful listening. The results—music that shines through clean and crisp—are worth it.

Hums and Ground Loops

What was that buzz? That strange hum? The digital hash from your computer that's showing up in the mic preamp? You may be a victim of ground loops, which can occur when using multiple AC-powered devices.

A ground loop means there is more than one ground path available to a device. In Figure 4, one path goes from device A to ground via the AC power cord's ground terminal, but A also sees a path to ground through the shielded cable and AC ground of device B. Because ground wires have some resistance (the electronic equivalent of friction), there can be a voltage difference between the two ground lines, thus causing small amounts of current to flow through ground. This signal may get induced into the hot conductor. The loop can also act like an antenna for hum and radio frequencies. Furthermore, many components in a circuit connect to ground. If that ground is "dirty," this noise might get picked up by the circuit. Ground loops cause the most problems with high-gain circuits, since massive amplification of even a couple millivolts of noise can be objectionable.

There are two main fixes: Break the loop by interrupting the audio ground, or break it by interrupting the AC ground line. The preferred method depends on the nature of the problem, so let's look at various options.

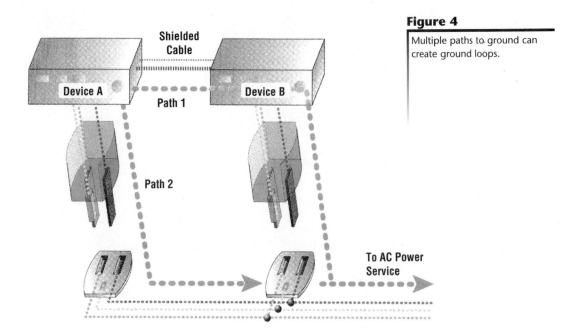

Figure 4

Multiple paths to ground can create ground loops.

Ground Lifters. Some musicians simply "lift" the AC ground by plugging a 3-wire cord into a 3-to-2 adapter. This is definitely not recommended since it eliminates the safety protection afforded by a grounded chassis. However, rather than spending another page or two explaining why you shouldn't do this, just don't do it, okay?

Solution No. 1: The Single Plug. You can solve many ground loop problems by plugging all equipment into the same grounded AC source, such as a barrier strip that feeds an AC outlet through a short cord, as this attaches all ground leads to a single ground point. However, it is crucial that the AC source is not overloaded and is properly rated to handle the gear plugged into it.

Solution No. 2: The Broken Shield. A solution for some stubborn ground loop problems is to isolate the piece of gear causing the problem and disconnect the ground lead (shield) at one end only of one or more of the audio patch cords between it and other devices. The inner conductor is still protected from hum by a shield connected to ground, yet there's no completed ground path between the two devices except for AC ground.

Sometimes a ground loop shows up as objectionable only if the grounded metal chassis of a piece of rackmount gear contacts the metal rail of a rack cabinet. There's an easy fix: HumFrees, from Dana B. Goods, are little plastic strips that attach to your device's rack ears and insulate the device from the rack (see Figure 5). They can be particularly effective with rackmount computer peripherals that dump a lot of garbage to ground.

Solution No. 3: Audio Isolation Transformer. Using a 1:1 audio isolation transformer is much more elegant than simply breaking the shield, but delivers the same benefit: It interrupts the ground connection while carrying the signal. Although a cord with a broken shield is less expensive, the transformer offers some advantages. If necessary, it can also change impedance or levels if you choose a transformer with different impedances for the primary and secondary windings (e.g., use the transformer to boost the level of a device with a fairly low output; this gives less noise than turning up the mixer's preamp gain).

For a commercial implementation, check out Ebtech's rackmount Hum Eliminator. This consists of audio transformers in a rackmount case, and uses TRS (tip-ring-sleeve) phone jacks that work with balanced or unbalanced lines. To "break" an audio ground line, just use one of the transformers in the Ebtech instead. (Ebtech also makes a

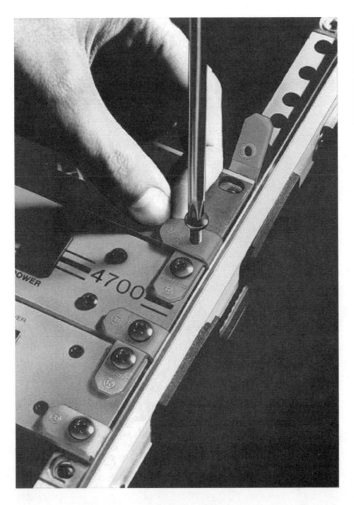

Figure 5

HumFrees non-conductive bushings (distributed by Dana B. Goods) help break ground loops by isolating rackmount devices from each other.

model that converts back and forth between +4 and -10 signal levels—see Figure 6.)

Solution No. 4: AC Isolation Transformer. Many times, you can also break a loop by removing the direct connection from a piece of gear to AC ground through an isolation transformer (see Figure 7). This doesn't always work because the ground loop may not involve the AC line but various ground-to-ground connections; however, loops involving the AC line generally seem to be more problematic and common. Breaking the audio connection is a simpler, lower-power solution (and can also minimize computer-generated "hash"), but an AC isolation transformer provides ancillary benefits (see "Studio AC Protection" in Chapter 3). In summary, an AC isolation transformer can clean up the AC line, reduce spikes and transients, and provide performance almost equal to that of a separate AC line. One such device is made specifical-

Figure 6

The Ebtech Hum Eliminator uses audio isolation transformers to break ground loops. The stereo model is shown.

Figure 7

The Furman IT-1220 isolation transformer is a new type of power conditioner that provides balanced power, greatly reducing ground loop hums and radiation from electrical cables into audio circuits.

ly for musicians: MIDI Motor's Hum Buster, which has a large transformer with 10 isolated AC outlets.

So which is better, breaking the audio connection or the AC connection? It depends. If you have a lot of microprocessor-controlled gear and less than ideal AC, adding isolation transformers can solve various AC-related problems and get rid of ground loops. If you just have a simple ground loop problem, then patching in an audio isolation transformer may be all you need.

Phase Problems

It is important to make sure your studio connections are in phase. But before we discuss detecting and solving phase problems, let's explain the concept of "phase."

Without getting into the mathematical details, in most cases we're really talking about a change in signal polarity. Reversing the polarity inverts the entire signal so that the negative-going parts of the waveform become positive-going and vice versa (see Figure 8). In practical terms, at any part of the waveform where the speaker cone would have been moving toward you, flipping the polarity causes the cone to move away from you.

Flipping polarity is independent of the wave's frequency, but there's another form of phase reversal (as used in phase-shifter effects) that is frequency-dependent. This creates the phase reversal by delaying the input signal and adding the delayed signal to the original. Most musicians and engineers understand what the term "phase reversal" means, so we'll call it that, even though "polarity reversal" is technically a more accurate term in most situations.

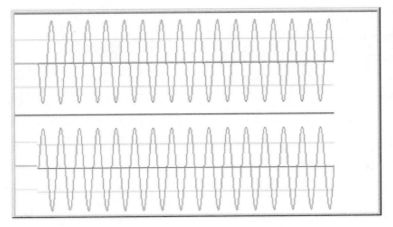

Figure 8

An in-phase and out-of-phase signal. Note how the peaks of the waveform on top correspond directly to the troughs of the waveform on the bottom.

Flipping a signal's phase may or may not mean too much by itself; that's a matter of debate. Some people feel you can definitely hear a difference with instruments like drums. For example, with a real kick drum, the first rush of air pushes out at you. If this signal goes through a system that doesn't change phase, the speaker will push air out to re-create the sound of the kick. But if the signal flips phase, then the speaker will pull in to move the required amount of air. It will still sound like a kick drum, although many people hear a subtle—but important—difference.

In any event, there's no debate that mixing an out-of-phase signal with an in-phase version of the same signal can cause a weakening and "thinness." Phase problems often occur when you're using two microphones, since, depending on their spacing, they can pick up a signal's waveform at different points, thereby creating phase differences at various frequencies. Problems can also occur with parallel effects. For example, if an echo signal is out of phase with respect to an in-phase dry signal and the two are mixed together, the echoed signal will tend to cancel the dry signal somewhat, resulting in a thinner sound.

There are many opportunities for phase problems in the studio. Balanced cables can be miswired, some balanced gear assigns pin 3 instead of pin 2 to the "hot" connection (even though an international standard defines pin 2 as hot), some "vintage" effects weren't too careful about phase, and even some new gear will have a design problem crop up from time to time that flips the phase.

Testing 1-2-3. Phase meters, which can detect an out-of-phase condition, are expensive. Fortunately, 2-track digital audio editors make a pretty good substitute. With such software you can determine not only whether a device's output is in phase with its input, but in some cases whether a signal is correctly phased or reversed.

To hook up your test setup, split the input signal and send it both to the input of the device being tested and to the digital audio editor's left channel input. This is your reference. Then feed the output signal of the device being tested to the digital audio editor's right channel. You can split this off to an audio monitor as well if you want to hear what's going on. Record a few seconds of stereo audio, then inspect the waveforms in the left and right channels.

As one example of how to use this technique, here's how you would test a mixer to make sure all outputs were in phase. Patch something like a drum sound generator into the mixer input, then test the output at a variety of points: master out, submaster out, monitor out, sends out, direct out, etc. Figure 9 shows a comparison of the input and the send output; the two waves are in phase. If they were out of phase, the peaks and valleys would have the same shape, but go in reverse directions—in other words, when the waveform rose on the upper channel, it would fall by an equal amount in the lower channel. Figure 10 shows what this would look like.

Vintage guitar effects are notorious for phase problems, and are well worth testing. It's also a good idea to test the entire input-to-speaker chain to make sure nothing's amiss. In particular, check that there isn't a phase difference between the left and right channels, as that can have disastrous results in a mix.

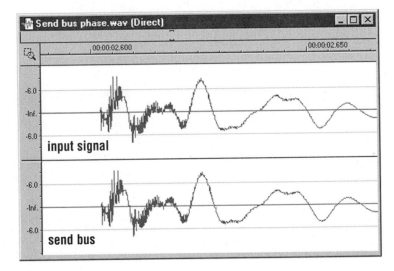

Figure 9

Comparing the phase relation-ship between a mixer input and the mixer's bus send output.

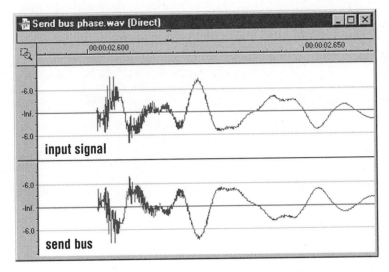

Figure 10

What the bus send output wave-form would look like had it been reversed.

Absolute Phase. Figure 11 shows an example of absolute and flipped phase with guitar. The top channel shows the guitar's original, in-phase signal; note how it starts by going positive. The bottom channel shows the same guitar signal, but flipped in phase. Note how it starts by going negative. It seems that you can identify the absolute phase of many drums similarly—look for an upward slope at the beginning of the signal. However, these are just a few examples; some signals do start off with negative transients.

Figure 11

Two versions of a guitar signal: in phase (upper) and out of phase (lower).

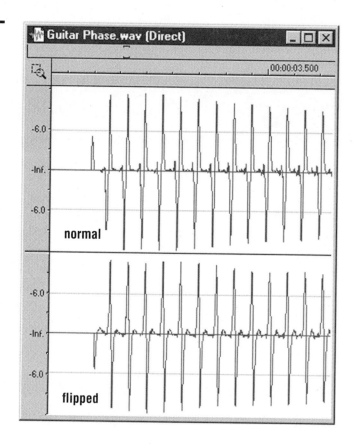

Fixing Phase Problems. If you feel that phase-flipping does matter, the same program that identified the problem can also provide the solution. Just about all digital audio editors let you select an audio region and reverse the polarity, so you can always import files from your multitrack hard disk recorder (or bounce signals over from digital tape), correct the polarity, then send it back from whence it came. Simple!

In any event, boot up your 2-track editor one of these days and take an hour or so to check out the phase integrity of your system. You never know what evil lurks in the wiring of cables.

For Further Reading

Anderton, Craig. *Home Recording for Musicians*. (revised and updated, Amsco Publishing, 1996.)

Anderton, Craig. *MIDI for Musicians*. (Amsco Publications, 1986.)

Anderton, Craig. *Multieffects for Musicians*. (Amsco Publications, 1995.)

Benford, Tom. *Welcome to PC Sound, Music, and MIDI*. (MIS Press, 1993.)

Chappell, Jon. *Build Your Own Recording Studio*. (McGraw-Hill, 2003.)

Chappell, Jon. *The Recording Guitarist: A Guide for Home and Studio*. (Hal Leonard, 1998.)

Chappell, Jon. *Rock Guitar for Dummies*. (John Wiley & Sons, 1998.)

Eargle, John. *Handbook of Recording Engineering*. (Van Nostrand Reinhold, 1996.)

Holsinger, Erik. *How Music and Computers Work*. (Ziff-Davis Press, 1994.)

Huber, David Miles. *Hard Disk Recording for Musicians*. (Amsco Publications, 1995.)

Luther, Arch C. *Principles of Digital Audio and Video*. (Artech House, 1997.)

McIan, Peter. *Using Your Portable Studio*. (Amsco Publications, 1996.)

Pahwa, Ash, Ph.D. *The CD-Recordable Bible*. (Eight Bit Books, 1994.)

Parker, Dana, and Robert Starrett. *CD-ROM Professional's CD-Recordable Handbook*. (Pemberton Press, 1996.)

Pohlman, Ken. *Principles of Digital Audio*. (second edition, SAMS Publishing, 1989.)

Rona, Jeffrey C. *Synchronization from Reel to Reel: A Complete Guide for the Synchronization of Audio, Film & Video*. (Hal Leonard Publishing Corporation, 1990.)

Rubin, David M. *The Desktop Musician*. (Osborne McGraw-Hill, 1995.)

Rumsey, Francis. *The Audio Workstation Handbook*. (Focal Press, 1996.)

Watkinson, John. *An Introduction to Digital Audio*. (Focal Press, 1994.)

Watkinson, John. *The Art of Digital Audio*. (Focal Press, 1994.)

Glossary

ADSR: Attack, Decay, Sustain, Release. The different stages of an envelope.

A/D converter: Analog-to-digital converter, also called an ADC. A device that changes the continuous fluctuations in voltage from an analog device (such as a microphone) into digital information that can be stored or processed in a sampler, digital signal processor, or digital recording device.

AES/EBU: This professional digital audio format is named after the acronyms of the Audio Engineering Society and European Broadcasting Union, two groups that define how the data will be transmitted electrically. Although it travels on a single cable, AES/EBU is a stereo signal and is very similar to the S/PDIF standard (see below). At the physical level, AES/EBU audio uses three-pin XLR connectors.

aftertouch: See *pressure sensitivity*.

AIFF: Audio Interchange File Format, a standard audio file format supported by Macintosh and some Windows applications.

aliasing: The unwanted frequencies which are produced when a sound is sampled at a rate which is less than twice the frequency of the highest frequency component in the sound. These unwanted frequencies are typically high-frequency tweets and whistles.

amplitude: The amount of a signal. It can relate to volume in an audio signal or the amount of voltage in an electrical signal.

analog: A signal or device that varies in a continuous, non-stepped manner.

attack: The first parameter of an envelope generator; determines the rate or time it will take for the event to reach the highest level before starting to decay.

balanced: An audio signal configuration in which two "hot" leads carry audio signals that are identical but of opposite polarity. Balanced connections are good for reducing interference induced into the cable.

bit: A single piece of information assigned a value of 0 or 1, as used in a digital computer. Computers use digital words which are combinations of bits. A 16-bit word can represent 65,536 different numbers.

bounce: When recording or sequencing, to bounce tracks means to combine (mix) several tracks together and record them on another track.

buffer: An area of computer memory that is used to temporarily store data.

byte: A computer word made up of eight bits of data. See *bit*.

cardioid: A directional microphone with a heart-shaped, narrow pattern, which picks up from directly in front of the mic and tends to reject signals from other directions. Good for recording drums.

CD-ROM: Compact Disc Read-Only Memory. A laser-encoded disc that can store large amounts of computer data.

cent: Unit of pitch equal to 1/100 of a semitone.

channel, MIDI: An information pathway through which MIDI information is sent. MIDI provides for 16 available channels, each of which typically addresses one MIDI instrument.

channel, output: The circuitry through which an instrument outputs individual notes.

chorus: A voice doubling effect created by layering two identical sounds with a slight delay (20-50ms) and slightly modulating the pitch of one or both of the sounds.

clipping: Distortion caused by recording at too high a level.

clock: A steady pulse from a generator which is used for synchronizing sequencers, drum machines, etc. Common sequencer timing clock rates are 24, 48, or 96 pulses per quarter note. MIDI timing clocks run at a rate of 24 ppq.

compression: The reduction of an audio signal's dynamic range, or loudest and softest points.

crossfade: To gradually fade out one sound while fading in another so that a seamless transition is made between the two sounds.

cutoff frequency: The frequency above which a low-pass filter will start attenuating signals present at its input.

cycle: One complete oscillation, period, or vibration of a signal.

DAT: Digital Audio Tape recorder (also refers to the actual tape cassette used by this format, resembling a miniature video cassette). DAT decks can record standard analog signals, but most also have digital inputs and outputs for direct recording of digital audio.

Data compression: Data reduction. Used to decrease file size and transfer time.

decay: The second stage in an ADSR type envelope generator.

decibel (dB): A reference for the measurement of sound energy. In theory, the minimum change in volume that the human ear can perceive.

delay: A controllable time parameter giving the ability to start an event only after a predetermined amount of time.

depth: The amount of modulation. Sometimes called amount, width, intensity, or modulation index.

digital: Voltage quantities or other data represented as binary numbers. Digital information is not audible and so must be converted to analog form by a DAC before it is output.

D/A converter (DAC): Digital-to-analog converter. A device which interprets digital information and converts it to analog form. All digital musical instruments must have a D/A converter so that we can hear their output.

DMA: Direct Memory Access. With DMA, a computer peripheral can access memory directly, bypassing the CPU, which saves time and frees up the CPU for other tasks. Different devices are assigned different DMA numbers for identification.

DSP: Digital signal processing.

dynamic range: The range of the softest to the loudest sound that can be produced by an instrument or playback/recording medium. This can also be the difference between the low and high signal levels obtainable by a velocity-sensitive keyboard. The greater the dynamic range, the more sensitive the keyboard.

envelope: A shape representing the changes in a sound's amplitude (or other parameter) over time.

envelope generator: A circuit, usually triggered by pressing a key on a keyboard, that generates a changing voltage (or data string) with respect to time. This voltage typically controls a VCF or VCA. An ADSR is one type of envelope generator. See *ADSR*.

EQ: Abbreviation for equalization.

equalizer: A device which allows attenuation or emphasis of selected frequencies in the audio spectrum. Equalizers usually contain many bands to allow the user a fine degree of frequency control over the sound.

Fast Fourier Transform (FFT): A computer algorithm which derives the fourier spectrum from a sound file.

filter: A device used to remove unwanted frequencies from an audio signal, thus altering the signal's harmonic structure. Low-pass filters are the most common type of filter found on music synthesizers; they only allow frequencies below the cutoff frequency to pass. High-pass filters only allow the high frequencies to pass, and bandpass filters only allow frequencies in a selected band to pass through. A notch filter rejects frequencies that fall within its notch.

FireWire (IEEE 1394): A high-speed communications protocol able to transfer data and multitrack digital audio in real time.

flange: An effect created by layering two identical sounds with a slight delay (1-20ms) and slightly modulating the delay of one or both of the sounds. The term supposedly comes from the early days of tape recording when delay effects were created by pressing on the flanges of the tape reels to change the tape speed.

frequency: The number of cycles of a waveform that occur in a second.

FSK: Frequency Shift Keying. An audio tone (frequency) modulated by a pulse wave, which is used both for data transfer and also for sequencer and drum machine synchronization.

fundamental: The first, lowest note of a harmonic series. The fundamental frequency determines a sound's overall pitch.

gain: The factor by which a device increases the amplitude of a signal. Negative gain attenuates a signal.

Green Book: The Compact Disc Interactive (CD-I) standard was released by Phillips in 1978 and allows for full-motion video on a standard 5-inch disc. This requires a dedicated CD-I player and is not compatible with an audio CD player.

ground loop: Hum or other noise caused by current circulating through the ground connections of a piece of equipment or system. This is due to different voltage potentials existing along different ground lines.

hard disk: A storage medium for digital data which can hold more information and access it faster than a floppy disk.

hertz (Hz): A unit of frequency equal to 1 cycle per second.

high-pass filter: See *filter*.

IRQ: Interrupt Request. In PCs, when a peripheral device like a sound card or a CD-ROM drive needs to communicate with the computer's CPU, it sends a signal called an interrupt via a specific IRQ, causing the CPU to stop what it's doing and pay attention. Problems will result if two or more peripherals are set to the same IRQ value.

jack: A receptacle into which a plug is inserted. See *plug*.

layering: The stacking of two or more sounds on the same keyboard range to create a denser sound.

LFO: Low Frequency Oscillator. An oscillator used for modulation used below the audible range (20 Hz). Example: Varying pitch cyclically produces vibrato.

loading: To transfer from one data storage medium to another. This is generally from disk to RAM memory or vice versa, as opposed to saving from RAM to disk.

looping: The process of repeating a portion of a sample over and over in order to create a sustaining or repetitive sound. The looped sound will continue as long as the key is depressed. A sound is usually looped during a point in its evolution where the harmonics and amplitude are relatively static in order to avoid pops and glitches in the sound.

lossless compression: A technique that reduces the size of a file without sacrificing any of the original data. (When expanded, the compressed file becomes an exact replica of the original file.)

lossy compression: A technique in which some data are deliberately discarded to reduce the size of the file. (When expanded, the compressed file is lower in quality than the original file.)

low-pass filter: A filter whose frequency response remains flat up to a certain frequency, then rolls off (attenuates signals appearing at its input) above this point.

memory: The part of a computer responsible for storing data.

merge: Combining sequences, sounds, tracks, MIDI data, etc.

MIDI: Musical Instrument Digital Interface. MIDI enables synthesizers, sequencers, computers, rhythm machines, etc. to be interconnected through a standard interface. MIDI is an asynchronous, serial interface, which is transmitted at the rate of 31.25 KBaud or 31,250 bits per second.

MIDI clock: Allows instruments interconnected via MIDI to be synchronized. The MIDI clock runs at a rate of 24 ppq. See *clock*.

MIDI continuous controller: Allows continuously changing information such as pitch wheel or breath controller information to be transmitted over a MIDI cable. Continuous controllers use fairly large amounts of memory when recorded into a MIDI sequencer. Some standard MIDI continuous controller numbers are listed below:

PWH = Pitch Wheel

CHP = Pressure

1 = Modulation Wheel

2 = Breath Controller

3 = (Pressure on Rev. 1 DX7)

4 = Foot Pedal

5 = Portamento Time

6 = Data Entry

7 = Volume

8 = Balance

10 = Pan

11 = Expression Controller

16–19 = General purpose controllers 1–4 (High Res.)

64 = Sustain Switch (on/off)

65 = Portamento Switch (on/off)

66 = Sustenuto (chord hold)

67 = Soft Pedal (on/off)

69 = Hold Pedal 2 (on/off)

80–83 = General purpose controllers 5–8 (Low Res.)

91 = External Effects Depth

92 = Tremolo Depth

93 = Chorus Depth

94 = Detune

95 = Phaser Depth

96 = Data Increment

97 = Data Decrement

mini-phone: An ⅛" diameter connector found on many portable tape players and computer audio setups, identical to the phone connector but smaller and shorter. See *phone*.

modulation: The process of one audio or control voltage source influencing a sound processor or other control voltage source. Example: Slowly modulating pitch cyclically produces vibrato. Modulating a filter cyclically produces wah-wah effects.

monophonic: The characteristic of a musical instrument that is capable of playing only one note at a time. Monophonic sound has only one voice part.

MP3: A lossy data compression format that stores audio in roughly one tenth the size of a WAV file, but yields remarkably good audio results. Used for music on the Internet and the Web because of its small size and good sound.

multitimbral: The ability of a musical instrument to produce two or more different sounds or timbres at the same time.

multitrack: Recording a musical piece by dividing it into tracks, and combining the tracks during playback. Also, a device with such capabilities.

normalize: A digital processing function that increases the amplitude of a sound file until the peak amplitude of its loudest sample reaches 100% of full scale.

Orange Book: The Orange Book defines the standard for writable or recordable media such as CD-Rs and magneto-optical discs. It defines where the data can be written and, in the case of the MO, how it is erased and rewritten.

OMS: Open MIDI System. OMS acts as a central MIDI driver between OMS-compatible hardware and software. Created by Opcode Systems.

panning: Moving an audio signal from one output to the other. Panning a sound between two speakers changes the apparent position of the sound in the stereo field.

patch: A particular sound created on a synthesizer. Comes from the use of patch cords on the original modular synthesizers. To route signals.

phone: A ¼" diameter connector, a.k.a. "guitar cord." Phone plugs and jacks come in both mono and stereo versions.

plug: A (male) connector that has one or more protruding pins and fits into a jack. See *jack*.

plug-in: Software that extends the functional capabilities of a host program.

polyphonic: The characteristic of a musical instrument that is able to play more than one note at the same time. Polyphonic sound has more than one voice part.

preset: A preprogrammed sound and control setup on a sampler or synthesizer. Presets can be made up in advance of a performance, stored in memory, then recalled instantly when desired.

pressure sensitivity: The ability of an instrument to respond to pressure applied to the keyboard after the initial depression of a key. Sometimes called aftertouch.

program change: A MIDI message that tells a synthesizer to change from one instrument sound to another.

proximity effect: When cardioid microphones are placed very close to the sound source, a boosting of the bass frequencies occurs which is known as the proximity effect. Mostly associated with dynamic microphones.

punch-in: When recording, punching in over-writes a previously recorded track starting at the punch in point.

punch-out: When recording, punching out stops the recording process started by a punch-in, thus preserving the previously recorded track starting at the punch-out point.

Q: The figure expressing a filter's resonance. Varying Q varies the sharpness of the filter sound.

quantize: Correcting rhythmic irregularities in sequenced music by moving notes to, or closer to, the nearest division of a beat.

RAM: Random Access Memory. The memory in a computer that stores data temporarily. Data stored in RAM is lost forever when power is interrupted to the machine if it has not been saved to another medium, such as floppy or hard disk.

RCA: A round single-pin connector with a protruding sleeve, commonly used in consumer audio gear. Occasionally referred to in consumer electronics circles as a "phono" connector.

Red Book: 16-bit, 44.1kHz audio. Red Book is the prerecorded CD audio standard as found in music stores today. Because of this standard, any CD will play in any audio compact disc player. Specified are the sample rate (44.1 kHz), type of error detection and correction, and how the data is stored on the disc.

release: The final part of a sound's envelope, when the amplitude returns to zero.

resonance: A frequency at which a material object will vibrate. In a filter with resonance, a signal will be accentuated at the cutoff frequency. See *Q*.

reverb: An audio effect that recreates multiple sound reflections in various acoustic environments.

ReWire: A method of running digital audio between software programs. "Virtual patch cords."

REX: A file format that allows audio to be broken up and stored as MIDI-triggerable slices for use in loop-based manipulation.

sample: A digitally recorded sound.

sample rate: The rate at which level measurements of the signal are taken when digitally sampling a signal. The higher the sample rate, the higher the sound quality.

sampling: The process of recording a sound into digital memory.

SCSI: Small Computer Systems Interface. An industry standard interface that provides high-speed access to peripheral devices such as hard disk drives, optical discs, CD-R drives, etc.

sequencer: A device that records and plays back a series of pre-programmed events. A digital sequencer may record MIDI keyboard data, program changes, or realtime modulation data to be played back later, much like a tape recorder or player piano. Digital sequencers use memory on the basis of events (key on, key off, etc.) while a tape recorder uses memory (tape) on the basis of time.

serial interface: A computer interface in which data is transmitted over a single line one bit at a time. The MIDI interface is an example of a serial interface.

signal processing: Using electronic circuitry to modify a sound.

signal-to-noise ratio (SNR): The SNR, measured in decibels (dB), is a way of describing how loud the signal is compared to the residual noise (static, hiss) in the recording.

SMPTE: Acronym for Society of Motion Picture and Television Engineers who adopted a standard time code in order to synchronize video and audio. SMPTE information is in the form of hours, minutes, seconds, and frames. There are two types of SMPTE time code: Longitudinal Time Code (LTC), which is typically recorded on audio tape, and Vertical Interval Time Code (VITC), which is often recorded on video tape.

software: The programs or sets of instructions describing the tasks to be performed by a computer.

Song Pointer: MIDI information that allows equipment to remain in sync even if the master device has changed location. MIDI Song Pointer (sometimes called MIDI Song Position Pointer) is an internal register (in the sequencer or autolocator) which holds the number of MIDI beats since the start of the song.

sound module: A synthesizer or sampler without an attached keyboard. Produces sounds via input from an external MIDI device.

S/PDIF: A consumer version of AES/EBU stereo digital audio. The acronym stands for Sony/Philips Digital Interface Format. S/PDIF (pronounced "SPIH-diff") is carried on unbalanced RCA connectors. S/PDIF signals can also be transmitted on optical cables.

split: Dividing the range of a MIDI keyboard or other controller into different sections, each of which controls a different instrument or sound. Also, the point at which this division occurs.

step time: A sequencer mode where events are entered one at a time.

stripe: Recording time code onto a tape.

surround sound: An audio system that uses six discrete channels of audio, plus bass management, to enhance the listener's experience with three-dimensional sound.

System Exclusive (Sys-Ex): A type of MIDI data that applies to a specific brand and model of instrument.

TDM: Time-Division Multiplexing. TDM allows many different signals to be sent along a common data highway, or bus, at a very fast rate. These signals are "time-sliced" into their own "time slots," and travel together as a single data stream. When they get to their destination, the receiver can split out the signal(s) it needs.

timbre: Tone color. The quality of a sound that distinguishes it from other sounds with the same pitch and volume.

time code: A timing reference used to synchronize different audio devices together, or to film or video.

tremolo: A cyclic change in amplitude, usually in the range of 7 to 14Hz. Usually achieved by routing a LFO (low frequency oscillator) to a VCA (voltage controlled amplifier).

TRS: Tip-ring-sleeve. TRS phone and mini-phone plugs are used for stereo audio connections, with one channel connected to the tip and the other connected to the ring (a metal region between the tip and the sleeve). The sleeve connects to ground. TRS connectors are also used for balanced mon-aural audio connections; in this setup, the tip and ring both carry the signal. See *balanced*. They are also used to split out loop send and loop return connections in mixers and signal processors.

undo: Canceling the results of a previous operation, or string ("multiple levels") of previous operations.

USB: Universal Serial Bus. A communications protocol that's fast enough for MIDI and limited audio use.

VCA: Voltage Controlled Amplifier. A circuit whose gain is determined by a control voltage.

VCF: Voltage Controlled Filter. A filter whose cutoff frequency or resonant frequency is determined by a control voltage.

velocity sensitivity: A keyboard which can respond to the speed at which a key is depressed; this corresponds to the dynamics with which the player plays the keyboard. Velocity is an important function as it helps translate the performer's expression of the music. Velocity data can be transmitted over the MIDI line.

VST: Virtual Studio Technology. A format developed by Steinberg for virtual-instrument and effects plug-ins to be shared amongst supporting applications.

vibrato: A cyclic change in pitch, usually in the range of 7 to 14Hz.

White Book: This is sometimes known as karaoke CD, and is used in applications where the combination of full-motion video and audio is needed.

XLR: An industry generic term for round, latching three-pin connectors. XLR connections are used for balanced audio, microphones, and AES/EBU digital signals.

Yellow Book: The CD-ROM standard for computer data.

Contributors

JIM AIKIN is former senior editor of *Keyboard* magazine and the author of *Software Synthesizers: The Definitive Guide to Virtual Musical Instruments* (Backbeat Books).

CRAIG ANDERTON coined the term "electronic musician," and is a musician and author of various books, including *Home Recording for Musicians, Do-It-Yourself Projects for Guitarists, Electronic Projects for Musicians,* and *MIDI for Musicians.* Craig has also written numerous articles for magazines such as *Guitar Player, Keyboard, EQ, Rolling Stone, Mix,* and *Byte.* In addition to playing with the Cologne-based band Rei$$dorf Force, Craig has played on, produced, mixed, or mastered several major-label releases. He also lectures all over the world on technology and the arts, consults to manufacturers in the music business, and is Executive Editor for *EQ* magazine. His web site is www.craiganderton.com.

MICHAEL BABCOCK's writing credits include *Music & Computers* and other publications.

JON CHAPPELL is a guitarist, composer, and author. Jon has authored two books in the successful *Dummies* series, *Guitar for Dummies* and *Rock Guitar for Dummies* (John Wiley & Sons), and has played and recorded with Pat Benatar and Graham Nash. He is a former editor-in-chief of *Guitar* and *Home Recording* magazines, and wrote *The Recording Guitarist—A Guide for Home and Studio.* He has published pieces in *Entertainment Weekly, Rolling Stone,* and *The New York Times.*

JULIAN COLBECK has played keyboard for Steve Hackett, ABWH, Yes, John Miles and Charlie, among others. He is the author of more than a dozen books, including the best-selling Keyfax series of buyer's guides, and is co-founder of Keyfax Software.

MITCH GALLAGHER is the editor-in-chief of *EQ* magazine. An industry veteran, he is a journalist, teacher, musician, recording engineer, and award-winning composer. His first book, *Make Music Now!,* was recently released by Backbeat Books.

SCOTT GARRIGUS is a multimedia musician, teacher, and writer as well as a certified MIDI maniac.

CHRIS GILL is a music writer who has served as associate editor of *Guitar Player* and editor of *Vintage Gallery*.

JOE GORE is a consulting editor for *Guitar Player* who has recorded and toured as guitarist with Tom Waits, PJ Harvey, and many others.

TED GREENWALD is the former editor of *Interactivity* magazine. He has also been an editor for *Guitar Player* and *Musician*, and he is author of *The Musician's Home Recording Handbook*.

DAVID MILES HUBER is widely acclaimed in the recording industry as a digital audio consultant, author, engineer, university professor, guest lecturer, and professional musician. He has authored numerous books on the subjects of recording and electronic music and is a contributing editor for *EQ* magazine.

BRENT HURTIG is a freelance writer specializing in multimedia and music. He is the former editor of *EQ* magazine.

MIKE HURWICZ is a writer and consultant based in Brooklyn, NY.

CAROLYN KEATING is an audio engineer, musician, and freelance editor who has worked for record labels, production companies, and has edited numerous music publications.

JEFF KLOPMEYER is a musician, writer, and consultant.

JOHN KROGH is technical editor for *Keyboard*. John is an active composer in the film and TV industries.

ROBERT LAURISTON co-authored *The PC Bible* and has written about computer hardware and software for many magazines.

MICHAEL MARANS is a former editor for *Keyboard*, as well as a guitarist and recording authority.

HOWARD MASSEY is a noted industry consultant and veteran audio journalist. Howard is the Software Reviews Editor for *Surround Professional* and author of eleven books, including *Behind the Glass* (Backbeat Books), a collection of interviews with the world's top record producers.

ROGER NICHOLS is a legendary engineer/producer who has toured with Steely Dan and has engineered all of their albums. His list of album credits is immense, including projects with Gloria Estefan, John

Denver, Frank Sinatra, Rickie Lee Jones, and Placido Domingo. Roger has three Grammy awards and six Grammy nominations.

DAVE O'NEAL plays and records with his band Industrial Soup and writes video game music and software for Electronic Arts.

MARTIN POLON is an internationally syndicated magazine columnist writing about audio, video, multimedia, and computing in the pages of *EQ, Studio Sound, One-To-One, Television Broadcast,* and numerous other publications. Polon has taught at the University of Massachusetts at Lowell and the University of Colorado and is a member of a curriculum body in the recording arts at the University of California.

GREG RULE is editor-in-chief of *Keyboard* magazine and a remixer, composer, music producer, and voting member of the National Academy of Recording Arts and Sciences. Greg's remix and recording work has earned him a #1 position on the *Billboard* Hot Dance Breakout chart, a gold record, and a pair of AXIEM awards.

MARVIN SANDERS heads Marvster Media, an advertising and marketing agency focused on the musical instrument industry. Former positions include vice president of publishing for Harmony Central, editor-in-chief of *Keyboard* magazine, and keyboard product manager for Roland U.S.

BENNET SPIELVOGEL, a.k.a. "The East Side Flash," owns Flashpoint Recording Studios in Austin, TX.

MARK VAIL is a former editor for *Keyboard* and author of *The Hammond Organ: Beauty in the B* (Backbeat Books).

GUY WRIGHT is the former technical editor of *Interactivity.*

Index

Produce Compelling Audio for Digital Video

www.cmpbooks.com

Producing Great Sound for Digital Video, 2nd Edition

Packed with hundreds of real-world techniques that range from pre-production through the final mix. You get step-by-step tutorials, tips, and tricks so you can make great tracks with any computer or software. This revised edition features expanded sections on choosing and using microphones, boom and lav techniques, and wireless. The companion audio CD contains sample tutorial and demo tracks and platform-independent diagnostic tools.

ISBN 1-57820-208-6
$44.95

Audio Postproduction for Digital Video

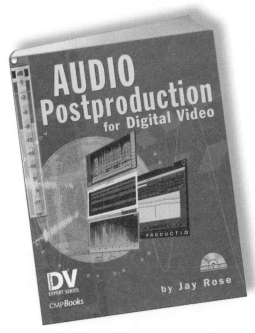

Perform professional audio editing, sound effects work, processing, and mixing on your desktop. You'll save time and solve common problems using these "cookbook recipes" and platform-independent tutorials. Discover the basics of audio theory, set up your post studio, and walk through every aspect of postproduction. The companion audio CD features tutorial tracks, demonstrations, and diagnostics.

ISBN 1-57820-116-0
$44.95

Find CMP *Books* in your local bookstore

www.cmpbooks.com • 800-500-6875 • cmp@rushorder.com

WHEN IT COMES TO MUSIC, WE WROTE THE BOOK.

Make Music Now!
Edited by Mitch Gallagher
If you're starting to set up a home studio or making one better, here's all the info and inspiration you need. This easy-to-read guide is a fun introduction to using computers to make and distribute original music. From the basics of MIDI, to choosing and using gear, putting your music online, burning CDs, and more, you get the guidance you need to make music now!
Softcover, 192 pages, ISBN 0-87930-637-8, $17.95

The Finale Primer
Mastering the Art of Music Notation with Finale
By Bill Purse
Second Edition
This easy-to-use guide will help you understand and use Coda Finale, the leading software program for music notation. It provides a solid foundation plus exercise drills for maximizing the benefits of Finale's invaluable capability to edit, reformat, and reorganize musical material. Covers Finale for the Macintosh and Windows.
Softcover, 256 pages, ISBN 0-87930-602-5, $24.95

Behind the Glass
Top Record Producers Tell How They Craft the Hits
By Howard Massey
George Martin, Glen Ballard, Phil Ramone, and 34 other world-class producers share their creative secrets and nuts-and-bolts techniques in this prime collection of firsthand interviews. These masters of the trade offer tips and tricks you can use in the studio—professional or at home—whether you're a musician, producer, engineer, or student, or just want to know how the hits are made.
Softcover, 336 pages, ISBN 0-87930-614-9, $24.95

Succeeding in Music
A Business Handbook for Performers, Songwriters, Agents, Managers, and Promoters
By John Stiernberg
When can you quit your day job? This user-friendly guide provides a solid understanding of how the fundamentals of business, finance, marketing, and strategy apply to the music world. Whether you're starting or strengthening your career, you'll learn why a business plan is key—and how to put one into action.
Softcover with CD-ROM, 208 pages, ISBN 0-87930-702-1, $24.95

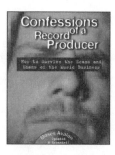

Confessions of a Record Producer
How to Survive the Scams and Shams of the Music Business
By Moses Avalon
Second Edition
If you're a musician, producer, engineer, or any other recording professional, this practical, provocative guide will help you protect your rights and assets. Using real-life examples drawn from 20-plus years' experience, this book reveals how producers dip into budgets, artists steal songs, labels skim royalties, and other unfortunate truths—and how you can survive them.
Softcover, 288 pages, ISBN 0-87930-660-2, $19.95

Secrets of Negotiating a Record Contract
The Musician's Guide to Understanding and Avoiding Sneaky Lawyer Tricks
By Moses Avalon
This is your streetwise guide to deciphering music recording agreements crafted by today's top major-label lawyers. To help you out-maneuver treacherous loopholes, hidden agendas, and other contractual land mines that drain your earnings, this book deconstructs actual record contracts clause by clause and translates them into plain English.
Softcover, 320 pages, ISBN 0-87930-636-X, $22.95

AVAILABLE AT FINE BOOK AND MUSIC STORES EVERYWHERE, OR CONTACT:

Backbeat Books • 6600 Silacci Way • Gilroy, CA 95020 USA
Phone Toll Free: (866) 222-5232 • Fax: (408) 848-5784
E-mail: backbeat@rushorder.com • Web: www.backbeatbooks.com